# PERSPECTIVES ON CONDUCTING

Rooted in research and practice, *Perspectives on Conducting* presents a multi-faceted exploration of the role of the modern-day conductor. Seeking to bring a more inclusive approach to understanding conducting as a career, this book expands beyond elite pathways to highlight the contributions made by conductors across different areas of musical engagement, including youth projects, community groups, and professional ensembles. Chapters by an international roster of authors address the challenges conductors face in working with a wide range of ensembles, including orchestras and choirs made up of young people, university and conservatory students, adult volunteers, and professional musicians.

The contributors draw on their experience and expertise as practising conductors and scholar–practitioners to explore both the core musical responsibilities and the additional administrative and social demands placed on today's conductors. With topics including pathways to conducting careers, the creative role of the conductor in shaping new music, conducting mixed-ability ensembles, the experiences of women and queer conductors, and more, the perspectives collected here reflect the versatility required of the contemporary conductor, giving students and emerging professionals a forward-thinking view of the conductor's role.

**Róisín Blunnie** is a choral conductor. She is Associate Professor of Music and Programme Chair of the MA in Choral Studies at Dublin City University, Ireland.

**Ciarán Crilly** is Associate Professor of Orchestral Conducting and Artistic Director of the UCD Symphony Orchestra at University College Dublin, Ireland.

"*Perspectives on Conducting* is a truly wonderful addition to the scholarship of choral and orchestral conducting. It is packed full of insightful and—perhaps more importantly—useful ideas for choral and orchestral conductors, and all of those who are interested in musical leadership."
—**Professor Paul Mealor**, composer, conductor, University of Aberdeen


"With practical insights from many fine contributors, *Perspectives on Conducting* is extremely useful to anyone wishing to explore what conducting means in today's world."
—**Alice Farnham**, conductor, author of *In Good Hands: The Making of a Modern Conductor* (2023)

# PERSPECTIVES ON CONDUCTING

*Edited by Róisín Blunnie and Ciarán Crilly*

NEW YORK AND LONDON

Designed cover image: © Getty Images

First published 2024
by Routledge
605 Third Avenue, New York, NY 10158

and by Routledge
4 Park Square, Milton Park, Abingdon, Oxon, OX14 4RN

*Routledge is an imprint of the Taylor & Francis Group, an informa business*

© 2024 Róisín Blunnie and Ciarán Crilly

The right of Róisín Blunnie and Ciarán Crilly to be identified as the authors of the editorial material, and of the authors for their individual chapters, has been asserted in accordance with sections 77 and 78 of the Copyright, Designs and Patents Act 1988.

All rights reserved. No part of this book may be reprinted or reproduced or utilised in any form or by any electronic, mechanical, or other means, now known or hereafter invented, including photocopying and recording, or in any information storage or retrieval system, without permission in writing from the publishers.

*Trademark notice*: Product or corporate names may be trademarks or registered trademarks, and are used only for identification and explanation without intent to infringe.

ISBN: 978-1-032-29028-7 (hbk)
ISBN: 978-1-032-29027-0 (pbk)
ISBN: 978-1-003-29966-0 (ebk)

DOI: 10.4324/9781003299660

Typeset in Sabon
by Apex CoVantage, LLC

# CONTENTS

About the Contributors     *viii*

Introduction     1
*Róisín Blunnie and Ciarán Crilly*

**PART I**
**Becoming a Conductor**     **5**

1  Teaching the Unteachable: Postgraduate Orchestral
    Conductor Training in European Conservatoires     7
    *Sinead Hayes*

2  The Conductor as Apprentice: The *Kapellmeister*
    Route to Opera Conducting     27
    *Killian Farrell*

3  Thoughts on the Role of the Assistant Conductor     40
    *Gavin Maloney*

4  The Kodály Route to Becoming a Choral Conductor     45
    *Bernie Sherlock*

## PART II
## Conductors in Practice: Orchestral Perspectives — 63

5  From Concept to Concert: A Journey of Choosing, Learning, and Performing a Score — 65
   *Rebecca Miller*

6  "This Will Be the One!": Strategic Programming and Repertoire Selection for Non-Professional Orchestras — 80
   *Ciarán Crilly*

7  The Role of the Conductor in US Orchestras: A Concise Guide — 92
   *Peter Shannon*

8  Fostering the Next Generation — 103
   *Gerhard Markson*

9  How to Help Musicians Feel More Valued and Fulfilled at Work — 107
   *Tiffany Chang*

10  Intuition: The Missing Piece? — 119
    *Hannah Baxter*

## PART III
## Conductors in Practice: Choral Perspectives — 133

11  Playing the Long Game: Strategies for Building Consistency in the Chamber Choir — 135
    *Orla Flanagan*

12  The Other Side of Programming: How to Shape a Choral Concert Programme — 146
    *Kari Turunen*

13  Together from the Start: The Collective Power of the Choral Warm-Up — 156
    *Róisín Blunnie*

| | |
|---|---|
| 14 Rehearsal Techniques for Contemporary Choral Music: The Use of the Movable-*Do* System in the Teaching of Non-Tonal Repertoire<br>*László Nemes* | 169 |
| 15 Facilitating Connections: Leading and Developing University Choirs<br>*Amy Ryan* | 184 |
| 16 Innovative Choral Approaches: 'The Intelligent Choir' and the 'HyFlex' Method<br>*Jim Daus Hjernøe* | 201 |

**PART IV**
**Changing Perspectives**     **213**

| | |
|---|---|
| 17 The 'Maestro Myth' Revisited<br>*John Andrews* | 215 |
| 18 "You Are Now One of the Boys": Congratulations?<br>*Nadya Potemkina* | 228 |
| 19 Cracking Open the Conducting Closet: Shared Experiences among Queer Conductors<br>*Thomas Dickey* | 241 |
| 20 Voices for Change: Socially Responsible Programming in Youth Choral Music Education<br>*Lynsey Callaghan* | 252 |
| *Index* | 264 |

# ABOUT THE CONTRIBUTORS

**John Andrews** is a British conductor specializing in rare and under-performed repertoire. He won the BBC Music Magazine Award for Best Opera Recording in 2021 and 2023. Alongside a wide-ranging freelance career, he is currently Principal Guest Conductor of London's National Symphony Orchestra.

**Hannah Baxter** is the founding editor of the journal *Notes from the Podium*. Collaborators include Sir Mark Elder, Benjamin Zander, JoAnn Falletta, Sir Andrew Davis, and Sir Roger Norrington. She was awarded a PhD from the University of Sussex for her thesis on Stravinsky's effect on the role of the conductor.

**Róisín Blunnie** is Associate Professor of Music and Programme Chair of the MA in Choral Studies at Dublin City University, Ireland. She conducts the mixed chamber choir Laetare Vocal Ensemble and the undergraduate student choir DCU Lumen Chorale.

**Lynsey Callaghan** is Head of Programmes, Research, and Academics at the Royal Irish Academy of Music, where she also oversees the development of conducting. She is founding Artistic Director of both Dublin Youth Choir and the Cross-Border Youth Choir, and Artistic Director of the Belfast Philharmonic Youth Choirs and Tallaght Choral Society.

**Tiffany Chang** is an orchestra and opera conductor whose mission is to help musicians feel valued, seen, and fulfilled. Via her leadership on the podium and blog called *Conductor as CEO*, she inspires transformation by challenging conventional thinking and applying perspectives from other industries.

**Ciarán Crilly** is Associate Professor of Orchestral Conducting and Artistic Director of the UCD Symphony Orchestra at University College Dublin, where he was Head of the School of Music 2018–23. He has been active as a freelance conductor, violinist, and violist for over twenty years.

**Jim Daus Hjernøe** is Full Professor at the Royal Academy of Music in Denmark. He leads the RAMA Vocal Center and is known globally for jazz/pop choir directing. Since 2002, he has focused on improvisational vocal art, developing the Intelligent Choir philosophy and Vocal Painting to foster shared musical responsibility through co-creation.

**Thomas Dickey** is Director of Orchestral Studies and Associate Professor of Music at Oklahoma State University. He conducts the OSU Symphony Orchestra and teaches graduate- and undergraduate-level courses in orchestral conducting, literature, and pedagogy.

**Killian Farrell** followed the traditional *Kapellmeister* route through German opera and is currently *Generalmusikdirektor* of the Staatstheater Meiningen, having previously been First *Kapellmeister* at the Theater Bremen and the Staatsoper Stuttgart. He has also worked with Komische Oper Berlin, De Nationale Opera Amsterdam, and Theater Heidelberg.

**Orla Flanagan** is Assistant Professor of Music at Trinity College Dublin. She conducts the mixed-voice choir Mornington Singers and is Artistic Director of the Sing Ireland International Choral Conducting Summer School.

**Sinead Hayes** is an Irish freelance orchestral and opera conductor. An alumna of the Royal Northern College of Music, Manchester graduate conducting programme, she is conductor of the Hard Rain SoloistEnsemble, Belfast and the Royal Irish Academy of Music Symphony Orchestra. She has conducted orchestras and ensembles in Ireland, the UK, and Europe.

**Gavin Maloney** is Associate Principal Conductor of the RTÉ Concert Orchestra. He has enjoyed a long-standing relationship with Ireland's National Symphony Orchestra, with whom he was appointed Assistant Conductor at the age of twenty-one. Gavin has conducted all the leading ensembles in Ireland, plus orchestras in Germany, France, Italy, and the UK.

About the Contributors

**Gerhard Markson** is a German orchestral conductor. From 2001 to 2009, he served as Principal Conductor of the RTÉ National Symphony Orchestra. Recordings dating from his tenure with the orchestra are available on several labels, including Naxos. He has worked with over 100 orchestras and opera companies worldwide.

**Rebecca Miller** is Principal Conductor of the Bishop's Stortford Sinfonia, Principal Conductor of the Royal Orchestral Society, Director of Orchestras at Royal Holloway University, and Principal Guest Conductor of the Orchestra of the Swan. She was Chief Conductor of the Uppsala Chamber Orchestra in Sweden 2019–23.

**László Norbert Nemes** is a choral conductor and music pedagogue, Co-Artistic Director of the National Youth Choir (The Netherlands), Artistic Director of the New Liszt Ferenc Chamber Choir (Hungary), and founder of the National Youth Choir of Hungary. He is currently Professor of Choral Music and Musicianship at the Royal Conservatory of The Hague and at the Liszt Academy of Music in Budapest.

**Nadya Potemkina** is a conductor, violist, and educator who directs Wesleyan University Orchestra and Concert Choir and teaches courses in instrumental conducting and orchestral literature. She is the music director of Connecticut FluteFest and Ad Hoc Bach Collective, both performance and community engagement initiatives in Middletown, CT (USA).

**Amy Ryan** lectures at the Royal Irish Academy of Music, Dublin, and is Artistic Director of University College Dublin Philharmonic Choir. She conducts Cuore Chamber Choir and the choir of St Stephen's Church, and has guested as conductor of UCD Symphony Orchestra and as Chorus Director for Irish National Opera.

**Peter Shannon** has been Artistic Director and Conductor of the Jackson Symphony in Jackson, Tennessee since 2015 and was Artistic Director and Conductor of the Savannah Philharmonic, in Savannah, Georgia 2008–19. He was previously conductor of the Collegium Musicum Orchestra in Heidelberg, Germany.

**Bernie Sherlock** is Artistic Director of the Irish Youth Choirs and New Dublin Voices. She has won prizes for her conducting in Finland, Hungary, Belgium, Italy, Slovenia, Wales, and Ireland, and she works internationally as a conductor, adjudicator, workshop leader, and teacher of conducting. She lectures at the TU Dublin Conservatoire.

**Kari Turunen** is the Artistic Director of the Vancouver Chamber Choir. He holds a DMus degree from the University of the Arts, Helsinki, and has taught choral conducting from university level to short courses in Europe, North America, and Asia. Presently he is on the faculty of the Vancouver Academy of Music.

# INTRODUCTION

*Róisín Blunnie and Ciarán Crilly*

There is a certain romanticism associated with the idea of a 'conductor.' Holding a singular position of leadership, the *chef d'orchestre* or *chef de choeur* is frequently revered, already on a pedestal by virtue of their natural habitat: the podium. Part of the mystique derives from conceptual uncertainty, as the most frequently posed question about conducting must surely be: "What does a conductor actually do?" or some variation thereof. A possible follow-up might incorporate the phrase: "It's just waving your arms about." Individual answers might conflate notions of leadership, impacting the sound of an ensemble, acting as a channel of communication between musicians and audience, interpretation, and vision, but it is likely that no two responses will be the same.

Such equivocation would not apply when contemplating what a conductor might *look* like, as, for much of the twentieth century, there was a persistent archetypal image that tended to be an older white male, always dressed in tails, directing an orchestra that in turn was predominantly male. This image may not be so far removed from the character played by Bugs Bunny in *Long-Haired Hare* (1949), a beloved Looney Tunes short that parodies the on-stage extravagances of superstar conductor Leopold Stokowski (1882–1977). The fundamental perception of the 'conductor' has broadened enormously in the last four or five decades, and for this we ought to celebrate the pioneering work of talented and resolute figures who have blazed a trail for progress regardless of gender, sexuality, or ethnicity. Gender imbalance in particular has been addressed via a number of prominent initiatives, yet a lot of work remains to be done in the service of greater equality.[1]

DOI: 10.4324/9781003299660-1

If the perception of the conductor is evolving, then so too is that of the conductor's role. Returning to the initial question about the conductor's function, common answers may remain conservative, with an emphasis primarily on the person who stands on a podium—usually in front of an orchestra—for a performance enjoyed by an assembly of music devotees. This, of course, is only one perspective. In this volume, we seek to bring multiple viewpoints of the conductor's art into a public forum. While presenting a wide range of contexts, we acknowledge that it is impossible to be entirely comprehensive, especially in terms of the types of ensemble that tend to require a conductor. However, the featured authors offer a transferability of skills and approaches that could be adopted right across the profession. There are established voices, progressive voices, and new voices, all with valuable experiences to share with others in this continuously evolving vocation. We have sought to present a multifaceted definition of the role of the modern-day conductor, rooted in both research and practice, bringing a more inclusive approach to the understanding of conducting than exists in previously published texts, which have often focused on the realm of elite professionals as an aspirational ideal. Clearly, this is not the whole story.

We highlight the activities of conductors in different arenas of musical engagement, including youth projects, educational institutions, voluntary societies, and professional organizations. Among the types of ensemble represented are orchestras and choirs with a membership comprising young people, university and conservatory students, adult volunteers, and professional singers or instrumentalists. All contributors are either practitioners or scholar–practitioners who are able to draw upon their expertise with empirical or heuristic outcomes. The versatility and adaptability often required of the contemporary conductor is reflected not only in terms of the types of ensemble and repertoire but also in extramusical areas of responsibility, be they administrative, managerial, social, or pastoral.

In structuring this collection, we were influenced by how each writer tended to frame their experiences. Some concentrated on the specifics of choral or orchestral conducting, while others approached broader organizational or societal issues. A selection of potential routes into the profession opens the volume, and this will be most enlightening for those contemplating a career as a conductor, or perhaps just setting out on their journey. These chapters examine some of the most orthodox pathways, namely postgraduate study in leading conservatoires, the *Kapellmeister* journey through German opera houses, and working as an assistant or associate conductor with a major symphony orchestra. The final chapter in Part I appraises an important foundational programme for choral conductors, or indeed all conductors, at the Kodály Institute in Hungary, where musicianship and highly developed aural skills are accentuated.

Parts II and III showcase conductors in practice, first from an orchestral then a choral point of view. Themes include how to work with a management team, devising suitable programmes for your ensemble, relying upon innate musical intuition, and how to build confidence and performance quality within rehearsals. One contrast between orchestral and choral conductors is in how the latter are often tasked with a more didactic role, especially when working with singers who are not professionally trained; thus there can be an onus to 'coach' singers in terms of vocal technique and sound production, as well as being able to deliver an accomplished musical product in performance. Thinking 'beyond the podium' is evident in these chapters, but is more conspicuous in Part IV, which considers perspectives that are necessarily changing, encompassing questions of gender, sexuality and sexual orientation, and social responsibility.

These discourses are assisted by the fact that public debate on the conductor's role has become increasingly mainstream. This is thanks in part to TV shows such as *Mozart in the Jungle* (2014–18) and *Philharmonia* (2018–19), and the movie *Tár* (2022), all of which deal with socio-political matters behind or beyond artistic duties in fictional settings.[2] In addition, two books on the art form by leaders in the field, Mark Wigglesworth and Alice Farnham, aimed at a general music readership, have emerged in recent years.[3] It is our hope that this collection shall make a positive contribution to the debate, assisting students, practitioners, and general readers in discerning a fuller picture of what conductors are and what they are capable of achieving.

In preparing this book, the editors would like to extend their sincerest thanks to the following: the UCD College of Arts and Humanities for funding support under the research strand Ireland in the World; UCD graduate students Fiona Baldwin and Tegan Sutherland for invaluable assistance in copyediting and proofreading; Shane Barriscale for the preparation of musical examples; the editorial team in Routledge for unwavering encouragement; our colleagues in the School of Theology, Philosophy, and Music in DCU, and the School of Music in UCD; and, finally, all our contributors.

## Notes

1 Examples of current initiatives for women conductors include the Taki Alsop Conducting Fellowship (https://takialsop.org/) and the Royal Philharmonic Society Women Conductors programme (https://royalphilharmonicsociety.org.uk/performers/women-conductors).

2 Bradley Cooper's Leonard Bernstein biopic *Maestro* was released at the end of 2023 to great acclaim, but the film's narrative is concerned more with his personal rather than his professional life.
3 Mark Wigglesworth, *The Silent Musician: Why Conducting Matters* (London: Faber & Faber, 2018); Alice Farnham, *In Good Hands: The Making of a Modern Conductor* (London: Faber & Faber, 2023). Going back a little further, there are other valuable 'insider' accounts, including Leonard Slatkin, *Conducting Business: Unveiling the Mystery Behind the Maestro* (Milwaukee: Amadeus Press, 2012) and Christopher Seaman, *Inside Conducting* (Rochester: University of Rochester Press, 2013).

# PART I
# Becoming a Conductor

# 1

# TEACHING THE UNTEACHABLE

Postgraduate Orchestral Conductor Training in European Conservatoires

*Sinead Hayes*

Leopold Stokowski's oft referenced quote that, "Conductors are born, not made,"[1] seems to point to a profession apart, one whose practitioners are endowed with unattainable gifts and qualities, summoning unseen forces as they weave musical magic with their white sticks, while contained on a small square box. The path to the box—the podium—has never been straightforward, and in the past, traditional routes involved working one's way up through the opera house system, as discussed in Killian Farrell's chapter in this volume, or playing in an orchestra, or acting as assistant conductor and taking the chance to jump in when the conductor was indisposed, with the most celebrated examples being Arturo Toscanini and Leonard Bernstein.[2] Today, completing postgraduate conductor training at a conservatoire has become yet another route into a profession that remains shrouded in mystique.

### Paths, Doors, Gatekeepers, and Spilled Coffee

My own route into working as a conductor was somewhat circuitous. Early study as a violinist was diverted initially into training as a structural engineer, with a bachelor's degree in civil engineering at the University of Galway followed by a one-year master's in structural steel design at Imperial College London. Music was always the goal however, and, after a few years as a full-time—and eventually part-time—engineer, I completed a BMus in violin and composition at City University, London. This was followed by postgraduate training (MMus) in conducting at

DOI: 10.4324/9781003299660-3

the Royal Northern College of Music, Manchester. International masterclasses and competitions followed, and through formative experiences conducting choirs, youth orchestras, and amateur orchestras, I have navigated towards my current career as a full-time freelance conductor of opera, contemporary music, and orchestras, mostly with professional groups, in Ireland.

And so, to November 2021, when, after a busy weekend of conducting, I came across an article by respected Irish music critic Michael Dervan in the *Irish Times*. One paragraph caught my eye:

> Conducting is probably the most mysterious and widely misunderstood of musical callings. Someone, usually a man, waves his hand in the air, the players respond and music is made. The technique is complicated, yet musicians who have no training in it can actually conduct with great artistic success. And highly trained conducting wizards can be as dull as dishwater.[3]

After mopping up the coffee sprayed on the kitchen table in sputtering indignation, I paused to reflect. Dervan's view is one that I have encountered time and again among orchestral musicians and audiences. Could there be some truth in his statement?

To stand in front of a professional orchestra as a conductor in a public performance, quite a few doors need to be opened. One needs to be invited by the orchestra's management, and before the invitation, competence, at the very least, must be assured. In the conducting business, the investigation of competence, and assignation of relative value is usually carried out not by the orchestra management but by the conductor's management team or agent. In return for commission, they choose to represent the conductor, based on many factors: the strength of recommendations from mentors and teachers, the approval of competition juries, the perceived potential of the conductor to succeed in the gruelling world of international guest conducting, and, in the case of acclaimed instrumentalists/singers, their existing profile within the classical music industry. The level of training a conductor has undergone is also considered, with completion of postgraduate training at a recognized conservatoire an advantage in verifying a baseline of technical and musical competence. But what exactly does this conservatoire training of conductors involve, and does it transform instinctive vibrant musicians into highly trained, dull automatons, as Michael Dervan might have us believe?

## Conductor Qualities

In his book *The Silent Musician: Why Conducting Matters*, conductor Mark Wigglesworth lists the traits of the ideal conductor, compiled from his own canvassing of orchestral musicians. Conductors need:

> Good baton technique, rehearsal technique, musicianship, knowledge, interpretive conviction, an ability to communicate, to stretch and challenge people, to make the performance better than the rehearsals, to be inspirational, to have a good ear, clear thoughts, reliability, competence, rhythm, an expressive face, sense of structure, ability to accompany, style, suitability for the repertoire, originality, knowledge of string bowing, an ability to collaborate, analyse and solve difficulties, explain why things need to be repeated, empower people, train people, make people listen.[4]

The list goes on to describe ideal conductor personality traits such as humour, respect, awareness, and many more. It is a "daunting job description," as Wigglesworth rightly points out.[5] Surely no one could be born with such a multitude of skills, leadership, and personal qualities. The end of Stokowski's truncated quote would seem to concur: "But musical education and general culture are of inestimable value to the born conductor."[6]

Wigglesworth's ideal conductor traits are broadly divided into musical and personal qualities. Of the musical qualities—taking musical talent as a prerequisite—baton technique, rehearsal technique, musicianship, and rhythm can all be evaluated, improved, and taught. The personal qualities of leadership and creativity are less tangible and, thus, can be taught to a lesser degree. Training can help develop a conductor by focusing on building musical and conducting skill levels, but what of the notion that great artistic success can be achieved without any training?

To answer this, we turn to noted conducting pedagogue Harold Farberman, who points to the increasing virtuosity of the orchestras of today, noting that, "Many orchestras are forced to create performances because conductors forfeit their leadership rights due to technical deficiencies."[7] This leads us to the conclusion that a conductor armed with the requisite musical and technical conducting skills has a better chance of consistently realizing a musical performance that rises above the mere mundane into something never to be forgotten than a conductor relying purely on instinct, although opinions can vary widely as to what might constitute an unforgettable performance.

## Industry Demand and Training Outline

There is a clear demand within the orchestral community for those with skills developed during postgraduate training. A survey of the full-time professional orchestras in the UK shows that, as of October 2022, twelve out of eighteen music directors or principal conductors and eight out of fifteen principal guest conductors have completed a master's in conducting.[8] A survey of assistant conductor positions in major orchestras in the UK and Europe shows that almost all assistant conductors have completed a master's in conducting. Many of these assistant conductors already have artist management in place.

But what does conductor training involve? The format, content, and means of delivery vary from conservatoire to conservatoire, but a high-level conducting postgraduate course will include the following elements:

- Weekly repertoire classes involving two pianos, small ensemble, or chamber orchestra.
- Individual lessons with the principal conducting teacher, as well as with guest musicians visiting the conservatoire, focusing on score preparation, technique, and so on.
- Supporting studies, including musicianship, ear training, score reading, analysis, and music theory.
- Opportunities to attend rehearsals and act as assistant conductors for projects internally within the conservatoire or externally with local professional orchestras and opera companies.
- Additional seminars on leadership, movement, body awareness, and so on.

Each conducting course is designed and developed by the main conducting teacher, so within these broad areas, there is much scope for variation and innovation. It is this variation, as well as the personality and strengths of the individual conducting teacher and students, that can help shape the typical graduate profile of the emerging conductors.

## Three Case Studies

To get a better idea of the distinction between postgraduate orchestral conducting courses, it is useful to compare three of the leading conservatoires. For the purposes of this exercise, I have chosen to concentrate on European institutions: the Sibelius Academy, Finland; Zurich University of the Arts, Switzerland; and the Royal Academy of Music, London. Graduates of all three institutions currently hold conductor and assistant conductor positions worldwide, and none of the three insists on high-level keyboard skills as a prerequisite for entry, which would be the case for most postgraduate courses in Germany.[9]

The postgraduate conducting courses in each institution will be examined by addressing the following themes:

- Audition process.
- Course content.
- Teaching philosophy of the principal teacher.
- Pathways from the conservatoire into the profession.

## Case Study 1: Sibelius Academy, Helsinki, Finland

### Background

The Sibelius Academy, Finland has provided advanced-level training for musicians since its establishment in 1882. Currently numbering 1,400 students and 500 teachers, the Sibelius Academy merged in 2013 with the Academy of Fine Arts, Helsinki and the Helsinki Theater Academy, under the umbrella of Uniarts Helsinki.[10] The Academy conducting department numbers a long list of international conductors among its alumni, including Esa-Pekka Salonen, Jukka-Pekka Saraste, Mikko Franck, and Hannu Lintu. The current principal conductor of the BBC Symphony Orchestra, Sakari Oramo, is also a graduate, and in 2020 took up the position of Professor of Conducting at the Sibelius Academy. He succeeded Atso Almila (2013–19), Leif Segerstam (1997–2013), Eri Klas (1993–97), and Jorma Panula (1973–93).[11] Of these distinguished teachers, Segerstam and Panula have had an immeasurable influence over the training of conductors in Finland. Panula, now in his nineties, continues to teach in masterclasses worldwide, as well as through his Panula Academy, established in Finland in 2014.

The Sibelius Academy currently offers a five-and-a-half-year bachelor's conducting degree and a two-and-a-half-year master's degree, taught through English and Finnish. Three conducting options are available: orchestral, wind band, and choral conducting. Fees for EU/EEA students are free (€5,000 per year for non-EU/EEA) which, when coupled with the renown of the department, means that competition is extremely high. In 2022, forty-four candidates applied for the master's in orchestral conducting, with just one student being accepted.[12]

### Audition

Auditions for the autumn semester take place in May, and candidates for both the bachelor's and master's degree are auditioned together. Candidates initially submit a video of themselves conducting an ensemble of at least seven musicians, demonstrating both playing through and rehearsing with the ensemble. From this, nine candidates were chosen for the live auditions in 2022. The live audition includes the following:

- Music theory and aural skills test (including four-part atonal dictation), score playing, an analysis of a score, and a group and individual aural test.
- An audition on main instrument or voice.
- A twenty-five-minute conducting test, during which candidates conduct and rehearse the orchestra on previously prepared repertoire. In 2022, test pieces were Mozart's Symphony No. 40, second movement, and Schubert's Symphony No. 5, second movement.
- A final interview.

By accepting just one conductor to the master's and one to the bachelor's course, class sizes are kept small, maximizing the possibilities for individual development and conducting opportunities. The repertoire for the 2022 auditions was chosen to demonstrate the candidate's musical abilities, rather than focusing on their time beating skills. During the auditions, the candidates were asked to vary their tempi and to solve particular musical issues as they arose in order to evaluate flexibility and listening skills. The main instrument audition is also very important in order to evaluate the musical potential of the conductors. In autumn 2022, the class numbers were eight orchestral conductors across all years, including two female students.[13]

*Course Outline*

Once accepted, students work to develop the skills to work as conductors at the highest possible level. A typical week will include two preparatory sessions of three hours duration each, with orchestra sessions on Friday or Saturday. Individual lessons are a recent and beneficial addition to the course. Students work regularly with the training orchestra, a twenty-six to twenty-eight-piece sinfonietta formed from current students of the Sibelius Academy who are paid an honorarium for their work. Although this is very useful for gaining experience, the orchestra's response does not compare with that of a professional orchestra. To help gain this valuable experience of working with professionals, students have regular conducting workshop opportunities with the many professional orchestras throughout Finland. Projects in 2022–23 included rehearsals and concerts with the Joensuu City Orchestra and the Oulu Sinfonia, as well as workshops with the Finnish Radio Symphony Orchestra and a concert with the Helsinki Philharmonic Orchestra for some students.

Group discussions also feature, with video analysis used after orchestral sessions to review areas for improvement. This use of video as a teaching tool was pioneered by Jorma Panula. Since the arrival of Arturo Alvarado as course coordinator in 2017, the conducting courses in the Sibelius Academy have been evolving, with current students benefitting from additional supporting studies in orchestral arranging and vocal coaching as well as organized rehearsal attendance and cooperation with the conservatoire's composition department. If weaknesses in other areas are identified, students can opt for additional modules. Students also continue to study their main instrument.[14]

## Main Conducting Teacher

Conductor Sakari Oramo's start as conducting professor was far from ideal, commencing just two months before the Covid-19 lockdown. Following a pivot to online teaching, some benefits became apparent, including the opportunity for online sessions with well-known conductors, who suddenly found themselves with time on their hands.[15] This supplemented the Sibelius Academy's well-established practice of inviting distinguished conductors and teachers to the course, ranging from noted Russian pedagogue Ilya Musin and conductor Arvīds Jansons in the 1980s and 1990s to Johannes Schlaefli, Nicolás Pasquet, and Sir Roger Norrington in recent years.

Oramo's path to conducting came via a distinguished career as alternating concertmaster with the Finnish Radio Symphony Orchestra. Aged twenty-four, he enrolled in Jorma Panula's conducting class, where he sought to learn how a conductor thinks. Panula's uncomplicated approach to music gave his students, including Salonen, Saraste, and Oramo, the means to conduct an orchestra by encouraging economy of gesture and discouraging excessive talking during rehearsals. Panula also fostered a broad engagement with the arts outside music, helping to create conductors who could look beyond the confines of the classical music world.[16]

Oramo is still developing his own teaching style and, away from the practice sessions with orchestra, uses individual lessons to focus on repertoire, score preparation, posture, breathing, and helping his students find their own strengths and weaknesses.[17] During his own highly successful career, Oramo has held positions with some of the most prestigious orchestras in the world, including the City of Birmingham Symphony Orchestra, BBC Symphony Orchestra, and Swedish Radio Symphony Orchestra.

*Bridge to the Profession*

Conducting students at the Sibelius Academy benefit from Sakari Oramo's high-level experience when seeking to bridge the gap between working with academy students and training orchestras and working with professionals. Oramo outlines the key to success: "Be there with the musicians, invite them to make music with you, and listen carefully to what they do. You don't need to play the orchestra so much—it plays itself when you do the right thing."[18]

It is in connecting conducting studies and the profession that the Sibelius Academy community excels, overtly acknowledging that developing conductors need focused support and guidance to acquire experience in the real world. There is a tradition among Finnish conductors of more established professionals actively helping emergent colleagues gain professional experience and secure engagements. Finnish professional orchestras also see the importance of investing in new conducting talent, actively creating opportunities for invitations, and more importantly, re-invitations, even if the musical results are less than perfect.[19] Within the music industry, Finnish conductors are seen as a safe bet, able to get the job done on very few rehearsals. Agencies such as HarrisonParrott have developed strong links with the Sibelius Academy, with young conductor Kristian Sallinen being the latest Finnish addition to the roster.[20]

In summer 2022, I had a chance to observe the collegial atmosphere among Finnish conductors when I was invited as an observer to Jukka-Pekka Saraste's LEAD festival in Fiskars, Finland. Here, three generations of Sibelius Academy graduates could be seen actively working together to develop and promote the next generation of conducting talents (including Kristian Sallinen).[21] This cooperative group atmosphere continues in Oramo's class today, maintaining the tradition of Jorma Panula, who's greatest talent was "to create an atmosphere in which people can learn from themselves and each other. He wanted us to express ourselves exactly as we wished."[22] It was very special to see Panula drop by during the LEAD Festival, sitting in the background, quietly making sure his legacy continues.

## Case Study 2: Zürcher Hochschule der Künste, Zurich, Switzerland

*Background*

From one of the most established conductor training programmes, we will now look at the programme in the Zürcher Hochschule der Künste (ZHdK). The ZHdK has existed since 2007, following the amalgamation of the Zurich Canton University of Design and Art and Zurich University of Music and Theatre, itself formed in 1999, following the amalgamation of the conservatoires of Winterthur and Zurich.[23] The conducting programme was established in 1999 with Professor Johanna Schlaefli as its director, representing an evolution from the joint conducting course of the music schools of Zurich, Bern, Basel, and Geneva under conductor Manfred Honeck.[24] The retirement of Professor Schlaefli in August 2023 signalled an inevitable change in direction for the ZHdK conductor's studio, with successor Christoph-Mathias Mueller teaching together with Schlaefli from August 2022 before taking over in August 2023. Nevertheless, the extraordinary success of the programme to date with alumni such as Mirga Gražinytė-Tyla, Philippe Bach, Kerem Hasan, and others means that it merits examination. A number of ZHdK graduates hold conductor and assistant positions worldwide, a remarkable achievement for such a relatively young training programme.[25]

The ZHdK offers a three-year bachelor's, two-year master's, and two-year specialized master's in conducting, affording students the potential for up to seven years of conducting study. During the bachelor's degree, students study both conducting and their primary instrument, fulfilling Professor Schlaefli's idea that "the best way is that someone becomes a musician first."[26] Very few students are accepted onto the bachelor's course specializing in conducting. Each year, one to three students are accepted on the master's and specialized master's course. Fees are relatively low (CHF1,440 for EU and CHF2,440 for international students annually),[27] so competition is high.

### Audition

Following submission of a conducting video, which can include conducting two pianos, selected candidates are invited to submit further conducting videos, as well as a videoed instrumental performance, and a short video explaining why they would like to study conducting. Approximately twelve applicants are then invited to an in-person audition consisting of:

- A twenty-five-minute conducting audition with ensemble. In 2022, the test pieces were Beethoven's Symphony No. 2, 3, or 7, first and second movements (to rehearse) and Bartók's Concerto for Orchestra, fourth movement (play through only).[28]
- A fifteen-minute aural/harmony test, including singing and playing piano, sight-singing an atonal melody, tapping or vocalization of the rhythm of an orchestral part, reproduction of metric-bound and free-metric rhythmic structures.
- Hearing tests to identify intervals, chords, and progressions.
- A ten-minute interview to discuss professional goals.

## Course Outline

In October 2022, there were eleven conducting students in ZHdK, five of whom were female. When accepted, students benefit from a weekly, forty-minute individual lesson, weekly group discussions, focusing on repertoire, and general conducting topics, as well as three hours of repertoire group lessons with an ensemble of string quintet, wind quintet, and two pianos. An important aspect of the course sees students participate in intensive project weeks three to four times per term with orchestras in Switzerland and Eastern Europe. These project weeks give valuable experience with different orchestras and the potential for professional engagements as guest conductors.[29] Students are also required to act as assistant conductors and to attend rehearsals for opera productions and symphony orchestra projects inside and outside the conservatoire.

Through the open, familial atmosphere of the class, each student's individual artistic personality is developed, as confirmed by alumnus Kerem Hasan, who enjoyed the dedicated work ethic that was fostered within the group during his three years as a student of Schlaefli.[30] As in the Sibelius Academy, video footage of the ensemble and orchestral sessions is used as a means of examining what worked and what did not during fortnightly one-to-one sessions.[31] For the master's course, supporting studies include weekly score reading (forty minutes), ear training (sixty minutes), and analysis (ninety minutes). Students can also choose from a wide range of elective modules to enhance their individual interests. At specialized master's level, the emphasis is on the development of conducting skills with no supporting studies but the addition of a master's project.

## Main Conducting Teacher

Following high-level training as an oboist, Johannes Schlaefli pursued conducting studies with Mario Venzago, Leonard Bernstein (at Tanglewood), and American conductor Kirk Trevor, with whom he subsequently worked as teaching assistant. A former chief conductor of Bern Chamber Orchestra among others, Schlaefli is now recognized as one of the leading conducting teachers in the world.[32] His approach of developing the individual artist's personality has much in common with Jorma Panula and Kirk Trevor, mirroring the latter's teaching philosophy of taking students from one level to the next by fostering a questioning approach and helping them to become their own teachers.[33]

It is a testament to Schlaefli's teaching style that all his students look completely different when conducting. Kerem Hasan summarizes Schlaefli's teaching style as gently nudging the student in the right direction.[34] Conductor James Lowe, music director of Spokane Symphony Orchestra, and a teaching collaborator of Schlaefli's, points out his ability to pick the correct moment to isolate an issue, without overloading the student.[35] I can also attest to this personally, having participated in a transformative ten-day masterclass with Professor Schlaefli in Teplice in 2010.

For Schlaefli, it is important to understand the structure, getting a sense of what the music wants to say. He considers himself a coach rather than a teacher, giving his students the tools to thoroughly master the scores they conduct, by scanning the landscape of the music. Everyone takes their own decisions on how they traverse that landscape, based on their understanding of potential obstacles, and who could need the conductor in what way. Where could there be a problem in the balance, in the ensemble, and why is it a problem? Where do you think musically it is in two, but maybe better in four? Why? For whom?[36]

Such questions become second nature with practice. The musical ideas and answers are then transferred into movement. Within Schlaefli's teaching approach, technique is a valuable means to an end, and control of gesture, allied with a complete knowledge of the score, is the means through which a clear musical vision or inner voice can be conveyed.[37] Schlaefli himself describes conducting as: "Fine tuning of different energies, collecting the energy of listening, inspiring, taking, helping, feeling the orchestra as a unit that has its own heartbeat."[38] He aims for absolute equity among his students, insisting that each be given exactly the same amount of time in front of the orchestra or ensemble, regardless of level. He is also aware of the gender balance in his masterclasses and class in Zurich, noting that for today's teenage female musicians, conducting will be a much more normalized career choice than for their older colleagues. In the coming years, Schlaefli will continue his teaching activities through the Conducting Academy Johannes Schlaefli, which launched in October 2022. Here, outside the formal structure of ZHdK, he will have the chance to work with more emerging conductors, as well as offering mentoring and score discussion to his students via Zoom.[39]

## Case Study 3: Royal Academy of Music, London, UK

### Background

From Zurich, we travel west to the Royal Academy of Music (RAM), London. Founded in 1822 as Britain's first conservatoire, the RAM has occupied its current premises in Marylebone Road since 1911. In 1999, the Academy was admitted as a full member to the University of London, and currently has 868 students, of whom approximately half are international.[40]

The conducting course was founded in 1983 by Colin Metters, who became Professor Emeritus of Conducting in 2013, following the appointment of Sian Edwards as Head of Conducting. Alumni such as Susanna Mälkki, Mark Wigglesworth, Edward Gardner, and more recent graduates, such as Ben Glassberg and Jonathon Heyward, occupy conductor and assistant conductor positions worldwide.[41] The conservatoire offers a two-year master's in conducting and recently introduced a one-year continuing professional development diploma aimed at professional musicians who want to move into conducting. Typically, one or two students per year are accepted for the master's course, with one further student accepted for the professional development year. Annual fees are £13,500 for UK/EU students and £29,000 for non-EU students.[42]

### Audition

The application process initially involves the submission of a conducting video, which can include two pianos. Following this, twelve to fourteen candidates are invited to the in-person audition held over two days, usually in February. The first day consists of aural tests, an interview and an audition conducting a wind ensemble. In 2022, the repertoire was Stravinsky's *Symphonies of Wind Instruments* (1947 revision) and Mozart's Serenade No. 10. For the second round of the audition, four or five candidates are invited for a forty-minute audition with two pianos, repertoire for which was Schumann's Symphony No. 2, third movement, and Janáček's Sinfonietta, third movement. Unlike the auditions in Helsinki and Zurich, auditionees do not need to perform on their instrument/voice. The longer session gives a chance for more interaction between the panel and the candidates, with questions around the audition from the previous day.

### Course Outline

In October 2022, there were four postgraduate conducting students, two of whom were women. Repertoire is studied in weekly two-piano sessions (two- to three-hour sessions) with supporting studies, including aural training, keyboard skills, and score reading. Further sessions include various combinations of small ensembles in addition to the two pianos. Students have regular individual lessons with Sian Edwards, with a small cohort meaning more flexibility in the time available. Additional seminars on analysis, music history, and programming are also available. Students collaborate with composers and the opera department on various projects to broaden experience, and there are frequent opportunities to observe rehearsals and act as assistant conductors for projects inside and outside the academy. Student conductors frequently prepare the academy orchestras and ensembles ahead of visits by outside guest conductors.[43]

## Main Conducting Teacher

The head of conducting in the RAM is Sian Edwards, who switched from French horn to conducting while a student at the Royal Northern College of Music in Manchester. Initial lessons with Sir Charles Groves, Timothy Reynish, and Norman Del Mar led to studies with Ilya Musin at the Saint Petersburg Conservatory. These were followed by success at the Leeds Conductors Competition and a flourishing career in the opera house and the concert hall. Alongside her conducting work, Edwards has always taught on an individual basis, and before her RAM appointment in 2013, she taught conducting at the Guildhall School of Music and Drama, London. In October 2022, Edwards commenced a conducting position at the University of Music and the Performing Arts, Vienna, and she divides her time between there and London. She continues to have an active career as a guest conductor, in addition to her teaching activities, and she is much in demand as a guest tutor on conducting courses and masterclasses.[44]

Edwards has spoken of her aim to share the legacy of her mentor, the legendary Russian conducting pedagogue Ilya Musin,[45] whose influence as a teacher can still be felt today, more than two decades after his passing. In a teaching career spanning over six decades, in addition to Edwards, he taught numerous conductors of international reputation, including Semyon Bychkov, Martyn Brabbins, Yuri Temirkanov, Tugan Sokhiev, and Alice Farnham.

Sian Edwards is one of the few female leaders of postgraduate conducting courses in the world. In an interview with the author, she noted that although the number of women applying for the RAM postgraduate conducting programme is high, the success rate for entry is low. Edwards is actively working to address this, establishing the Glover–Edwards Conducting Programme,[46] which focuses on equipping female conductors with the skills and confidence to compete at audition with their male counterparts.[47] Recent RAM graduate and alumna of the Glover–Edwards Programme, Charlotte Corduroy is currently forging a successful career with a number of assistant conductor posts.

Edwards asks her students to study the scores in great detail in order to "show me something that you own—even if it is just the first two bars." The underlying teaching principles of her former teacher Ilya Musin are still an influence, although enhanced by Edwards's thirty-five years of global experience. She points to the immediacy of response from working with two pianos as a litmus test for gestural efficiency, but not at the expense of the interplay between conductor and orchestra, the intangible interaction between gestural intent of rhythm, character, and idea that comes from the *auftakt* (upbeat) and the resultant sound.

She supports her students in their conducting projects within the RAM, and also externally, deliberately avoiding overloading them with an unmanageable volume of repertoire. The emphasis is on deep engagement, rather than rattling through the music. The door is always open for graduates who would like some support, and an outside eye in those delicate years between graduation and gaining a career foothold. It is an 'aftercare service' that can make all the difference in the competitive conducting profession. The approach is clearly successful, with recent graduates Jonathon Heyward and Ben Glassberg, among others, winning high-profile conducting appointments and international conducting competitions.

### Bridge to the Profession

The RAM conducting alumni form a solid network, with students benefiting from alumni connections in London, the UK, and further afield. Edward's ongoing mentoring relationship with her conducting graduates has extended into the profession. One recent example is Chloe Rooke, who worked as assistant to fellow RAM graduate Ben Glassberg at Glyndebourne and Rouen before undertaking her own opera engagements in the Netherlands.[48]

## Looking at All Three Programmes

### Choice of Programmes

Each postgraduate course differs slightly in its approach to preparing conductors for the profession. The three programmes chosen have a proven international profile within the orchestral community, hence the decision to focus on these particular institutions, but others such as the Royal Northern College of Music (RNCM), Manchester,[49] Hochschule für Musik, Weimar, and the Vienna University of Music and Performing Arts could equally have been chosen.

### Choosing the Students

In each conducting programme, the audition process is an important initial filter. Audition success, as a verification of sorts, reassures industry professionals that the postgraduate student has a baseline of musical and technical skill, as well as a robust support system for their development, at least for the duration of their course. Both Johannes Schlaefli and Sibelius Academy conducting course coordinator Arturo Alvarado admit that the audition process is flawed in its short time frame,[50] with some talented conductors inevitably falling through the cracks of the selection process. Schlaefli, among other teachers, uses the longer external masterclass format to identify potential students before inviting them to apply for his course in ZHdK.[51] In Finland, Jorma Panula's 'sandbox,' in which young musicians come for an informal conducting session with an ad hoc ensemble of their peers, has proved to be a very effective way of identifying talent at an early age. From the sandbox, potential conductors as young as twelve years old have been spotted and mentored by Panula and the Finnish conducting fraternity, emerging onto the international stage in their early twenties with a decade of conducting experience already accumulated.[52]

The conducting profession has always relied upon mentorship and connection to ensure that emerging conductors gain experience, opportunity, and exposure. Postgraduate conducting courses could be seen as a systemized extension of this, graduates emerging with a guaranteed baseline of the requisite skills necessary to "manage and get out alive" from professional guest conducting engagements.[53]

*Some Reservations*

The welcome rejection of the old, dictatorial conducting style has been replaced with a new, collegial approach to the conductor–orchestra relationship. But where does collaboration end and complacency begin? Are traditions passed down from the batons of Strauss and Mahler being lost because high-profile careers have been embarked upon too early? As Mark Wigglesworth points out, conductors set the standard for how orchestral music is performed, and, whether they admit it or not, orchestral players look to the conductor to achieve the highest possible standards.[54] These standards can only be achieved through effective and, hopefully, inspiring rehearsals. It is a source of immense frustration for orchestra members to listen to poetic descriptions of interpretive fancies when glaring issues of ensemble, balance, and articulation have not been addressed by the conductor, but, equally, the magic of the music must never disappear.

*Possible Training Additions*

Rehearsal technique is something that is acquired on the job, and each conductor finds their own way to the best performance possible with the ensemble. In my own work, particularly with contemporary music, I find myself drawing on my training as an engineer, in particular, the problem-solving abilities honed over eight years of combined study and postgraduate experience. The ability to create a hierarchy of technical issues swiftly, home in on one that will potentially solve others, and effect solutions from a number of options has saved much gnashing of teeth among the ensembles with which I work. As in everything, the key is to balance this cerebral approach with an artistic one, while always listening, gauging the level of ensemble resistance, and comparing the results to a musical idea informed by good taste. I am not advocating for the addition of engineering studies to the already challenging range of support studies included in postgraduate conductor training, but perhaps a semester of problem solving targeted at developing faster aural analytical responses would form the basis for a systematic approach to rehearsing more effectively.

It is no coincidence that many of the celebrated conductors of the past were also composers. My own undergraduate composition training really helped in understanding the process by which a piece is created. The advantages of thinking like a composer are abundant, according to conductor and pedagogue Harold Farberman, whose conducting students at Bard Conservatory, New York were required to complete one full composition for orchestra during their training.[55] Composition still features in the Bard conductor training programme today, and is something that could also be considered for European conducting courses.

As we work to maintain and build audiences, a certain level of improvisational creativity would go a long way towards more spontaneity in the performance of the familiar canonic warhorses. Perhaps an exploration into the training and working practices of the Association for the Advancement of Creative Musicians (AACM) would give a much-needed change of perspective when appraising possibilities for the creative training of conductors.[56]

**The Future?**

Following Covid-19, we find ourselves in a very changed musical world. The Black Lives Matter movement has prompted a welcome re-evaluation of how and what we programme in orchestral concerts. Schemes to promote diversity and inclusion within the orchestral community will hopefully start to reap meaningful results in the coming years. At the heart of these developments is a broadening of the potential for new ideas and directions within the classical music industry. Yet, if everyone working at the upper levels of the industry has gone through roughly similar training, the potential for thinking outside the box is lessened. The proliferation of postgraduate conductor programmes, all offering variations on a similar training path to the profession, could be seen as a double-edged sword in this regard—on the one hand improving general skill levels within the profession, but, on the other hand, strengthening the insider culture that is a by-product of graduate mentor–mentee networks.

## In Conclusion

Real diversity will only come when the classical music industry becomes a true meritocracy. For this to occur, huge power and financial shifts are necessary in the industry, and barriers such as age, gender, and training need to be re-evaluated. In this utopian environment, widespread and wide-ranging music education programmes would empower audiences and orchestra management teams to decide for themselves what is good, rather than deferring to the industry public relations machine to decide on their behalf. In this ideal world, orchestra management and artistic planners would have access to specialist training in critical comparative listening, as well as sitting in on at least two conducting masterclass sessions every year. With knowledge would come the confidence to reach outside the powerful music agency machinery, to find conductors who would really help orchestras reach new musical heights.

Sadly, this is a highly unlikely scenario, and, in the end, it is the artform itself—and our experience of it—that is slowly being eroded by ordinary performances lauded as extraordinary. Audiences have been slow to return to the live concert experience, and as conductors we find ourselves on the frontline in the fight for the future of music-making. In many ways, diversity and new ideas represent the best hope for the continued survival of 'classical music.' Changing how conductors are trained at conservatoire level, equipping them with gestural and musical skills, while also developing their creativity, is part of the solution. But until the classical music world truly begins to look outward and orchestra management dares to reach beyond the established industry networks for conducting talent, we risk going around in ever decreasing circles until inevitable disappearance.

## Notes

1 Cited in Liz Garnett, "The Conductor's Charisma," Mastersinger, Winter 2011, https://www.abcd.org.uk/storage/Mastersinger_archive/The_Conductors_Charisma_Liz_Garnett.pdf.
2 Italian Arturo Toscanini (1867–1957) was principal conductor of the New York Philharmonic and NBC Orchestra among others. He got his big break by stepping in for the conductor of a production of Verdi's *Aida* while touring as part of the cello section of an opera orchestra in Rio de Janeiro in 1886. American composer and conductor Leonard Bernstein (1918–90) was Assistant Conductor of the New York Philharmonic when he stepped in for Bruno Walter in 1943, conducting without a rehearsal, and launching his international career.

3. Michael Dervan, "Leader of the Pack: The Strange Art of Conducting," *Irish Times*, 15 November 2021.
4. Mark Wigglesworth, *The Silent Musician: Why Conducting Matters* (London: Faber & Faber, 2018), 221.
5. Wigglesworth, *The Silent Musician*, 221.
6. Garnett, "The Conductor's Charisma."
7. Harold Farberman, "Training Conductors," in *The Cambridge Handbook of Conducting*, ed. José Antonio Bowen (New York: Cambridge University Press, 2003), chap. 18, Kindle, https://doi.org/10.1017/CCOL9780521821087.019.
8. Survey carried out by author using orchestra database on Musical Chairs and internet research. The table of results is available at Sinead Hayes, "Perspectives on Conducting: Teaching the Unteachable: Conducting Chapter Resources," accessed 22 June 2023, https://www.sineadhayes.net/perspectives-on-conducting-teaching-the-unteachable-conducting-chapter-resources.
9. For a more thorough examination of orchestral postgraduate training in Europe and the United States, see Luke William Dollman, "Orchestral Conductor Training: An Evaluative Study of Current International Practice at the Tertiary Level" (PhD diss., University of Adelaide, 2013), https://docslib.org/doc/13427449/orchestral-conductor-training-an-evaluative-survey-of-current-international-practice-at-the-tertiary-level.
10. "Merger of the Arts Universities," Uniarts Helsinki, updated 15 February 2023, https://www.uniarts.fi/en/general-info/our-history/.
11. Dollman, "Orchestral Conductor Training," 87–88.
12. "Sibelius Academy Admission Statistics," Uniarts Helsinki, accessed 15 September 2022, https://www.uniarts.fi/en/documents/admissions-statistics/.
13. Zoom Interview with Sibelius Academy Conducting Course Coordinator Arturo Alvarado, 16 November 2022.
14. Interview with Arturo Alvarado, 16 November 2022.
15. "Sakari Oramo," interview by Michael Seal, A Mic on the Podium, podcast, episode 36, broadcast 29 November 2020, https://www.listennotes.com/podcasts/a-mic-on-the-podium/episode-36-sakari-oramo-Xt52HyUqb6E/, 1:40.
16. "Sakari Oramo," 11:00.
17. "Sakari Oramo," 54:00.
18. "Sakari Oramo," 1:02:00.
19. Esa-Pekka Salonen highlights this as a major factor in the success of Finnish conductors: "The professional established musical life has the guts to invest in young people, with the risk that this entails." "Esa-Pekka Salonen on Radical Success in Music Education," ArtistsHouseMusic, YouTube, video, 14:29, published 16 November 2011, https://youtu.be/B_IxARWyMIA.
20. "Finnish Conductor Kristian Sallinen Joins HarrisonParrott for Worldwide General Management," News, HarrisonParrott, published 7 June 2023, https://www.harrisonparrott.com/news/2023-06-07/finnish-conductor-kristian-sallinen-joins-harrisonparrott-for.
21. Conductors Esa-Pekka Salonen, Jukka-Pekka Saraste, Hannu Lintu, and Dalia Stasevska.
22. "An Interview with Hannu Lintu," Eatock Daily, blog, published 19 March 2013, https://www.colineatock.com/eatock-daily-blog/an-interview-with-hannu-lintu.
23. "Predecessor Institutions of Zurich University of the Arts," Zürcher Hochschule der Künste, accessed 25 September 2022, https://www.zhdk.ch/en/aboutus/history-575.
24. Dollman, "Orchestral Conductor Training," 139.

25 "Christoph-Mathias Mueller Appointed New Lecturer in Orchestral Conducting at ZHdK," Zürcher Hochschule der Künste, accessed 25 September 2022, https://www.zhdk.ch/en/news/christoph-mathias-mueller-appointed-new-lecturer-in-orchestral-conducting-at-zhdk-5491.
26 Dollman, "Orchestral Conductor Training," 40.
27 €1,483 and €2,513 as of October 2022.
28 Zoom interview with Johannes Schlaefli, 2 November 2022.
29 "Kerem Hasan," interview by Michael Seal, A Mic on the Podium, podcast, episode 36, broadcast 6 June 2021, https://www.listennotes.com/podcasts/a-mic-on-the-podium/episode-63-kerem-hasan-UX-E_jKOPeH/, 17:00.
30 "Kerem Hasan," 19:33.
31 "Kerem Hasan," 19:10.
32 "Johannes Schlaefli," Conducting Academy Johannes Schlaefli, accessed 24 September 2023, https://conductingacademy.ch/johannes-schlaefli-2/.
33 "A simple, consistent philosophy of teaching," Kirk Trevor, accessed 25 September 2022, https://kirktrevor.com/main/teaching/.
34 "Kerem Hasan," 18:52.
35 Interview with conductor James Lowe, 10 September 2022.
36 Zoom interview with Johannes Schlaefli, 2 November 2022.
37 "Gstaad Conducting Academy – Prof. Johannes Schlaefli," Gstaad Menuhin Festival, Facebook, video, posted 15 August 2021, https://www.facebook.com/GstaadAcademy/videos/373869574260373, 0:18.
38 "Gstaad Conducting Academy – Prof. Johannes Schlaefli," 3:04.
39 Zoom interview with Johannes Schlaefli, 2 November 2022.
40 "Royal Academy of Music," University of London, accessed 27 September 2022, https://www.london.ac.uk/ways-study/study-campus-london/member-institutions/royal-academy-music.
41 "Alumni," Royal Academy of Music, accessed 27 September 2022, https://www.ram.ac.uk/alumni/meet-our-alumni?departments=conducting.
42 €15,255 and €32,770 as of October 2022. "Fees," Royal Academy of Music, accessed 27 September 2022, https://www.ram.ac.uk/study/fees-scholarships-and-bursaries/fees.
43 Zoom interview with Sian Edwards, 9 October 2022.
44 "Sian Edwards," Royal Academy of Music, accessed 27 September 2022, https://www.ram.ac.uk/people/sian-edwards.
45 "Sian Edwards," interview by Marie Claire Breen, Artistic Futures, podcast, episode 4, broadcast 24 November 2021, https://www.operanorth.co.uk/news/artistic-futures-episode-4/, 22:00.
46 Previously called the Sorrell Conducting Course.
47 "Sorrell Women Conductor's Programme," Royal Academy of Music, accessed 27 September 2022, https://www.ram.ac.uk/news/sorrell-women-conductors-programme.
48 Ben Glassberg and Chloe Rooke, "Conductors Ben Glassberg and Chloe Rooke," interview by Annette Isserlis, Tea with Netty, podcast, broadcast 19 August 2022, https://www.listennotes.com/podcasts/tea-with-netty/tea-with-netty-conductors-L4yK_QXY0lu/, 22:00, 13:27.
49 The RNCM conducting department continues to go from strength to strength and in January 2021 was a partner in the creation of a comprehensive online conducting teaching resource ConductIT (https://conductit.eu/).
50 Dollman, "Orchestral Conductor Training," 147.
51 The author has observed this first hand, as well as hearing from other Schlaefli students who initially applied to masterclasses and were invited to apply for the master's in Zurich.

52 The author first heard about the 'sandbox' during conversations with Finnish conductors at the Fiskars Festival 2022.
53 "Sakari Oramo," 16:00.
54 Wigglesworth, *The Silent Musician*, 220.
55 Farberman, "Training Conductors."
56 "Mission Statement," Association for the Advancement of Creative Musicians, accessed 24 September 2023, https://www.aacmchicago.org/.

# 2
# THE CONDUCTOR AS APPRENTICE
## The *Kapellmeister* Route to Opera Conducting

*Killian Farrell*

> The *Kapellmeister*: An indication of all things that one must fully know and be able to do, who wishes to stand before an ensemble with honour and integrity.
>
> Johann Mattheson (1739)[1]

The coaching of singers from the piano, the preparation of an orchestra for an operatic production, the conducting of off-stage musicians, rehearsing the chorus, editing orchestral parts, and of course, conducting performances in an opera house—these are just some of the many tasks that comprise the duties of a *Kapellmeister*, the German word meaning 'master of the band.' The '*Kapellmeister* tradition' refers to a career path that begins with various positions as a staff conductor, typically in regional opera houses, as a method of developing a conductor's skill and repertoire.[2] As a young conductor training in Ireland, I was fascinated by this word. I read it for the first time in biographies of my favourite composers: Mendelssohn, Wagner, and Mahler are among the many composers to have held the title of *Kapellmeister* during their careers. I became aware that it referred to a system prevalent in German-speaking opera houses, a sort of apprenticeship that trained young conductors in all aspects of the operatic craft and gave them the skills they needed to become competent opera conductors. However, beyond this vague beginning, I found it impossible to find any literature in English that comprehensively explained the structure of a German opera house, and the route that would lead one to become a *Kapellmeister*. My hope is that this chapter will serve precisely this need, explaining the role of the *Kapellmeister* as a craftsperson in the modern-day opera house, and also the unique organizational structure of a German theatre.

## Background

The conducting profession has undergone a marked change since the second half of the twentieth century. Before the advent of conducting competitions, fellowships, and assistant conductor positions, there was only one route available to the aspiring conductor in the "Central European Tradition"[3]—the long and arduous path through provincial theatres, taking positions as repetiteur, chorus master, and junior conductor to gather experience and develop a repertoire. Almost every major conductor of the late nineteenth and early twentieth century made the so-called *Ochsentournee* through the provinces, a German word that translates as 'hard slog.' Richard Wagner in Würzburg and Riga, Richard Strauss in Meiningen and Munich, and Gustav Mahler in Kassel and Prague are just three examples of major musical figures who started their careers as conductors in the opera house. A later generation of conductors, who became known almost exclusively for their work in the concert hall, still served their apprenticeships in the theatre; George Szell, whose reputation rests on his astonishing achievements with the Cleveland Orchestra, was *Kapellmeister* at the Berlin Hofoper (the present-day Staatsoper unter den Linden), where he assisted Richard Strauss. The early careers of Fritz Reiner in Dresden and Bruno Walter in Cologne and Hamburg were similarly dominated by positions in the theatre, which laid the basis for their later work in the symphonic field.

The advent of the 'star conductor' has done much to change the way conductors are educated, and careers are made. The creation of conducting competitions made overnight success a possibility, and it is somewhat fitting that Herbert von Karajan advised the jury at the inaugural International Conducting Competition in Berlin in 1969 that "it isn't a question of filling a Second *Kapellmeister*'s post, but of finding an explosive new talent. Whether that talent is already fully formed or not is completely irrelevant."[4] It is an irony typical of this transformation in the conducting profession that Karajan, himself a product of the theatre system, would use the term *Kapellmeister* in such a disparaging fashion. The qualities that the word *Kapellmeister* represents—a long apprenticeship, a service to the work at hand, a hard-won mastery of craft—are still ideals to which all conductors should aspire. Indeed, the qualities of musical literacy, linguistic ability, and a deep knowledge of the operatic repertoire that were identified by Erich Leinsdorf as essential to the conducting profession are precisely those honed by daily work in the opera house.[5] And yet, the perception of a *Kapellmeister* as a staid functionary devoid of inspiration is deeply embedded in our contemporary musical culture. Christian Thielemann, one of the foremost living exponents of the *Kapellmeister* tradition, identifies this issue with an anecdote from his early career:

> I was conducting . . . in London, and I heard someone saying about a conductor . . . "oh, he is only a *Kapellmeister*." I was surprised, because I had grown up with a very positive meaning of *Kapellmeister*, and then they explained to me, "*Kapellmeister* means that it's a very boring . . . conductor with no fantasy."[6]

The concept that, in the words of Leopold Stokowski, "conductors are born and not made" has contributed to the mythology surrounding the figure of the conductor as an *Übermensch*.[7] A Promethean struggle against opposing forces in the form of a conducting competition, or a meteoric breakthrough, is much more attractive to promoters and orchestral managers than a steady rise through the opera house. However, in the Central European conducting tradition that we are discussing, the role of the *Kapellmeister* as conductor and servant of the work at hand has been evolving since the beginning of the eighteenth century—as we shall see later, initially as composer–conductor, and later evolving into solely performing conductor.

## The History of the *Kapellmeister*

One of the first recorded usages of the term *Kapellmeister* was in Johann Mattheson's treatise on the *Vollkommener Kapellmeister* (the complete *Kapellmeister*). He considered the term a "general indication of all things that one must know and be able to do, who wishes to stand before an ensemble with honour and integrity."[8] Mattheson also assumed the words '*Kapellmeister*' and 'Composer' to be synonyms, an assumption common in literature of the time.[9] Heinrich Christoph Koch, in his *Musikalisches Lexikon*, describes a *Kapellmeister* as:

> The foremost member or leader of an ensemble (*Kapelle*). In courts with ensembles, in the realms of sacred music or the opera, or both together, the *Kapellmeister* is he who is to compose works specifically required for court events, to choose and perform other works, and to lead the direction of the entire musical performance.[10]

The definition of the term *Kapellmeister* remained remarkably consistent until the middle of the nineteenth century, at which point the compositional elements of the position began to recede, and the *Kapellmeister* was considered primarily as a performing musician, albeit one who remained the disciplinary leader of an ensemble.[11] The period of greatest development in the craft of conducting took place around this time, between 1820 and 1850. This was the period in which the baton, or a similar implement for time-beating, became commonplace for the leadership of an ensemble. Felix Mendelssohn Bartholdy and Ludwig Spohr were the figureheads of conducting in a period which led to the standardization of visual signals instead of auditory time-beating, and insistence on rehearsal conditions that would be conducive to a high standard of performance.[12]

The musician to exert the greatest influence on the Central European conducting tradition was undoubtedly Richard Wagner. In his treatise *On Conducting*, he described the state of music-making around 1850 as suffering under the "increasing negligence [of our arts institutions] in their choice of conductors."[13] He writes of his admiration for the "*Kapellmeister* [of an older generation who] was a formidable personage, who knew how to make himself respected at his post; sure of his business, strict, and far from polite," and disparages the contemporary trend to appoint conductors to the court operas in:

> An erratic manner—grand personages [who] begin to flourish under the protection of the lady in waiting to some princess, etc. It is impossible to estimate the harm done to our leading orchestras and opera theatres by such nonentities.[14]

It is unsurprising that such polemic would have stemmed from the pen of Wagner, a figure who heralded a revolutionary change in music history, both as a composer and as a conductor. His subjective approach to musical interpretation, believing that performance is a creative and not merely a recreative act, inspired the next generation of *Kapellmeisters*, who were, in the words of Raymond Holden:

> Nurtured by [the culture fostered by Wagner] as young musicians as they rose through the opera-house system, provided with a repertoire of works that was the basis for their programme policies, and were given a sense of belonging that was unique in the history of performance.[15]

The foremost musician among the acolytes of Wagner was Hans von Bülow, perhaps the prototype of the modern conductor.

Hans von Bülow (1830–94) was a true disciple of Wagner, conducting the premieres of *Tristan und Isolde* and *Die Meistersinger von Nürnberg*, as well as assisting him earlier in his career in Zurich, where Wagner was working as a conductor while in exile after the May Uprising in

Dresden in 1849. As Wagner himself had done, von Bülow worked in a number of opera houses at the beginning of his career in a variety of positions: as repetiteur, chorus master, and later *Kapellmeister*. He held the successive positions of *Hofkapellmeister* (the chief conductor of a court opera house or orchestra) in Munich, Hannover, and Meiningen, and most particularly in Meiningen was responsible for a number of orchestral reforms, chief among them being the introduction of pedal timpani and the five-string double bass.[16] He played a key role in further developing the modern profession of the *Kapellmeister*, and also took a keen interest in promoting younger colleagues. The position of assistant conductor in Meiningen was highly coveted, and in 1885 the then twenty-one-year-old composer and conductor Richard Strauss was appointed.[17] It was to be the first in a series of *Kapellmeister* positions for Strauss, culminating in his appointments as the *Generalmusikdirektor* of the Hofoper in Berlin and the Staatsoper in Vienna.[18] In Vienna he had been preceded by Gustav Mahler, a further example of the tradition of the conductor–composers who, like Wagner and Strauss, had forged their careers in the opera house. Mahler had a particularly itinerant path through provincial theatres, holding positions in Bad Hall, Ljubljana, Olomouc, Kassel, Leipzig, and Hamburg, before finally taking the position of director of the Vienna Hofoper. Strauss and Mahler marked the last of the great conductor–composers who presided over the opera in Vienna, and they both succeeded in instigating reforms and improving musical standards.[19]

Conductors from the following generation were known primarily as performers, although many of them continued to compose during their performing careers. This generation was heavily influenced by their predecessors, Mahler and Strauss, and includes Bruno Walter, Otto Klemperer, and Wilhelm Furtwängler. These three conductors each held positions as *Hofkapellmeister* or *Generalmusikdirektor* in German opera houses, although they are better known today for their recordings in the symphonic field. Perhaps the first conductor to serve as a model for the *Kapellmeister*-as-performer was Herbert von Karajan. He had no aspirations to compose his own music, but was determined as a young musician to become a conductor, and worked in Ulm and Aachen as *Kapellmeister*, building a large repertoire under adverse conditions.[20] His later success as principal conductor of the Berlin Philharmonic led him to become the most recorded conductor of his generation. Since Karajan, countless conductors have followed his path as purely recreative artists, working in a series of smaller opera houses to learn repertoire before becoming the music director of a major institution. These include such figures as Wolfgang Sawallisch, Christoph von Dohnányi, and Kirill Petrenko.

## The Role of the *Kapellmeister* Today

The modern *Kapellmeister* works within the constraints of the German repertoire system, a method of planning the productions of a theatre to perform a large number of pieces in constant rotation. It stands in direct contrast to the *stagione* system, which is used in Ireland and the United Kingdom. In the *stagione* system, a production is rehearsed and performed over a short period of time, normally six to eight weeks, before the next production is rehearsed and performed, and there is no rotation of different operas at the same time. In a *stagione* theatre, singers and conductors will be engaged on short-term contracts to perform individual productions. The advantage of this system is that it can lead to very high artistic quality—every production is rehearsed extensively, and the performers, chorus, and orchestra have the luxury of only having to focus on one operatic production at a time. The disadvantage is that it can lead to a lack of variety in the season and offers the public only a limited number of productions.

In a repertoire theatre, an ensemble of singers is engaged as resident artists to perform a number of operatic roles each season, depending on the *fach* or categorization of each singer.[21] As the ensemble is permanently employed by the theatre, and theoretically available at all times during the season, the theatre can schedule productions of multiple operas that run concurrently. This provides the audience with a wide choice of operas to attend in any given week—it is not unusual to see up to five different operas being presented over the course of seven days in a German theatre. However, from an artistic standpoint, there are two main challenges presented by the repertoire system:

1. There can be many weeks, or perhaps even months, between performances of a particular opera, without rehearsals between.
2. The orchestra does not consist of the same players for each performance. Instead, there is a pool of musicians, meaning that each performance has a different group of musicians playing.[22]

In the modern German opera house, the engagement of a *Kapellmeister*, a conductor familiar with the entire repertoire of the house and with a close relationship to the ensemble, chorus, and orchestra, is a safeguard to ensure that the musical quality of each performance is maintained under these often-adverse conditions. The repertoire system developed in a time when the standards of musical performance, and the expectations of the public, were very different to those of today. In the 1850s, for instance, at the dawn of the modern theatre system, it was not unusual for the viola section to consist primarily of wind players who had had only basic training on a string instrument.[23] Some 170 years later, the standard of musical execution is exceptionally high and thoroughly professionalized, and audiences expect a degree of technical competence in every operatic performance, even within the constraints of the repertoire system. The training of a *Kapellmeister* produces a conductor with a toolkit to facilitate a performance under these adverse conditions, with little to no rehearsal time.

### The Structure of a German Opera House

The theatre system in Germany, Austria, and Switzerland is built upon the model of a *Mehrspartenhaus* (multi-department theatre). This refers to the disciplines of *Musiktheater* (opera), *Schauspiel* (spoken-word theatre), and dance or ballet that co-exist together under the umbrella of a larger theatre organization. These theatres are known as *Stadttheatern* (municipal theatres) or *Staatstheatern* (state theatres) depending on the source of the theatre's funding.[24] Each theatre with a *Musiktheater* department can be further divided into one of five categories, referring to the number of full-time positions in the orchestra.[25] These categories are:

A. More than ninety-nine full-time positions.
B+. Between seventy-eight and ninety-eight full-time positions.
B. Between sixty-six and seventy-seven full-time positions.
C. Between fifty-six and sixty-five full-time positions.
D. Fewer than fifty-six full-time positions.

These categories are considered as approximate markers of the budget, and therefore the regional or national significance, of an opera house.

The music department of a German opera house is organized in a strict hierarchy with clearly defined roles, as outlined in the following sections.[26]

### *Generalmusikdirektor*

The chief conductor of an opera house, and the person responsible for the musical standards of the orchestra and ensemble. They are involved in the planning of the repertoire and the selection of singers during auditions, and also decide on the allocation of conducting assignments within the opera house, among guest conductors and *Kapellmeisters*. When the orchestra of the opera house plays symphony concerts, the *Generalmusikdirektor* will typically be the conductor of these concerts, and will invite soloists to take part in the concert series.

### First *Kapellmeister*

This is the next most senior conductor in the hierarchy of an opera house, and they often conduct more performances per season than the *Generalmusikdirektor*. They will typically rehearse and perform two to three of their own productions in an operatic season, as well as conducting performances of a production that the *Generalmusikdirektor* has rehearsed when he or she is not present—this is known as a *Nachdirigat* ('conducting after'). The position of First *Kapellmeister* is more common in smaller theatres—many larger opera houses have eliminated the position and instead rely on a roster of guest conductors.

### Second *Kapellmeister*

This position is normally occupied by a repetiteur who will spend part of their time playing for musical and scenic rehearsals, and part of their time conducting. They are seldom responsible for their own productions, but will take over many performances of the productions of the *Generalmusikdirektor* and First *Kapellmeister*, typically without rehearsal. This position is often combined with that of the *Studienleiter*, *Chordirektor*, or perhaps the musical assistant to the *Generalmusikdirektor*.

### *Studienleiter*

The word *Studienleiter* translates as 'director of studies,' and they are the head pianist or vocal coach of a German opera house. They are responsible for the daily planning of the music department, including the coaching that each singer in the ensemble will receive to ensure that they are fully prepared for a role by the beginning of each rehearsal period. They are often responsible for conducting backstage music, and during orchestral rehearsals they take notes for the singers on diction, articulation, and expression to help them optimize their performances.

### *Chordirektor*

The *Chordirektor* is responsible for the preparation of the professional chorus in an opera house. They will lead musical rehearsals to teach the chorus singers the pitches and rhythms of works they are to perform, and will attend all rehearsals and performances in which the chorus sings, to make any necessary corrections and adjustments. It is not unusual, particularly in smaller theatres, for the *Chordirektor* to conduct choral concerts in conjunction with the orchestra, or perhaps some performances of operas with extensive chorus parts.

## The Training of a *Kapellmeister*

There are as many routes into the so-called *Kapellmeister* system as there are conductors, and in particular those conductors coming from outside the German-speaking world may have varied educational backgrounds. Here, however, I will describe the typical path taken by conductors who start their undergraduate training in Germany. The training of orchestral conductors and repetiteurs goes hand-in-hand in German music conservatories. A study of the conducting curricula of various German conservatories indicates the importance placed on basic repetiteur skills, even if the students are not advanced pianists.[27] The skills developed during the education of a *Korrepetitor* are precisely those required by a conductor working in the operatic field: playing vocal scores on the piano with an awareness of orchestral texture, coaching singers on their roles, and a broad knowledge of the operatic repertoire. The opposite is also true; *Korrepetitors* need to develop a basic conducting technique in order to be able to conduct rehearsals, off-stage music, and perhaps even performances if necessary.

An undergraduate education in a German conservatory consists of eight semesters, with a further four required for a master's qualification. In addition to weekly lessons in conducting and *Korrepetition*, the students also receive lessons on an orchestral instrument, singing, foreign languages, music history and analysis, and composition.[28] At the end of up to six years of study, there are many options available to graduates; some will work as freelance conductors and take part in competitions, and others will apply to be assistant conductors, a position which is becoming increasingly common in concert and radio orchestras. However, many graduates choose to apply for jobs in theatres, as it is a guaranteed form of employment that allows a conductor at the beginning of their career to gather practical experience quickly. For the majority of these young conductors, the first step on the ladder is a position as a *Korrepetitor*, perhaps with conducting responsibilities. The audition for this type of position consists of several parts: playing selections from the operatic literature and singing (or 'marking') the singers' lines at the same time, coaching a singer on an aria or recitative, sight-reading, and playing operatic excerpts with a conductor.[29] If the candidate is successful, they can expect to receive a two-year contract as a repetiteur, and perhaps the chance to take their first steps as a conductor with a handful of performances.

For a position as a *Kapellmeister*, the audition process is more extensive than that of a *Korrepetitor*. The process consists of at least two rounds. The first round is a short rehearsal with the orchestra, known as a *Vordirigat*, after which the orchestra will vote to progress their preferred candidates to the second round. The second round is typically a performance of an opera or operetta in the theatre, without orchestral rehearsal. The difficulty of the work to be performed is dependent on the type of position available and the size of the opera house, but the work will often be a lighter opera in the standard repertoire, such as *L'elisir d'amore* or *Il barbiere di Siviglia*. In addition, the candidate may have to demonstrate their abilities to coach singers from the piano, and also discuss their approach to organizational matters in an interview with the *Intendant* (general manager) of the theatre. As First *Kapellmeister*, a young conductor can begin for the first time to take charge of their own productions and rehearsal processes, while also assisting the *Generalmusikdirektor* and being part of the management team of the theatre.

The length of time it takes for a conductor to progress from *Korrepetitor* to *Kapellmeister*, and perhaps *Generalmusikdirektor*, can vary widely depending on individual career development and opportunity. Many well-known conductors became a *Generalmusikdirektor* at prodigiously young ages: Herbert von Karajan in Aachen at the age of 27, and Christian Thielemann in Nürnberg at the age of 29 are two such examples.[30] Other conductors who achieved fame in the opera house never rose above the position of First *Kapellmeister*, such as Carlos Kleiber, who held that position at the State Opera in Stuttgart from the age of 36 to 42.[31]

**The Future of the *Kapellmeister* System**

There is no doubt that the classical music industry is in a state of change. The German Association of Professional Orchestras (*Deutsche Orchestervereinigung*) publishes a record each season of the number of permanent positions in German orchestras. Since 1992, the number of positions has fallen from 12,159 to 9,749, a decrease of almost 20 per cent.[32] There has also been a decline in the number of attendees in German opera houses, from 4.4 million visitors in the 2008–09 season to 3.8 million visitors in the 2018–19 season.[33] Both of these trends point to a somewhat concerning future for the opera industry in its Teutonic heartland, in a country traditionally regarded as the modern crucible of operatic tradition. Perhaps the most immediate challenge for young conductors in the coming years is the paradigmatic shift in repertoire-planning in Germany: opera houses are concentrating more on individual productions as 'happenings,' or unique artistic events, to the detriment of the repertoire system. This means fewer revivals of older productions, and a smaller repertoire of works to be conducted. Traditionally, a young conductor beginning in the *Kapellmeister* system would start with repertoire performances of technically less-challenging operas or operettas. The quantity of repertoire in a season allowed managers to take greater risks on young conductors; if a conductor's first performance was unsuccessful, it was not a serious failure, because the number of pieces in the season meant that not every performance was expected to function without fault. However, at the time of writing, German opera houses, particularly at the international level, tend to hire guest conductors, rather than relying on in-house *Kapellmeisters*. Indeed, this position no longer exists at the State Operas of Hamburg, Munich, and Dresden, among others, with these opera houses relying on a roster of rotating guest conductors.

However, the opportunities afforded to a young conductor by the *Kapellmeister* system remain arguably unparalleled in any other part of the world. In 2012, the German Theatre Yearbook (*Deutsches Bühnenjahrbuch*) listed 743 personnel as *Musikvorstände*, an umbrella term which refers to positions as *Generalmusikdirektors*, *Kapellmeisters*, and *Chordirektors*.[34] This remarkable figure points to a thriving industry of conductors in full-time employment, who continue to facilitate the daily work of more than eighty opera houses in Germany. These opportunities for employment, and the chance to receive the 'podium time' so necessary for the development of young conductors, continue to attract candidates from all over the world. Despite the changes in the German theatre landscape, the comprehensive apprenticeship that has formed so many conductors over the preceding centuries still offers an unparalleled training in the often mysterious art of operatic conducting. I can only echo the preceding sentiments of Mattheson, that the word *Kapellmeister* indicates "all things that one must know and be able to do, who wishes to stand before an ensemble with honour and integrity." Such honour and integrity, forged over many years in the living tradition of the opera house, are the qualities upon which the *Kapellmeister* system is founded.

## Notes

1 Johann Mattheson, *Der vollkommene Capellmeister* (Kassel: Bärenreiter, 1989; first published 1739).
2 Wolfgang Schreiber, *Große Dirigenten* (Munich: Piper Verlag, 2005), 354.
3 The term coined by Raymond Holden to describe conductors working primarily in the German-speaking world and descending from the conducting lineage of Richard Wagner. See Raymond Holden, *The Virtuoso Conductors: The Central European Tradition from Wagner to Karajan* (New Haven: Yale University Press, 2005), 1.
4 Richard Osborne, *Herbert von Karajan: A Life in Music* (London: Chatto and Windus, 1998), 573.
5 Erich Leinsdorf, *The Composer's Advocate: A Radical Orthodoxy for Musicians* (New Haven: Yale University Press, 1981), 1–19.
6 Christian Thielemann, "A Conductor's Point of View," Weidenfeld-Hoffmann Trust, YouTube, video, 1:03:02, published 27 January 2016, https://youtu.be/efJAPlpkMNQ.

7 Harold Farberman, "Training Conductors," in *The Cambridge Companion to Conducting*, ed. José Antonio Bowen (Cambridge: Cambridge University Press, 2003), 252.
8 Peter Gülke, "Dirigieren," *Musik in Geschichte und Gegenwart*, sachteil 2, ed. Ludwig Finscher (Kassel: Bärenreiter, 2008), 1259.
9 There are many examples of this. See Leopold Mozart to Anna Maria Mozart, in *Mozart: Briefe und Aufzeichnungen*, vol. 1, ed. Wilhelm A. Bauer and Otto Erich Deutsch (Kassel: Bärenreiter, 2005), 413–14.
10 Heinrich Christoph Koch, *Musikalisches Lexikon, welches die theoretische und praktische Tonkunst, encyclopädisch bearbeitet, alle alten und neuen Kunstwörter erklärt, und die alten und neuen Instrumente beschrieben, enthält* (Frankfurt am Main: August Hermann der Jüngere, 1802), 825.
11 Arnold Jacobshagen, "Positionen des Dirigierens," in *Maestro!: Dirigieren im 19. Jahrhundert* (Würzburg: Königshauses & Neumann, 2017), 18.
12 Leon Botstein, "Conducting," *The New Grove Dictionary of Music and Musicians*, vol. 6, ed. Stanley Sadie and John Tyrrell (London: MacMillan, 2001), 261–75.
13 Richard Wagner, *On Conducting*, trans. Edward Dannreuther (New York: Dover Publications, 1989), 2.
14 Wagner, *On Conducting*, 5–6.
15 José Antonio Bowen, "Mendelssohn, Berlioz and Wagner as Conductors: The Origins of the Ideal of 'Fidelity to the Composer'," *Performance Practice Review* 6, no. 1 (Spring 1993): 77–88 (85); Holden, *The Virtuoso Conductors*, 8.
16 Holden, *The Virtuoso Conductors*, 26.
17 Strauss won the position over several highly regarded musical figures of the time, including Felix von Weingartner and Gustav Mahler, who had written an application letter to Bülow that read: "At the concert yesterday [of the *Meininger Hofkapelle* in Kassel] I felt myself in the presence of the greatest beauty that I had ever divined or hoped for, everything became clear to me. I thought: here is your home, here your master; today or never you must end your search." Henri Louis de la Grange, *Mahler* (New York: Doubleday & Company, 1973), 112.
18 Raymond Holden, *Richard Strauss: A Musical Life* (New Haven: Yale University Press, 2011), 95–106.
19 Holden, *Richard Strauss*, 93.
20 Holden, *The Virtuoso Conductors*, 227. He conducted works such as Strauss's *Arabella* in Ulm, a piece that normally requires an orchestra of eighty musicians, and yet he had to somehow perform the work with a contingent of only thirty-two.
21 The categorization of each role in the standard operatic repertoire is laid out in the standard reference work by Rudolf Kloiber and Wolf Kunold, *Handbuch der Oper* (Kassel: Bärenreiter, 2019).
22 The absurdity of this system has been well known for centuries. Carl Maria von Weber, upon his appointment as conductor of the opera house in Wrocław in 1804, sought to schedule rehearsals before every revival of an older production (known as a *Wiederaufnahme*) to raise the standards of performance. The theatre director was, understandably, dissatisfied with the added cost of these rehearsals, and this appears to have been a factor in Weber's departure from the theatre in 1806.
23 Wagner, *On Conducting*, 4.

24 There are a handful of opera houses in larger cities that exist independently, without being attached to other artistic disciplines, such as the State Operas of Hamburg, Berlin, and Munich.
25 "Statistik Planstellen und Einstufung der Berufsorchester," Unisono, accessed 5 October 2022, https://uni-sono.org/klassikland-deutschland/statistik-planstellen-einstufung-berufsorchester.
26 For a more detailed elucidation of the structure of a German opera house, see Arthur Werner-Jensen, *Oper intern* (Mainz: Schott, 2010).
27 The study plans and credit point assignments of the orchestral conducting undergraduate programmes of the Hochschule für Musik, Weimar (https://www.hfm-weimar.de/fileadmin/user_upload/Studienplaene_und_Ordnungen/Studienplaene/SP_BMus_Orchesterdirigieren.pdf), Hochschule für Musik und Theater, Leipzig, https://www.hmt-leipzig.de/home/fachrichtungen/klavier-dirigieren/studiendokumente_klavier/fileaccess_item_820404/view/sap/ba_di_sap_221026.pdf; and the Hochschule für Musik, Berlin (https://www.hfm-berlin.de/fileadmin/user_upload/Studium/Bachelor/Bachelor_PO_2012/AM_BA_Fachspezifische_Pruefungsordnung_1.pdf#page290), all accessed 12 January 2023, are just three examples that show the heavy weighting attached to repetiteur competencies in orchestral conducting training.
28 This is taking the aforementioned study plans as examples, although all German Hochschulen follow similar study plans.
29 These excerpts are almost invariably the second-act finale from Mozart's *The Marriage of Figaro*, the opening of Puccini's *La Bohème*, the opening scene of Strauss's *Elektra*, and the so-called 'Smugglers' Quintet' from Bizet's *Carmen*.
30 Both conductors had already held positions as *Korrepetitors* and *Kapellmeisters*. For biographical accounts, see Osborne, *Herbert von Karajan*; Christian Thielemann, *My Life with Wagner*, trans. Anthea Bell (London: Weidenfeld & Nicholson, 2015).
31 Charles Barber, *Corresponding with Carlos: A Biography of Carlos Kleiber* (Toronto: Scarecrow Press, 2011), 47–64.
32 "Planstelle der öffentlich finanzierten Orchester," Deutsche Orchestervereinigung, Deutsche Musikinformationszentrum, accessed 4 January 2023, https://miz.org/de/statistiken/planstellen-der-oeffentlich-finanzierten-orchester.
33 "Anzahl der Besucher von Opern in deutschen Theatern in den Spielzeiten 2008/09 bis 2019/20," Statistika, accessed 14 January 2023, https://de.statista.com/statistik/daten/studie/205067.
34 *Deutsches Bühnenjahrbuch 2012. Das große Adressbuch für Bühne, Film, Funk und Fernsehen* (Hamburg: Genossenschaft Deutscher Bühnenangehöriger, 2012), 14.

# 3
# THOUGHTS ON THE ROLE OF THE ASSISTANT CONDUCTOR

Gavin Maloney

During the twenty years of my professional conducting career, I have observed changes, in both type and prevalence, of assistant conductor schemes and fellowships. Historically, the assistant conductor role has been a central pathway into the profession. Notably, three of Gustav Mahler's associates were assistant conductors who went on to become great conductors *tout court*. They were Bruno Walter (1876–1962), Otto Klemperer (1885–1973), and Willem Mengelberg (1871–1951).[1] What do today's assistant conductors have in common with predecessors such as these? Is the role still rooted in the traditional *Kapellmeister* system?[2]

Nowadays many assistant conductor positions are open to applicants, while others are awarded to winners of conducting competitions,[3] and some are made by appointment. The kinds of work entailed in the assistant conductor role vary greatly between regions and organizations. Training schemes typically aspire to connect aspiring conductors with established artists and institutions and to provide a practical learning framework. While conductors must spend a great deal of their time preparing scores in advance of mounting the podium, they, unlike instrumentalists and vocalists, cannot practise alone. Hence, their first steps in gaining practical experience occur, by necessity, in the manner of a public spectacle. Conducting is an activity in which what matters most—experience—is not easily gained, especially at the early stages of professional formation.

Readiness to replace a more senior conductor at a moment's notice is foremost among the assistant conductor's responsibilities. It may be specified contractually which conductor(s), and what repertoire, fall under the assistant's remit. For example, she may solely shadow the principal or chief conductor, or be required to cover guest conductors as well. Faced with a lengthy season's repertoire list, the assistant conductor may well wonder, "how on earth do I manage so very many scores?" This challenge is, in a way, the gift of the position. Many aspiring conductors got their big break through the unexpected cancellation of an established figure. One such case is that of Leonard Bernstein. Aged 25, he was assistant conductor of the New York Philharmonic Orchestra. The first signal of his forthcoming success came on 14 November 1943, when he was summoned unexpectedly to substitute for the conductor Bruno Walter.[4]

The rapid pace of technological advancement impacts the working life of the symphony orchestra in myriad ways, some of which impact the duties of the assistant conductor. The trend away from paper, towards screens, is noticeable among performing musicians globally.[5] One imagines the day when orchestral musicians no longer read from printed pages. As one of the duties of the assistant conductor is to 'mark-up' the parts on behalf of the conductor, this type of technology may well make life a good deal easier in the future. In the meantime, however, the manual labour of inserting dynamics, phrase marks, corrected notes, and sometimes even bowings will continue to take a considerable amount of time. Depending on the repertoire, this area of responsibility also extends to re-orchestration, researching historically informed ornamentation, and even solving metrical problems that a new score may throw up.

Technology has also transformed the way backstage music is performed. The original occasional distant trumpet call (e.g., in Beethoven's *Fidelio* and *Leonore Overture No. 3*) became a striking feature of some nineteenth-century repertoire. One finds enormously effective examples of musicians *in der Ferne* (in the distance) in Mahler's Symphony No. 2 and Richard Strauss's *Eine Alpensinfonie*, for example. The latter is performed with twelve horns, two trumpets, and two trombones *hinter der Scene* (behind the scenes). These ensembles are typically placed in the assistant conductor's charge. Co-ordinating them with the main orchestra is a challenge, aided in recent decades by closed circuit television cameras and television monitors. Ives's Symphony No. 4 is an altogether different example of an orchestral work requiring more than one conductor. In this, "one of his most definitive works,"[6] the conductors must manage off-stage musicians, simultaneous combinations of differing time signatures, and simultaneous combinations of differing tempi.

Depending on the approach and availability of the principal conductor and guest conductors, the assistant conductor will typically be required to take rehearsals. In this respect, as in others, her role and responsibilities often resemble that of a junior conductor in the German *Kapellmeister* system. Rehearsing for another conductor is a unique task: enormously beneficial in terms of the experience gained, and challenging in that it requires one to achieve ends determined by another musical mind.

When the assistant conductor assumes responsibilities for outreach and education, he is given an opportunity to contribute value in domains of considerable importance. Any orchestra interested in its own future cares deeply about cultivating audiences and communicating the wider value of orchestral music generally. In this respect, the role of assistant conductor can be twofold, involving both the design of workshops, performance-presentations, and concert programmes and their subsequent delivery. Such work is significant in that several stakeholders—manager, orchestral musician, child, teacher, patient, prisoner, conductor—may be brought together through the power of music.[7]

Aside from conducting concerts, the main role of the assistant conductor is that of a ready replacement; most of their time is spent preparing to stand in. Depending on the appointment, this, unsurprisingly, demands a great deal of time. A cycle of Bruckner symphonies, a series of Stravinsky ballets, or—perhaps even more challenging—a season without a thread running through it, is the workaday stuff of many an experienced conductor. For the assistant conductor, there is nothing to do but prepare as best as possible. The occasion to conduct a rehearsal or performance will likely arise, but there is no predicting when or in what circumstances. Following time spent at the desk and the piano, the next biggest expenditure of time involves attending rehearsals. After direct conducting experience and private study, rehearsals are the aspirant's main occasion for learning and development. The assistant conductor is in the unique position of being able to speak to the conductor and the members of the orchestra about the contents and events of rehearsal. In this regard, even seemingly trivial details can shed light on musical and interpersonal difficulties, and the sometimes surprising connections between the two.

In recent years the media landscape has been transformed for conductors, and musicians generally, at all stages of their careers. Social media has, to some degree, put paid to the overbearing influence of the broadsheet critic. That said, being media savvy in general is ever more important to the young conductor who has achieved their first title. Fora in which to promote one's brand and image are newly available to upcoming generations of assistant conductors.[8] The question of how online presence connects to the aforementioned 'stakeholder' relations (concerning concert halls, classrooms, public spaces, hospitals, and prisons) is complex.[9] The confluence of social media gain and cultural loss may or may not concern new generations of assistant conductors. There is a new world to be navigated, as well as the gift of a remarkable musical inheritance.

A central activity to which an assistant conductor must devote considerable time is that of observing rehearsals. There is no more valuable way to learn than through reflecting on the successful, and occasionally unsuccessful, methods of more experienced colleagues. The intelligent observer will glean important information about time-management, rehearsal techniques, and communication styles. Contrasting approaches to phrasing, tempo manipulation, and balance also provide food for thought. The duty to attend rehearsals presents a unique opportunity to learn by observation. This aspect of the assistant conductor's routine is at the core of the role and is of manifold value. Complementarily, many senior conductors benefit from having a second pair of conductor's ears in the rehearsal hall. Discerning wrong notes, poor intonation, and dynamic imbalances requires attentive listening of unusual refinement. Attending rehearsals provides the opportunity to develop this skill. Although there is a long list of abilities the 'compleat' conductor must acquire, listening is primarily what a conductor does.[10]

Learning opportunities are not confined to the auditorium, however. According to a BBC report, some young employees lack exposure to the workplace norms that set them up to succeed.[11] The assistant conductor has the advantage of being able to observe and participate in the wider life of the orchestra. Depending on the organization, the role grants access not only to other conductors and orchestral musicians, but also to managers, planners, marketing professionals, librarians, and front-of-house staff.

Part artist, part apprentice, part intern, the assistant conductor occupies a unique position. Much has changed since Otto Klemperer assisted Gustav Mahler. Conducting and composition no longer fit together hand in glove. In the past century or so, technology, media, and politics have transformed the public-facing aspects of the role. At the time of writing, the sole conductor training position advertised on Musical Chairs is for a "Female Conductor Traineeship aimed at addressing the gender imbalance within classical music."[12] Assistant conductor programmes proliferate, however, as do assistant conductors. While assisting can be the best training possible, it is not a qualification to conduct. A legendary conductor once said to me that conducting could not be taught. There is more than a grain of truth in that. How might we make sense of this? The difference between learning by instruction and learning by discovery is primarily a difference in the materials on which the learner works. So it is with conducting.

## Notes

1 Roger S. Gordon, "Gustav Mahler, *Symphony No. 4*: A Historical Perspective," *Positive Feedback*, no. 8, August/September 2003, https://positive-feedback.com/Issue8/mahler.htm.

2 Anthony Tommasini, "Setting Bartok's Craggy Beauty within Its Contemporary Landscape," review of concert performance by Pierre-Laurent Aimard (piano) and Bamberg Symphony Orchestra, directed by Johnathan Nott, *New York Times*, 22 May 2009, https://www.nytimes.com/2009/05/23/arts/music/23nott.html.
3 For example, the winner of the Siemens Hallé International Conductors Competition "becomes Assistant Conductor of the Hallé, with the opportunity to work alongside the Hallé's Music Director, Sir Mark Elder CH CBE, for a minimum 2-year period in a meaningful and varied role." Siemens Hallé International Conductors Competition, accessed 29 August 2023, https://www.conductors-competition.com/.
4 *Britannica Online*, s.v. "Leonard Bernstein," updated 28 September 2023, https://www.britannica.com/biography/Leonard-Bernstein.
5 Albert Frantz, "iPad for Sheet Music," key-notes, accessed 22 September 2023, https://www.key-notes.com/blog/ipad-for-sheet-music.
6 John Kirkpatrick, "Preface," Charles Ives, *Symphony No. 4*, facsimile edition (New York: G. Schirmer, Inc., 1965), vii.
7 "Orchestre de l'Agora Begins a Partnership with Bordeaux Prison," Orchestre de l'Agora, accessed 20 September 2023, https://orchestreagora.com/en/community-projects/concert-workshops-at-bordeaux-prison/.
8 "Promoting Yourself and Your Music Online," Musicians' Union, updated 1 March 2022, https://musiciansunion.org.uk/career-development/career-guides/marketing-and-promotion/promoting-yourself-and-your-music-online.
9 Ariana Todes, "How Social Media Has Changed the Way Famous Musicians Communicate with Their Fans," *Classical Music*, 10 January 2023, https://www.classical-music.com/features/artists/pen-to-pixels-the-development-of-classical-music-fandom/.
10 In reference to the title of Gunther Schuller's *The Compleat Conductor* (Oxford: Oxford University Press, 1997).
11 Alex Christian, "Why Gen Z Workers are Starting on the Back Foot," Work: In Progress, BBC, published 10 April 2023, https://www.bbc.com/worklife/article/20230405-why-gen-z-workers-are-starting-on-the-back-foot.
12 "Opera North: Female Conductor Traineeship," Musical Chairs, accessed 5 June 2023, https://www.musicalchairs.info/jobs/39066?ref=48.

# 4

# THE KODÁLY ROUTE TO BECOMING A CHORAL CONDUCTOR

*Bernie Sherlock*

It was never my plan to become a choral conductor. It was not until after my initial teacher-training that I first properly encountered conducting. This did not happen until I went to Hungary. I felt, following my undergraduate music degree in Trinity College in Dublin, Ireland, and my subsequent Higher Diploma in Education, that I remained less than fully prepared for teaching music effectively in the classroom.[1] Not realizing at the time that it would lead into a somewhat random, unplanned route into conducting, I attended a week-long Kodály course given in Dublin by visiting pedagogues from Hungary. I realized then that what I needed to be a good teacher was to immerse myself in Hungary's world-renowned system of music education. Zoltán Kodály (1882–1967) had been the chief driving force behind its development, and I was inspired by his words: "It is the bounden duty of the talented to cultivate their talent to the highest degree, to be of as much use as possible to their fellow men."[2]

I subsequently went to Hungary and spent two years in the city of Kecskemét, at the International Kodály Institute (since then incorporated into the Franz Liszt Academy of Music).[3] Coming after five years of predominantly academic music study, the orientation around active music-making in music education in Kecskemét was exactly what I needed. Actual music-making was the foundation of every subject on the syllabus, whether music literature or teaching methodologies, solfège, theory, or folk music.

The syllabus also included conducting as a core subject. I had no conducting experience and was assigned to the beginner-level class of Ildikó Herboly Kocsár, who turned out to be one of the best music educators I would ever encounter. I did not see this at the outset; I was often bored during classes, as well as ignorant of the value for a teacher of detailed training in conducting. As the year progressed, however, and as Herboly Kocsár presented the class with increasingly difficult challenges, I became intrigued and took a deeper interest. This was the moment—not anticipated—when I fell in love with conducting. Thanks to Herboly Kocsár's brilliant teaching, I finished strongly in my first year and was moved to the advanced class for my second. Here I had another extraordinary teacher, the Director of the Kodály Institute, Péter Erdei. Among Hungarian choral conductors he is perhaps the best known internationally, having started the earliest of his extensive international travels for conducting and teaching at a time when permission to travel outside the Communist bloc was still very difficult to obtain. He assigned repertoire of ever-increasing difficulty and developed our technique with steeply sequential and intensive individual instruction.

It was not until I had been back in Ireland for two years that my first conducting opportunity arose. It was with a small mixed choir of staff and students from what was then Kevin Street College of Technology in Dublin. The members were people studying or lecturing in science and engineering who also happened to enjoy singing. I was delighted to be working with them, my first choir, and I strove to find ways for us to create as much musical magic as possible despite limited means.

That was how it began. What happened after that was very gradual. I became conductor of the chamber choir in Dublin's College of Music (now the TU Dublin Conservatoire), where I was already teaching.[4] Now I could explore more ambitious music and was able to programme masterpieces such as Poulenc's *Un soir de neige*, Debussy's *Trois chansons*, Vaughan Williams's *Fantasia on Christmas Carols*, Monteverdi's *Beatus vir*, and Vivaldi's *Gloria*, and also works by living composers such as Miklós Kocsár, Antonín Tučapský, Eibhlís Farrell, and David Fennessy. I began to conduct large choirs, starting with the DIT Choral Society at Dublin Institute of Technology, followed by the University of Dublin Choral Society (at Trinity College) for nine years, and then the Culwick Choral Society for twelve.

The standard repertoire for these large-scale choirs obliged me to take an additional step in my unplanned journey into conducting: learning how to work with orchestras. I approached Gerhard Markson, principal conductor of what was then the RTÉ National Symphony Orchestra, and he agreed to work with me on orchestral conducting technique. He was the ideal mentor: innately musical, hugely knowledgeable, and a model of clarity and economy in his conducting technique. He taught me without recordings or piano, just the two of us with copies of the score, me conducting in silence and him interrupting from time to time to say: "What character should you indicate to the first horns in bar 75?" Or, "It might be a good idea to look towards the cellos before you cue the *tutti* in bar 112." We were reading the same scores and hearing the same music inside our heads 'in sync,' reinforcing how grateful I felt for how the Hungarians had developed my 'inner hearing' (also known as 'audiation') during my two years at the Kodály Institute.[5] Markson analysed my technique and interpretation with great insight, and followed up by recommending and demonstrating the various improvements needed. Working with choral societies allowed me to study, rehearse, and perform numerous great works from the oratorio repertoire including Monteverdi's *1610 Vespers*, Vaughan Williams's *Sea Symphony*, Verdi's *Messa da Requiem*, Bach's Mass in B minor, Brahms's *Ein deutsches Requiem*, Handel's *Messiah*, Mozart's C minor Mass, and Poulenc's *Gloria*.

It always felt like an honour—and hugely fulfilling—to be conducting such music. And yet, if I had to choose, I would say that working with chamber choirs continued to hold the edge for me. This was chiefly because of my particular love of *a cappella* repertoire, music that I had grown increasingly acquainted with during my initial eight years as conductor of the College of Music Chamber Choir.[6] We performed frequently, presenting interesting concert programmes, and earning a high profile and a wide range of prizes at national competitions including Dublin's *Feis Ceoil* and the Cork International Choral Festival. In 2005, the College of Music decided to experiment with rotating the post of conductor of the Chamber Choir, so the choir was no longer mine.

I realized that the way forward was to create my own chamber choir. This would give me full freedom over all artistic programming, including new commissions, and over all decisions about where to go, and when, and how many performances to give. And so, in October 2005, I founded New Dublin Voices. After three years of performing and competing successfully around Ireland, the choir was ready to go abroad, winning our first international prize in France in 2008.[7] A year later, we were travelling to competitions in Germany, Hungary, and Finland, winning prizes in each one.[8] Quite quickly, then, New Dublin Voices grew into a high-level amateur choir and has continued to win prizes at competitions across Europe.

While prize money is great, and an important lifeline, the most valuable of our prizes have been invitations to appear as guests at some of Europe's most prestigious choral festivals, usually with all expenses paid. Some personal highlights include the European Festival of Youth Choirs in Basel in 2014, the 23rd Festival des Chœurs Lauréats in France in 2015, the 11th World Symposium on Choral Music in Barcelona in 2017, and the Aachen Internationale Chorbiennale in 2023.

It was inevitable that the rising international profile of the choir led to the rising profile of its conductor. I began receiving invitations from outside Ireland to sit on the juries of conducting and choral competitions, to give conducting masterclasses and choral workshops, or presentations on choral music in Ireland. Obviously, this felt like a long way from being bored in my first conducting classes in Hungary, but I remain very grateful for my accidental route into conducting. I had gone to Kecskemét with no ambition beyond becoming a better music teacher; yet here I am, and very thankful for what happened; both for the opportunities it has provided for getting deeply inside some of the most beautiful music in existence and for lasting friendships and connections with conductors, composers, singers, and other practitioners in Ireland and across the international choral community.

## Kodály and Conducting

The legacy of Zoltán Kodály is well known. As a composer, he left his mark on the world with a significant body of work. As an ethnomusicologist, he helped assemble huge collections of traditional folksongs preserved from recordings he made in the field. As a pedagogue, he was a key figure behind the establishment of a superlative national system of music education in his native Hungary.

Kodály was not known as a conductor. Yet his beliefs and ideas—and how they have been codified into a system of music education—offer the same kinds of all-pervasive, foundational benefits to the study of conducting as they do to the study of an instrument or the voice, or to music teaching or composition. These benefits are what I experienced during my two years of training at the Kodály Institute. But what are they? If we are asking what distinguishes a 'Kodály route' into conducting from other routes, then we need to identify where it is that Kodály-based music education and the skills needed for conducting interconnect.

One way or another, this interconnection relates primarily to Hungarian music education's highly developed concept of musicianship. The foregrounding of musicianship is the root of the whole system. Addressing the question, "Who is a good musician?" Kodály said:

> The characteristics of a good musician can be summarized as follows: a well-trained ear, a well-trained intelligence, a well-trained heart, and a well-trained hand. All four must develop together, in constant equilibrium.[9]

In Hungarian music education, these ideals are realized by the meticulous detail and sequencing of the methodology that was developed to teach them effectively. The methodology is immersively practical: learning by doing, like language-learning. The practical aspect of the methodology is predicated on singing and movement, beginning in pre-school and continuing through primary and post-primary school and into higher education.[10] Singing and movement are what provide access to the specifically Hungarian application of solfège, a concept that, while not exclusive to Hungary, in Hungary represents the pre-eminent and complete suite of skill-training activities for the development of musicianship.

Versions of what is called solfège are not the same in every country. In many areas of France, for example, solfège is strictly a reading system based on fixed-*do* where *do* is always the note C. Sometimes in my own context of Ireland, solfège is reduced to nothing further than 'writing in' the sol-fa names under notes on a stave. In Hungary, however, solfège goes far beyond mere reading. It is something comprehensive, where reading fluency via sol-fa represents only the gateway to the music universe. Hungarian conductor and pedagogue László Nemes defines solfège as:

> The training of music students' general musicianship through singing and other forms of music-making encompassing *all areas of musical knowledge and skill development* such as singing, rhythm, meter, form, melody, intonation, polyphony, harmony, notation, sight-reading, dictation, transposition, improvisation, and memory. The subject of solfège involves aspects of music theory (harmony, polyphony and form) as well as placing a strong emphasis on ear-training.[11]

Hungarian solfège leads—organically and empirically—to a breadth and depth of musicianship skills to be admired in any instrumentalist, singer, composer, or musicologist. Or conductor. Solfège classes for the international students in Kecskemét occur twice weekly for a total of five hours, plus intensive, practical homework assignments. During my own studies there, I saw this training as something that would support my original ambition to become a better music teacher. What I did not foresee was how it would later prove to be the foundation of my practice as a conductor.

Indeed, apart from one or two modules, every course we were required to take at the Kodály Institute was just as suited to someone intending to become a conductor as it was to music teachers: solfège, theory, methodology, score-reading, music literature, piano, chamber music, and voice training, in addition to the three classes every week in conducting itself. There is a seamless overlap in the institute between the implementation of Kodály's definition of the good musician and the development of all the skills and knowledge needed to be a good conductor.

The same skill training we received in the institute was on display during our weekly observation mornings in the local 'singing' primary school.[12] So many of the capabilities we saw being developed in those classrooms are identical to ones that are beneficial or essential for the good conductor. The children's advanced music literacy is an obvious example. Even more striking, however, was their highly developed capacity for inner hearing. This means that they could not only transcribe what they heard—I observed 12-year-olds writing down passages from Palestrina motets or Bach chorales or three-part inventions—but also 'inner hear' what they read, or what they composed. And this was all manifested in the various dictation, composing, memorization, and sight-reading exercises and games in which their teacher led them. Obviously inner hearing/audiation is an essential skill for the conductor, and we were observing it in schoolchildren.[13]

The ability to conduct was like the ultimate expression of Kodály's ideal of the well-trained ear, intelligence, heart, and hand. In Kecskemét, it did not matter whether you had any intention of becoming a conductor or not. Conducting represented an exercise for your musicianship, and a means for demonstrating the level attained. While there were several aspiring orchestral, choral, and opera conductors among my international classmates, the rest of us were primary school teachers, music teachers, instrumentalists, and singers. But we *all* studied conducting. This symbiotic connection between musicianship and conducting is also reflected in Hungarian teacher-training colleges, where conducting is compulsory. Training in conducting is not seen purely as something a teacher needs for directing the music-making in their classroom or choir. Conducting is seen as an important activity for the teacher's own development as a musician. It pulls together and consolidates, and exercises and enhances, all the key musicianship skills in which they have been immersed from an early age.

After two years, what I came away with from the Kodály Institute was akin to what people often acquire after moving to a new country where they do not speak the language. They learn the language both by studying it formally and by being immersed in it all around them every day. What Kecskemét's Kodály-based training gave me was a set of highly developed and advanced musicianship skills. Furthermore, the insistence on conducting as a basic element of that training not only reinforced my development as a musician, but also planted the seed of an idea about becoming a conductor.

## The Kodály-Trained Conductor in Practice

In this section, I will attempt to give some idea of what being a Kodály-trained conductor looks like in practice. I have selected various scenarios from my work which might illustrate how a challenge was overcome, or a target achieved, using skills and knowledge rooted in the training I received in Hungary. To be clear, I am not trying to suggest or imply that my methods in any of these scenarios are superior to those used by conductors trained via routes different from mine. Rather, I seek to demonstrate how the training that I happened to receive informs the conducting that I do. For reasons of space, I have confined my selection to examples covering only four elements: rhythm, melody, efficiency, and sequencing.

## Rhythm

*Snow Dance for the Dead* is a piece in ten voice parts by the Irish composer Seán Doherty.[14] It powerfully contrasts images of children playing in the snow with images of brutality from the Russian Revolution. To bring about the piece's full impact, the conductor and their choir must overcome a number of challenges, above all rhythmic ones.

The piece opens with a series of suspensions that are presented in polyrhythms, canonically, and that set the tone and character of everything that follows. The opening is in six parts without lower voices—SSSAAA (Example 4.1). The polyrhythmic pattern of four beats sung against a pulse of three beats (4:3) is established by the Alto 3 and Soprano 3 lines. This pattern eventually spreads to all ten parts and features throughout the piece. For many singers, feeling this rhythm and performing it accurately do not come naturally and immediately. How I address this provides a good illustration of the way my Hungarian training helps me to help the singers.

A general principle in Hungarian music teaching is to overcome difficulties like these by first removing complexity, and then comfortably establishing something simpler into which you re-insert the complexity. The philosophy behind this is that it is generally preferable to prepare challenges so that they never go wrong, rather than fix them when they do. Hungarian music teachers use this principle with all ages and levels, from very young children learning to sing their intervals with almost flawless intonation, to academy students singing orchestral extracts from the orchestral score of Stravinsky's *Rite of Spring*. To apply this principle specifically to the polyrhythms in *Snow Dance*, I strip away the rhythmic complexity—the 4:3 polyrhythms—so that all that remains is a simple recurring pattern of a descending three-note figure (Example 4.2). However, even after taking out the complexity there remains one small but disruptive stumbling block that cannot be removed: the minim tied to the semiquaver (see Soprano 3 and Alto 3).

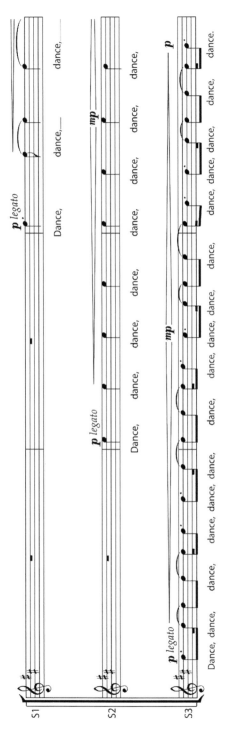

EXAMPLE 4.1  Seán Doherty, *Snow Dance for the Dead*, bb. 2–7.

# The Kodály Route to Becoming a Choral Conductor 53

**EXAMPLE 4.1** (Continued)

**54** Bernie Sherlock

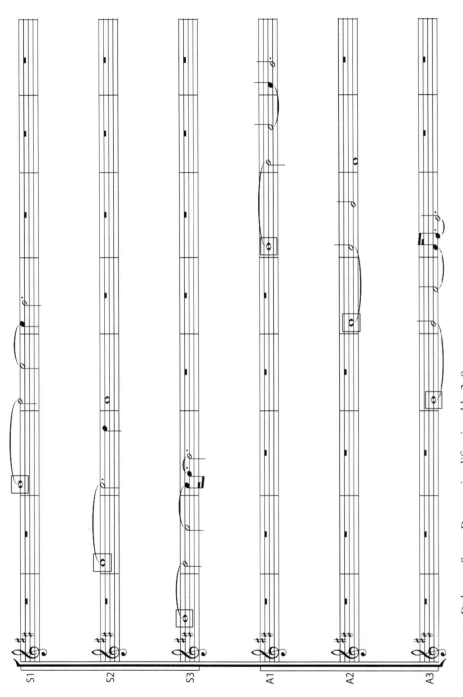

EXAMPLE 4.2 Doherty, *Snow Dance*, simplification, bb. 2–9.

Now that this stumbling block has been isolated, it will not take the singers long to attain security singing it. Since the figure will eventually appear in each of the ten voice parts, there is an important economy to be gained by asking the whole choir to work on it at once, initially with everyone singing the Alto 3 version in unison, on a loop. Hungarian schoolchildren are often asked to tap or beat one thing while singing something else. I find it a useful tool to use, and for this passage in *Snow Dance*, I have the choir tap semiquavers while at the same time singing the figure. This helps the singers place the first note after the tie over the barline accurately, which then helps them to 'sit into' the 'funkiness' they should feel against the polyrhythms when we put it all back together. Such reduction of complexity before progressing through building blocks is a standard pedagogical step in Hungarian music teaching. It quickly became a critical component of how I work with choirs.

## *Melody*

For many people, including many teachers, sol-fa is synonymous with the reading or sight-reading of melody.[15] In fact, as I tried to show earlier when describing the Hungarian system, reading melodies is only the starting point when it comes to sol-fa. A grounding in sol-fa goes far beyond mere melody and creates an intimate, highly informed, and fully practical acquaintance with elements such as harmonic function and large-scale musical forms such as sonata or fugue. Intermediary elements include intervals and chords of all kinds, all of it rock-solid in a Hungarian student's musical literacy. A number of these elements feature in the particular challenges that arise in a piece such as *Éjszaka* ('Night') by György Ligeti, so that using sol-fa can help me to help my singers succeed. Sol-fa has even proved helpful with choirs that have little or no familiarity with it.

What amounts to melody in *Éjszaka* is initially only a small, two-bar ostinato that ascends the major scale one note at a time, bar by bar. In short, melodic content is at first only a basic major scale in a dotted rhythm. It looks easy enough. However, these scales soon begin to overlap, creating tonal clusters that themselves overlap, and the strictly step-by-step movement then evolves into chains of small sequential cells. The effect, once all eight parts have entered, is of a huge, seething mass of sound, intended to evoke the text's '*rengeteg tövis*' (numerous thorns).[16]

It looks simple on paper, yet singers can become disoriented, and their accuracy and intonation suffer. To prevent or remedy this, I ask them to put the text aside and sing the notes in sol-fa. As preparation, they sing the scale of C major in unison using sol-fa, ascending and descending. Then we try doing this with Ligeti's rhythmic cells. Even for singers not used to sol-fa, using it here helps them both to feel anchored around *do* (= C) and to develop a strong sense of how each of the eight pitches of the scale relates to the others. This helps secure intonation and accuracy and prevent disorientation. In addition, parallel thirds are a prevailing feature of the piece, and even a small increase in familiarity with sol-fa can help singers solidify their orientation by 'locking into' them.

*Efficiency*

Efficiency, notably in rehearsal, has proved to be one of the lasting cumulative outcomes to emerge from all the interconnected strands of my Kodály-based training. Again, this is not to say that Kodály provides the only route. For me, however, it was the two years in Hungary that gave me the tools to make efficiency one of the foremost assets of my conducting. These tools enabled me to build an approach to conducting that matches certain aspects of my musical personality. For example, I think I am both artistically restless—always seeking new repertoire, never wanting to find myself dwelling for too long in any one stylistic neighbourhood—and someone who likes to move quickly when working with choirs. Not every stage in the process, of course, is fast. The slow part is exploring the vast and ever-expanding world of choral music, searching for the next work that is exactly right for one of my choirs and for myself. This involves a lot of sifting and reading, and sometimes interactions with composers or other conductors or singers, all of which takes time and cannot be rushed.

The fast part comes once I have committed to a piece. Speed and efficiency were for me natural by-products of all the close reading, inner hearing, and rhythmic, harmonic, and formal understanding that resulted from two years of advanced Hungarian solfège. It means that my analysis of a new work, how I prepare it for the choir, and also my preliminary ideas about how I might want to interpret it, all happen quickly. The next steps—introducing it to the choir and rehearsing it—happen quickly as well. The Kodály training I received helps me teach the choir using a pedagogically sequenced approach that minimizes the need for 'note-bashing' while optimizing rehearsal time. The highly developed ear-training inherent in Hungarian solfège also facilitates identifying and pinpointing issues; for example, regarding intonation or with rhythmic or melodic accuracy. And then, as soon as an issue is identified, the necessary problem-solving comes readily.

One of the obvious offshoots of this efficiency is how it increases the amount of music and number of projects I do. This can be seen in the work undertaken by my chamber choir New Dublin Voices in the twelve months from September 2016 to September 2017. If identifying and fixing an issue with the second tenors in bar 38 demonstrates efficiency at the micro level, then a full year with the choir demonstrates it at the macro level. In other words, a conductor's overall efficiency results from an accumulation of individual efficiencies—of preparation and rehearsal—that allows a choir and conductor to work quickly and effectively enough to be able to cover a lot of ground, engage in a busy schedule, and fulfil more of their ambitions. The year 2016–17 was a typically busy one for New Dublin Voices, with plenty of variety and some distinctions and competitive success, all facilitated by efficiency in conducting:

*September 2016*

- Harald Andersen Chamber Choir Competition, Helsinki (2nd prize).

*December 2016*

- Guest choir with RTÉ National Symphony Orchestra (*Video Games Classic*, conducted by Eimear Noone).
- Christmas concerts at the John Field Room of the National Concert Hall, Christ Church Cathedral, and Draíocht Arts Centre, Dublin.
- Performance on RTÉ Radio 1's arts programme *Arena* with the Irish Defence Forces Army No. 1 Band (conducted by Mark Armstrong).

*January 2017*

- Recording sessions for New Dublin Voices Christmas CD, *Make We Merry*.

*March 2017*

- Joint concert with King's Voices from Cambridge, UK (conducted by Ben Parry).

*April 2017*

- Concert, Hugh Lane Gallery, Dublin.
- *Evocations* concert, 2017 Cork International Choral Festival.
- Concert, *Féile na Bealtaine* (May Festival), Dingle, Co. Kerry.

*June 2017*

- Concert, Music in Wexford series.
- Concert, Limerick Sings Choral Festival.

*July 2017*

- Concert, Wood Quay Sessions (for the Contemporary Music Centre), Dublin.
- Guest choir, Tarragona Singing Week, Spain.

- Guest choir and concerts, World Symposium on Choral Music, Barcelona.

*September 2017*
- Final recording session for New Dublin Voices Christmas CD, *Make We Merry*.
- Concert in support of Sing Ireland bid to host the 2021 Europa Cantat Festival.[17]
- Baltic Sea International Choir Competition, Latvia (1st prize).

The singers in New Dublin Voices are good musicians with good voices; they are committed and enthusiastic, full of positive energy, and they tap into a certain momentum that the choir has built up over the years. They have day jobs or are students and have all signed up for something that they love, something they are good at. But they are not superheroes. And neither is their conductor. Yet, clearly, for an amateur choir that rehearses once a week to be this busy and successful over the course of twelve months, a great many things have to fall into place. One of the most important of those things is the efficiency that resulted from the musicianship training I received in Hungary.

*Sequencing*

There are many endeavours in life that benefit from a sequenced approach, and sequencing is obviously not something over which Kodály holds a monopoly. However, the sequencing that underpins the Hungarian system of music education is painstakingly empirical and methodical, with results that speak for themselves in the impressive musical literacy and understanding of the young musicians it generates. It is possible for conductors in other countries to import certain key aspects from Hungary and apply them productively to their work with choirs. Aspects which I have imported in my own context are illustrated in my final scenario here and include various tools for the development of reading and other musicianship skills, and, in particular, Hungarian-style sequencing.

Back in the academic year 2002–03, my programme for the DIT Choral Society included a performance at the National Concert Hall of Carl Orff's *Carmina Burana*. Since Orff includes passages for children's voices, programming *Carmina Burana* gave me the opportunity to do something I had been intending to do for some time: form a children's choir. The prospect of their children appearing at the National Concert Hall helped attract parents to my initial recruitment drive, and the Dunboyne Children's Choir was formed in October 2002.

The date of the concert was 4 February 2003, meaning we were limited to roughly just twelve one-hour rehearsals. Therefore, drawing out good projection from these young singers, and achieving good vowel sounds, pronunciation, phrasing, blend, and balance, as well as teaching the notes and imparting the confidence to sing them on the big occasion, was going to be challenging. It would prove to be an instance where all the interconnections between musicianship, pedagogy, and conducting within Kodály-based training were of vital importance. From the outset, even though time was short, I used various Hungarian tools—relative sol-fa, hand signs and other movement, and rhythm names[18]—and was able to start the children on the road to musical literacy, good inner hearing, and relatively developed general musicianship skills.

Sequencing played a crucial part. It needed to be child-centred, empirical, and based on Hungarian models. We started with pentatonic melodies in unison before eventually adding semitones, progressing onto melodies with ostinato or pedal-notes, then canon, two-part material with a simple second part, two-part material with parts of equal difficulty, and so on. In fact, the passages for children's chorus in *Carmina Burana* are all in unison. However, for the children to be able to engage musically and with security when they sang accompanied by orchestra, it was important that during their training they were singing, thinking, and listening in parts. The end result was a confident group of children ready to take their place on the crowded stage at the National Concert Hall and perform their part at a high level with good tone, intonation, ensemble, pronunciation, and presence.

Sequencing like this can be applied universally, irrespective of the age of a choir or its singers. For *Carmina Burana*, these were first-time choristers, highly dependent on effective sequencing to get them to the finish line. But in fact, this Hungarian kind of sequencing always comes into play with any choir I conduct—whether children or adults—particularly when we are approaching new material for the first time.

## Conclusion

No one in the audience would watch me at one of my concerts and think: "That is a Kodály conductor." It is not something you can observe in a conductor's gestures or in the artistic decisions they make, their interpretation. Features like these are the blended outcome of tutoring and experience and musical personality. They are features of *every* conductor, regardless of the route they travelled.

Yet in my case, all of it has been informed from the very beginning by the training in musicianship—as well as in conducting itself—in which

I was immersed for two years in Hungary. It has pervaded my entire career in music. It was the bedrock of both my master's and doctoral degrees in conducting and came full circle once I started teaching students who themselves went on to spend a student-exchange semester in Kecskemét or complete the institute's full master's programme. In addition, my own regular visits back to Hungary allow me to observe excellent practice once again. Or I can see it when Hungarians come to Ireland to teach on Kodály Ireland's summer courses, or at the Sing Ireland International Choral Conducting Summer School, which I directed from 2008 to 2019. Connections new and old are sustained when I find myself teaching or presenting alongside Hungarian teachers, or adjudicating with them, or being adjudicated by them. There is always something to share, something to learn.

What started with a small but life-changing course in Dublin, leading to two years of study and training in Hungary, has resulted in the career I enjoy as a conductor. For me, *that* is what it means to become a conductor via the 'Kodály route.'

## Notes

1 The Higher Diploma in Education, a teaching qualification, was the precursor to the current Postgraduate Master's in Education.
2 Zoltán Kodály, "Who is a Good Musician," in *The Selected Writings of Zoltán Kodály*, ed. Ferenc Bónis, trans. Lili Halápy and Fred Macnicol (London: Boosey & Hawkes, 1974), 197.
3 The current name is Kodály Institute of the Liszt Ferenc Academy of Music.
4 The College of Music was, at that time, run by the governmental education body known as the Vocational Education Committee (VEC). The college subsequently became part of Dublin Institute of Technology, which more recently has become the Technological University Dublin, or TU Dublin.
5 Inner hearing, or audiation as it is also known, particularly in North America, is the ability to hear—in your mind—the music you read. The corollary is being able to write down what you hear (or imagine if you are composing).
6 It has changed names several times from the College of Music Chamber Choir, the DIT Adelaide Singers, the DIT Chamber Choir, and now the TU Dublin Chamber Choir.
7 Special Prize for the First Performance of a New Work, Florilège Vocal de Tours, Enda Bates's *Sea Swell*.
8 The prizes were: 3rd prize, overall, and Special Prize, best interpretation of the set work (Bernie Sherlock), International Harald Andersen Chamber Choir Competition, Helsinki; 3rd prize overall, International Chamber Choir Competition Marktoberdorf; Grand Prix and Interkultur Special Prize for best conductor, 12th Budapest International Choir Competition.
9 Kodály, "Who is a Good Musician," 197.
10 The Dalcroze method, developed from 1886 by Émile Jaques-Dalcroze emphasizes dance and kinaesthetic rhythm games as a means of teaching various elements of music.
11 László Norbert Nemes, "'Let the Whole World Rejoice!' Choral Music Education: The Kodály Perspective," in *The Oxford Handbook of Choral Pedagogy*,

ed. Frank Abrahams and Paul D. Head (Oxford and New York: Oxford University Press, 2017), 100. Italics mine.
12 In the singing primary school, the students have four classes of solfège per week, plus choir. There are now approximately eighty of these schools, where there were approximately 250 in the 1970s and 1980s (figures from discussion with Hungarian music teacher Borbála Szirányi, 12 April 2023).
13 Over the years, I have had the opportunity to observe more music classes in Hungary and I have been equally impressed with the advanced musical literacy and inner hearing.
14 Seán Doherty's *Snow Dance for the Dead* was published in 2018 by Cailíno Music Publishers (CMP 418 11 037).
15 Guido d'Arezzo, an eleventh-century monk, was the first to use sol-fa syllables for the notes of the scale in his hymn *Ut queant laxis*. Sol-fa expresses the relative pitch and tonal function of each note.
16 György Ligeti, *Éjszaka · Reggel (Night · Morning): Two Unaccompanied Choruses on Texts by Sándor Weöres for 5–8-part Mixed Choir* (Mainz: Schott, 1973).
17 Sing Ireland was rebranded from the Association of Irish Choirs in 2019. It is Ireland's national body for the support, development, and promotion of all forms of group singing.
18 Rhythm syllables replace notes with the syllables making rhythms easier to read, perform, and audiate/inner hear.

# PART II
# Conductors in Practice
## Orchestral Perspectives

# 5

# FROM CONCEPT TO CONCERT

A Journey of Choosing, Learning, and Performing a Score

*Rebecca Miller*

A brand-new score. What could be more exciting? I sit down at my desk, my coloured pencils, ruler, and eraser are ready. I open the volume, take in the smell of new paper, and take inordinate amount of pleasure from cracking the binding. What an extraordinary amount of information I see in front of me—it is almost overwhelming. I must learn all the notes, absorb all the markings, make hundreds of decisions, and then persuade and enable an orchestra to play it. Where do I start? Page one seems obvious, but perhaps I should flip through and see what happens? After all, my job is to have a big vision of the piece, and how can I make decisions on page one to shape that vision if I do not know what happens later? And so, I embark on a remarkable journey.

In this chapter, I will bring you on this journey, from opening a score through to performance, and all the myriad skills and broad knowledge required for the voyage. In performance, our audience sees only the end result, the tip of the iceberg. But the journey from concept to concert is disproportionately skewed: the vast majority of a conductor's work happens before we even get to the podium, perhaps before we even get to the notes. So, this chapter is structured as such. It will discuss the long process of learning and preparation, leading to the performance, at which point the hard work is mostly done.

## Tools for the Job

To be a conductor is to be a great leader; to have vision and purpose, honesty, and integrity; to trust in those you lead; to have transparency, confidence, and communication skills; to have accountability and humility; to be able to delegate and empower; to have empathy, resilience, and emotional intelligence.

To be a conductor is to be a swan. The elegant gestures above the water belie the mad paddling occurring underneath. Conductors must be enablers: we enable the musicians in front of us to do their job. Conductors are listeners: we are the eyes and ears of the orchestra, we have the widest perspective, and we are a listening guide for both orchestra and audience. On stage, it is only the conductor who is silent, so we each must be completely dedicated to listening. Conductors are decision-makers: we must have a Big Vision and make the many decisions that shape it. Conductors must be intellectuals, researchers, analysts, multi-taskers, workhorses, teachers, students, leaders, followers, collaborators, negotiators, politicians, visionaries, philosophers, performers, and compassionate human beings. We are 'orchestra chefs.' We have the recipe, and it is our job to read it, understand it, interpret it, internalize it, sprinkle a little more spice here, bake a bit longer there, and ultimately bring it off the page, through the musicians, and out to the audience.

To be a conductor requires a broad and extensive set of skills and knowledge: technical skills such as baton technique, plus aural, rhythmic, and communication skills, and rehearsal techniques; and general musical knowledge such as orchestration, repertoire, music history, theory, and analysis. But beyond these skills, to be better musicians we also need a broad general knowledge (e.g., of history, philosophy, literature, art, and politics), and an awareness of context and relevance. As leaders, our industry-specific knowledge is a platform, but the wider our knowledge and broader the context, the stronger and more relevant will be our vision, and the bigger will be the purpose and impact of our leadership and ideas. I have found through my experience that the most important skills required are often left out of conducting textbooks and courses: those of general leadership, management, collaboration, negotiation, dialogue, and persuasion. Because no matter how great our ideas, we need to persuade others to bring them to life.

### Which Score?

Leaders are decision-makers. The first decision a conductor has to make concerns what to play. Like most aspects of conducting, choosing a programme is usually a collaborative process involving the orchestra manager/artistic administrator, and sometimes the musicians. But as is our job on and off the podium, we must work through details, but maintain perspective, asking how does this programme fit into the wider activity of the orchestra, and who is the audience?

Crafting a programme can be almost as important as the rehearsals and performances themselves. Consider the following questions: Who is the orchestra? Have the musicians played this music before? Are we bringing something new to them, or to the audience? It is good to balance new with familiar, straightforward with challenging, and create a programme that has a variety of styles, characters, colours, moods, and even of keys. And consider the connection between the pieces, be it historical, aesthetic, national, or cultural. Think about the context. Is the concert part of a series, or does it stand alone? Does it need a theme? Is it a family concert, requiring lots of shorter works with spoken introductions? Is it an education concert that ties in with school curriculum? Is it celebrating a composer's anniversary?

There are also bigger questions in programming. Should art serve to shine a light on the big issues of the world, such as climate change, diversity, politics? If so, how prominently should these issues play in our decision-making? We must prioritize the quality of the music we offer, and not programme just to tick boxes. But priorities of diversity and relevance can be set in our minds, while still bearing in mind aesthetic choices. I ask myself: "Can I find a work by a female composer for this programme?" I have found that most of the time it is possible, as there is no shortage of high-quality music by female composers. But we must also consider for whom is the diversity important? For the orchestra? For the audience? For posterity?

Our big ideas are, however, often overshadowed by practical considerations; for example, the venue (size of the stage and acoustic). Programme length and orchestration are crucial, and budget must be considered, as you inevitably have to make efficient use of limited funds (i.e., not too many extra musicians, avoiding hiring extra musicians for only a single work, instrument and music hire costs).

Finally, marketing and audience should always be borne in mind. What is our target audience? What is the orchestra's relationship to its audience, and does the orchestra have the audience's trust, in which case can we be a little more bold? Are we trying to push the programming envelope, or are we in a delicate time when safe is better? Presuming that the orchestra wishes to attract a new audience, do we need to provide musical access points for first-time concertgoers? We must balance programmes of lesser-known works with more popular works, or with a popular soloist, or even with a theme, an extra-musical feature (film, narration, dance), pre/post-concert discussions, or food and drink.[1]

## Behind the Score

Once we have decided what to perform, we must learn the scores. But what to do first? Should we head to the *New Grove* to learn about the composer? Or should we crack open the binding and let the dots speak to us themselves? Should we know what is behind the score before we get to know what is in it? Do great works of art require an understanding of context to be appreciated? Shakespeare's works perhaps elicit a negative response: his writings can stand on their own and pass the test of time, as they have for centuries, and contain universal truths about human nature and the human condition. The same could be said for many pieces of music: many great works can simply survive based on aesthetic qualities. But many cannot. Does one need to understand the historical or conceptual context of Bach's preludes and fugues or Brahms's symphonies to appreciate their greatness? Can Shostakovich's Symphony No. 5 be truly understood without knowledge of its political context? Is our understanding of Beethoven's works limited without knowledge of his political passions or his hearing loss?

One can surely appreciate a work of art on the surface for its beauty or innovation. But to fully understand a work of art, and to justify presenting it to an audience, we must know as much as possible about the context—be it historical, cultural, political, philosophical, or aesthetic—as ultimately these aspects are intricately linked to the decisions we need to make. But our quandary of 'where to start' remains, so perhaps we should try to have the 'best of both.' Knowing the context or history of a work is essential for developing our big vision, but it is also helpful to be able to detach from this information to provide much-needed perspective and distance.

Apart from historical or cultural context, there are other reasons we cannot simply rely on the dots on the page to understand and present the music we play. Many decisions reach beyond the notes, and the tempo, phrasing, balance, and structural decisions can all portray very different meanings depending on these decisions. Just as in the theatre, a phrase with different emphasis can completely change its message. Our job is to try to understand the composer's intentions, and then to interpret them according to our own aesthetic sensibilities. A broad knowledge of the composer, historical context, and his/her writings will inform decisions about our realization. For example, when approaching a Beethoven symphony, and contemplating the metronome marks at the start, it is important to know that he added metronome marks for his first few symphonies retrospectively. We should also read what Beethoven wrote on the topic, one with which he struggled greatly.[2] Brahms actually refused to use metronome marks altogether, saying, "I myself have never believed that my blood and a mechanical instrument go well together."[3] Conversely, Stravinsky is quoted many times saying that his metronome marks were to be strictly adhered to, even though his own recordings often fail to follow the tempo indications in the score.[4] When confronted with the shocking, extreme, and vividly contrasting nature of C.P.E. Bach's works, we should contextualize his belief in Enlightenment philosophy and his desire to express real human emotions.[5]

Music can be unburdened by words, and is therefore widely open to interpretation, which is simultaneously liberating and daunting. We may interpret a passage as humorous, when in fact it may be sarcastic in its intention. I have encountered several instances of conductors making assumptions based on the notes alone, only to have these assumptions clarified, or even contradicted reading the composer's programme note or having the composer present. The issues of tempo, metronome marks, interpretation, and the role of the recordings, are topics for a separate volume, with many relevant writings available already. All we can do is try to acquire the information that is available to us and make decisions on account of—or sometimes despite—such knowledge and awareness.

## In the Score

Finally, we reach 'the dots.' Our job is to know the score, inside and out, and the skills in absorbing it are wide-ranging. To truly know something, we need to know how it is put together: so, skills in musical analysis are key. Understanding a work's structure and harmony—where are the big pillars, where is the climax, where are the points of harmonic tension, where does the music need to be pulled back, and where does it need to flow—are all essential to developing an artistic vision. As we try to hear the composer's voice and why he/she made the decisions we see on the page, we need a deep knowledge of harmony, form, counterpoint, and orchestration. The composer has already made many decisions about what they put in the score, but we still have many choices to make of our own on how to 'speak the words.' Information is written in varying degrees of detail, but even with composers who pack the score with detail (such as Mahler) there is still the need for interpretation. How quiet is *piano*? How loud is *forte*? How short is short? What's the difference between a dot and a dash? Who has the primary line? The latter is one of a conductor's essential questions in preparation, rehearsal, and performance, and this hierarchy of line or balance of orchestration can be a defining element of conductor's interpretation.[6] In the eighteenth century, it was customary to play a note with a dot or dash at half its length.[7] But does this practice change over time? And does staccato really refer to the length of a note, or is it about the attack or the release?[8]

And what about the metronome marks? Should we follow them literally, as we do with the notes on the page? What if the orchestra cannot play the piece at the specified speed? Should they not play the piece at all, or is it better to have flexibility? My experience with living composers suggests that most of them are flexible with their tempo markings, that they support changes necessitated by acoustics or ability, and that the metronome marks are a guideline. Most say that they would prefer that the performers take ownership of the piece, rather than try to squeeze into an ill-fitted suit. So, whilst we should try our best to realize what is written on the page, we must 'realize' with flexibility and circumstantial understanding. But what does our experience with living composers say about how we should interpret those to whom we cannot pose our questions?

At this point—since we seem to have gotten a bit stuck at interpreting the printed information—we should perhaps pause to consider performance practice. If we are playing early music, should we imitate how it would have sounded at the time of its composition? Is it incongruous to ask a modern audience to listen with historical ears? Or perhaps such a request is one way of drawing us out of ourselves, into another time/life/country; after all, is performance not at least partially about taking the audience on a journey outside the concert hall and outside of themselves? Whatever the answers to these questions, understanding historical practice undoubtedly helps to inform our decision-making. Discerning the qualities, colours, limitations, and advantages of historical instruments can help us divine the composer's intentions. For example, comprehending how to use the harpsichord's limited attack and dynamic range to obtain desired musical results can inform the phrasing, dynamic range, colour, and character of playing the same piece on the piano; using a Baroque bow can help understand Bach's unwritten phrasing and dynamic intentions; trying a Baroque flute, with its peculiarities of intonation and varying registrational characteristics, can guide a flautist in decisions of phrasing and dynamics. Similarly, as a conductor, we must understand the instruments for which the piece was written in order to make informed decisions for the present day. And so, we ought to consult instrumental treatises, collections of letters, and manuscript facsimiles. We must explore harpsichords, bows, natural horns, and period instruments. Then, armed with the knowledge of what was done at the time, we make our own decisions, employing or integrating this knowledge accordingly.

## Developing Our Vision

How does one really learn a score? We cannot play it at home in our living room, as an instrumentalist can, so we must try anything and everything to learn it, hear it, absorb it, into our head, and eventually into our body and our arms. We should play the score at the piano, sing individual lines, hear the music in our head, analyse the harmony, the structure, the orchestration. "But," you say, "what about recordings? Do I not just conduct along to my stereo?" It would be much easier if we could. There are so many recordings available at our fingertips, it would be so easy to pop one on and wave our arms to it and rid ourselves of the endless hours trying to hear the music on the page in our head. Listening to recordings can be very helpful and it is a great tool, especially for research and comparison, but recordings must be used wisely and with awareness. Conducting to a recording will only teach you to follow, not to lead, and our main job as a conductor is to lead. We must anticipate, prepare, and connect with the sound of the orchestra. We cannot lead the orchestra if we are not connected with their sound; leaders must be connected with their team. We can never connect with the orchestra on a recording: it will never respond to us, it has zero flexibility, and we cannot lead it. We should absolutely use the wealth of recordings available, and listen to them, compare, contrast, learn from the greats, learn from the obscure, from the historic, and from the contemporary. They can even help us decide what we like and do not like, to unlock our imagination, to help solidify how we want the music to sound. But be careful not to get stuck listening to only one as this could lead (perhaps inadvertently) to copying someone else's interpretation, rather than developing one's own. We need complete integrity, belief, and confidence in our own tempos, ideas, and interpretation to communicate these to an orchestra, and such conviction cannot come from imitation.

For me, the score-learning process starts with a wide-angle lens, with the big picture, the structure, the content, the arch. Then I zoom in further, looking more and more in detail at the orchestration, the harmony, the melodic content, then the articulation, dynamics, phrasing, and balance. I am constantly asking questions, imagining and trying passages in different ways, with a variety of sounds and phrasings. And gradually, zooming in and out again, a picture begins to develop, a concept emerges. As I explore individual lines, I consider many questions of orchestration and instrumentation details, that is, is this passage difficult for this instrument? Knowledge of string technique and bowing is essential: should this passage be on or off the string? Is it playable off the string at my tempo? As for bowing, many conductors provide their own bowings, but if not, be sure you can at least review the orchestra's existing bowings, make sure it supports or does not conflict with your interpretative decisions, and suggest changes. Having bowing issues resolved in advance can save an enormous amount of time in rehearsal.

Decision-making is a crucial part of leadership. Leaders in all fields must put pen to paper, sign statements and contracts. For me, deciding what to mark in the score is an essential part of the learning process, and involves long and detailed decision-making. Before I put pen (actually, coloured pencil) to paper, I carefully consider the options before making any mark, and through this exploration I am also learning the score. Though they are part of the learning experience, I am ever conscious that markings serve as a 'road map' during rehearsals and performance: one cannot 'read' a score when conducting. For me at least, the markings are only a reference for looking down occasionally as one needs to be using the eyes for looking at the orchestra instead. Markings should be organized, clear, consistent, and relatively minimal. We want to let the notes, the original text, and the composer's presence always shine through. And the way we mark a score can reflect (and affect) our conducting and leadership style. I recall seeing George Szell's scores in the library of the Cleveland Orchestra. I was astonished at how meticulous and detailed they were, and thought they reflected the detail that we know was part of his character and that we can hear in his recordings.

Developing gesture is also a key part of the learning process. Codifying our musical ideas into illustrative and clear gestures is a crucial part of our preparation. We must continually balance our score study with gesture and mirror work, as both are crucial parts of preparation. We must be completely confident in our ideas and gestures: they must be so ingrained and internalized that we are not thinking about them on the podium, so our rehearsal head space can be reserved for listening, shaping, balancing, and communicating. When we finally meet the orchestra, we want to have in our arsenal as wide a 'toolbox' of gestures as possible so that we can adapt, adjust, respond, and communicate effectively, as a leader in any industry should be able to do. In honing our stick technique, mirror and technical practice with hands moving together and separately is crucial. For developing gestural repertoire, I recommend singing a passage whilst experimenting with gesture, or identifying specific descriptors for the music and finding gestures to match. Often describing the passage to someone else can help develop gesture. Practising a passage in many different ways, just as an instrumentalist would, is also helpful. I recall the violin lesson of a young student who could not decide which fingering to use in one passage: the teacher suggested practising one fingering on Monday, Wednesday, and Friday, and the second on Tuesday, Thursday, and Saturday (Sunday was a day off). I thought it was an insightful and playful way of building into technique the key skill of flexibility, so that we can, like top sportspeople, pull out those amazing shots when thrown a curveball.

Last, but certainly not least, listening skills—both on and off the podium—are indispensable to a conductor, and to any leader. We are the Chief Listener on stage, the only one without an instrument in hand or a voice part to sing, and we are the only ones who can be 100 per cent dedicated to listening. Aural training is a crucial part of our education and experience. We must continually listen for pitch and ensemble accuracy, intonation, sound, blend, balance, and details of articulation, dynamics, and phrasing. We need to quickly and confidently identify and diagnose problems in order to maintain an efficient rehearsal process. We are often there as 'listening guides,' mostly for the orchestra, but for the audience as well.

**Realizing Our Vision**

After weeks or months of singing, playing, imagining, and gesturing, it is nearly time to meet the orchestra and conduct. I offer here a few final pieces of advice before the first rehearsal. A good leader or manager should always come to a meeting prepared—by knowing the names of who will be there, their backgrounds, and the situation—and so should the conductor. I always ask for the personnel list and try to learn as many names as possible. We must remember the musicians are humans, not instruments, and we should integrate this approach into everything we do as a conductor. Knowing the strengths and weaknesses of your ensemble, and as much as possible about them (i.e., regular or guest, professional or amateur), feeds into our effectiveness as leaders and can have a bearing on rehearsal planning and management. Be sure to prepare a clear rehearsal plan that integrates flexibility as well as efficiency, know the timing and length of breaks for the orchestra, and minimize any occasions when musicians might sit around unused.

Presentation is also key to leadership, and the seemingly trivial question of "What should I wear?" is actually quite important. How we present ourselves communicates much about our character, and especially in conducting. The body is our instrument, and our facial expressions, gestures, tone of voice, and what we wear all affect the overall impression we give. We must as leaders set a guide for standards: if we are organized and clear in our ideas, we should look organized and tidy as well. Clothing that is smart, tidy, comfortable, subtle, and not distracting is probably best. Wrists should always be visible, as they are key tools for illustrating articulation, phrasing, and expressivity, and the face and eyes should also be clear (i.e., hair tied back), as these are key tools of communication.

Creating a positive working environment is important for any leader. I endeavour to create a hardworking, challenging, yet positive rehearsal atmosphere, rather than one that dwells on mistakes, and I try to embody positivity and confidence from the moment I walk into the room. We only have one chance at a first impression, and an orchestra's first impression of a conductor comes from the way we walk in and take to the podium, and from our first words and gestures. We must leave our baggage at the door as our mood can easily affect the working environment. We need to try to overcome any first rehearsal nerves, and a smile can go a long way; many musicians have mentioned to me the effectiveness of a conductor's smile on the room. Remember, your musicians may also be jittery for the first rehearsal, as they, too, are making their first impression on you and their colleagues.

Language skills are also important and a crucial part of a conductor's education to understand scores, writings on music, and perhaps to communicate with orchestras in different languages. Even if a conductor is not fluent, most orchestras will appreciate at least an attempt at a few words in their language.

Now it is time to conduct. Our first gesture is crucial; it can, in fact, be a dealmaker or a dealbreaker. The first gesture must be full of energy, character, and confidence. But as our primary role is to enable and empower, the gesture must also be one that is inviting and leaves space for response and interpretation. As a leader, we must continually persuade our team of our ideas, and we therefore must invite the group to come with us. The importance of trust in leadership cannot be overstated. We must trust our team, even if meeting them for the first time. To trust is to place your confidence in something, to be reliant on the character, ability, or strength of someone. If we give our first upbeat with trust—that is, we have full confidence in each musician's ability to play just as we show them—they can (and likely will) give their trust in return. We can only shape, craft, and realize our ideas if we have such trust. Trust should not, however, be confused with affection. Developing a rapport with an orchestra has nothing to do with whether they like us, or indeed, whether we like them. We can trust and be confident in each other regardless of personal feelings, which should be put aside. Music is at once very personal, but at the same time often requires us to distance ourselves from its realization to let the composer shine through.

The first run-through is always a thrill of nerves, excitement, and uncertainty, a bit like a long-awaited first date. The orchestra will be at their most attentive and observant, and this crucial stage of relationship development is to be savoured for the wealth of information it provides and for its potential for spontaneity and communication. I try to use this first run not only to impart my vision and musical ideas, but also to absorb how the orchestra plays, how they respond to my gestures, how I respond to their playing, how they communicate between themselves, their strengths, and their weaknesses, and what I need to adjust or improve. This is crucial acquaintance time, setting up communication for the rest of the week.

But we must remember that leaders must first listen and observe, so we need to let the orchestra play, let them speak, let them show us what they have to offer, not dive into detailed rehearsal work straight away. When a new leader moves in, they listen first, and move furniture later, that is, if you rip things apart and move all the furniture before you have even listened, it may risk disrupting the whole relationship and make the orchestra feel disenfranchised. The first run is a little like test-driving a car: we guide it, but we also see how it responds to our actions. And this is especially why we must be supremely confident in our ideas and gestures. The first run-through must clearly impart the tempo, the character, the articulation, the sound, giving the orchestra clarity of your ideas, clear leadership, and safe hands from the outset, increasing and solidifying confidence. With the initial run-through complete—or at least a long enough expanse of playing to gain an understanding of how the group plays and responds to your gestures—the detailed work can begin. But move the furniture carefully and methodically, not everything at once. We want to our team to feel enabled, empowered, and involved; maintaining a balance of playing and detailed work can go a long way to achieving such engagement.

Verbal strength and economy of words should be part of any leader's skillset and are especially important in an orchestral rehearsal. When stopping, there may be dozens of things to say to the orchestra, but we must choose only a few, and the ones that are going to make the biggest difference. A conductor can lose an orchestra's attention very quickly with too many words. Many things fix themselves on second run, especially if you adjust your gesture next time. Sensing which matters require immediate attention and which can be left alone comes with experience, but we should be aware that correcting mistakes the musicians themselves know will 'autocorrect' can erode trust and even appear condescending, albeit inadvertently. Comments should be efficient and clear (what the problem is, how to fix it), delivered in an articulate, confident voice, and framed positively if possible. For example, instead of saying, "You were too loud at bar 54," try instead, "Could you be quieter at bar 54?" A small language adjustment such as this can help maintain positivity; suggest an action for the next time, instead of emphasizing the criticism. As leaders, we must empower our team, and I embrace opportunities to give musicians the chance to self-assess. It keeps them engaged, empowered, and encourages critical listening. For example, let a section leader speak to their section first, before immediately jumping in with your correction. Of course, we must know what needs fixing and how to do so efficiently, but as leaders we must give our teams both strong leadership and independence: strong leadership enables and builds confidence, but independence can foster a sense of collaboration, group ownership, and collective commitment.

Humanity must be central. We are leading a team of highly talented, highly trained artists, who are human beings. Many decisions are already out of their artistic hands. They must play the music chosen by someone else, take someone else's tempo, follow someone else's phrasing, and abide by many requests of their sound, articulation, dynamics, and character. My experience with speaking to many musicians is that they want their talent and experience to be appreciated and utilized. They like to maintain some autonomy over their artistic work, dislike micromanagement, and want to be allowed to share ownership of a collective 'product.' So, we must guide but not dictate, lead but allow freedom—a delicate balance in leadership. Any leader must engrain self-reflection and self-assessment into their leadership, and conductors must often do this in a very short space of time, sometimes with only one rehearsal. As a conductor, one must learn from and reflect upon every moment with an orchestra and use it to change or improve matters the next time around. Personally, I find the time just after a rehearsal essential for self-reflection. I generally dislike any meetings or interviews during that time: while the rehearsal is freshest in my mind, I take the opportunity to make careful notes of what went well and what needs work, and then to sketch out a plan for the next rehearsal.

The balance of the individual and the collective is simultaneously one of the greatest attributes and one of the biggest challenges of the orchestral environment. When a player has a solo, this issue comes into greatest relief. An individual needs encouragement, support, and leadership, but also independence and flexibility. Absence of leadership can be frightening, but too much can be stifling. This is where negotiation and persuasion come into play. The soloist and the conductor must allow leadership and listening to flow in both directions, like duo partners: first one leads, then the other, with ebb and flow, give and take. Conductors need flexibility and adaptability. We must come with strong artistic vision, but what if the orchestra seems to want a different tempo than the one in our head? Or a soloist wants a passage vastly different than we envisaged it? As leaders, we must choose our battles, balancing confidence with flexibility, and remembering that we developed most of our ideas before we even met the orchestra. Some built-in flexibility can go a long way, especially in terms of the orchestra's confidence and self-reliance, and once we have met them and heard them play, we must be prepared to acknowledge that some of our ideas may or may not work.

Great leaders have empathy, self-awareness, and humility, and admit when they make mistakes. We must be aware, however, that as conductors our mistakes—even small ones—can be costly, for we can easily derail an entire performance. If mistakes do occur, we can first look at ourselves, thinking carefully before placing blame. Was I clear? Did I give a confident cue? In fact, before asking musicians for something, we must always try first to show it with our hands and be aware of whether we have done so. Did I clearly prepare that *subito piano*? Did I really show those accents?

If we are not sure, best to hold our tongue, and ensure you show it the next time. Many mishaps, initially assumed to be a musician's fault, can actually be (at least partially) a result of our actions. For example, if a horn splits a note, it is easy to simply blame the player, but we must understand that split notes occur for many reasons (insecurity, lack of support, insufficient breath) and occur even with seasoned professionals. Our job is to enable confidence in our musicians, often when it is lacking in the player themselves, and we must have empathy for their situation and give them the best possible chance to do their best. If they are insecure, it is possible that our beat was ambiguous or insufficiently confident, or that our baton suddenly disappeared below a violinist's head. And if a musician does make a mistake, we must try not to visually react, as they will likely be reacting enough themselves, and it is hard enough for musicians to shrug off a mistake and move on. They do not need any grimace from us that might create more insecurity. Of course, not every split note or wrong rhythm is our fault, but we must remember that with leadership comes responsibility. Knowing the difference between what is our fault and what is not is part of being a great leader.

## The Performance

The rehearsal process, much like the entire preparation process, can be like a zoom lens: starting on day one with a wide angle, then zooming in for detailed work, and gradually zooming out again in time for the dress rehearsal. But the dress rehearsal should have a different mentality as the others and can be a golden opportunity to mix consistency with spontaneity, to solidify the work done in rehearsal but also to push the envelope a little, keeping everyone concentrating, and preparing for the unexpectedness of performance. As conductors, we should be 'zoomed out' at a dress rehearsal, letting the details emerge, guiding and shaping the bigger picture with more of an audience perspective on the podium. Musicians usually like to save performance energy for the concert, so it is important not to demand full exertion for the entire dress rehearsal.

As to the performance itself, it is the first time that no one is allowed to stop, which can be simultaneously terrifying and liberating. In performance, the gesture becomes paramount, not only for the orchestra's listening, but also as guide for the audience. If we want to bring out an inner voice or a less obvious line, our gesture can help guide the audience's ears. In our modern visual society, purely auditory experiences are becoming fewer, thus our gestures can help visually aid those with less concert-going experience. Furthermore, in performance, a conductor's listening becomes less 'focal' and more 'peripheral.' We now need to listen, not with our mind on 'correction,' but with perspective and concentration on the whole. We must exist in three time zones: the future (preparing everyone for what comes next), the present (connecting with the sound), and the past (acknowledging what just happened and learning from it or applying it to the next event).

Charismatic and effective public speaking is expected of great leaders. Even though conductors primarily communicate non-verbally, we do need such skills to speak to the orchestra, and it is also becoming the expectation for us to speak to audiences, and at community and fundraising events. But we must remember that speaking in this way needs to be rehearsed. During my training, I practised on my friends and family, filmed myself, and very often educated my plants and pets (who are now very knowledgeable!). It is important to try making the same points in a variety of ways, not just to memorize. Just as an instrumentalist might practise various fingerings or bowings to enable flexibility in performance, flexibility and adaptability in speaking allow greater freedom and naturalness, and we will be less likely to sound scripted.

## Off the Podium

We have clearly established that to be a conductor is to be a great leader, with all the aforementioned qualities. But to be a conductor is also to be a community leader, a fundraiser, and an artistic citizen, sometimes standing up for the big issues in our society such as politics, climate change, and diversity. We must understand the workings of the organization that we lead. We might have a big idea of a programme, but we must understand the practical implications of realizing it, how the marketing team will sell it, how the development team will fund it, how the operations team will implement it, how the artistic team will source the best people to pull it off. We need to let deep organizational understanding shine through in our requests, our plans, and our leadership in general, so that those behind the scenes feel as valued and invested as those on stage. Our understanding, both organizational and humanitarian, must also shine through in our leadership on stage. Orchestral playing is a distinctly human thing: to take the inanimate ink, written by a human, and bring it to life through human collaboration, in a unique and fleeting artistic experience. What could be more human? Indeed, the qualities that make a great orchestra—listening, collaboration, communication, talent, determination, creativity, flexibility, and respect—are what make a great society. And great societies need great leaders.

## Notes

1 See Chapter 6 by Ciarán Crilly and Chapter 12 by Kari Turunen in this volume on approaches to programming.
2 See Clive Brown, "Historical Performance, Metronome Marks and Tempo in Beethoven's Symphonies," *Early Music* 19, no. 2 (May 1991), 247–58.
3 George Henschel, *Personal Recollections of Johannes Brahms* (Boston: Richard G. Badger, 1907), 78.
4 For example, "A piece of mine can survive almost anything but wrong or uncertain tempo." Igor Stravinsky and Robert Craft, *Conversations with Igor Stravinsky* (Garden City, NY: Doubleday, 1959), 135.
5 William S. Newman, "Emanuel Bach's Autobiography," *Musical Quarterly* 51, no. 2 (April 1965): 363–72, https://doi:10.1093/mq/li.2.363.
6 Schoenberg recognizes this quandary and attempts to clarify it for us with his *Hauptstimme* and *Nebenstimme* markings; but with most composers, it is up to the conductor.
7 As described by Quantz and Leopold Mozart. See Clive Brown, *Classical and Romantic Performing Practice 1750–1900* (New York: Cambridge University Press, 1999), 214.
8 See the assessment of string articulation in Robin Stowell, *The Early Violin and Viola: A Practical Guide* (Cambridge: Cambridge University Press, 2001), 93–94.

# 6

## "THIS WILL BE THE ONE!"

Strategic Programming and Repertoire Selection for Non-Professional Orchestras

*Ciarán Crilly*

### Introduction

Much of what I am drawing upon in this chapter is related to my twenty years managing and conducting the student symphony orchestra of University College Dublin (UCD) alongside instructive experiences with a wide range of professional, youth, and community ensembles. It is intended as a practical guide for conductors who are working with non-professional orchestras and are regularly faced with the challenge of programming music that is appropriate to each individual group.

UCD is the largest university in Ireland by student population,[1] but it had lacked an established symphony orchestra, despite a reasonably healthy culture of student music-making. I was invited to help remedy this situation when I joined the Department (now School) of Music in the 2002–03 academic year, with the foundation of what was to become the UCD Symphony Orchestra.[2] A steep learning curve—for myself and the members—became increasingly less precipitous as the years progressed, and it would be reasonable to suggest that the orchestra had successfully taken root by 2004–05, when the university was celebrating its 150th anniversary. Since that time, it has stabilized as an ensemble of around eighty to ninety members, performing a mixture of symphonic repertoire from the nineteenth and twentieth centuries, with excursions into programmes featuring popular music, film, and other media. The fact that it is offered as a taught module for students from any discipline in the university has encouraged the orchestra's success, but it is the appetite

DOI: 10.4324/9781003299660-9

for and commitment to high-quality music-making from its members that really maintains the group's momentum.

Running an ensemble that also functions as a module for students means taking ownership of the content in much the same way as a lecturer for any other academic module. Therefore, responsibility sits very much with the artistic director. This contrasts with how a professional or community orchestra operates, where the conductor will no doubt have to plan in tandem with a management team or committee. Programming is at the heart of such planning, and you need to negotiate different parameters for each type of ensemble.[3] The least restrictive circumstances will be found with professionals, as the technical challenge of an individual work shall not be a predominant factor. With non-professionals, whether they be voluntary adult musicians or young students, technical elements can make or break a performance, especially in the case of works that are just too demanding. On occasion, a less challenging choice can be a poor one, as this might engender disengagement or complacency, but there is always room to work on finer points of detail in this circumstance. A major work—or at least a sizeable proportion of it—that is beyond the reasonably expected capabilities of the ensemble, can actually be harmful to collective morale; or even individual morale, as there may be exacting solos that place undue pressure on particular members of the orchestra. So, how do we commence the task of making such a crucial decision?

**Planning Ahead**

While preparations are ongoing, concrete planning for seasonal programmes tends to, or should, happen well in advance. For the orchestra in UCD, as with most university orchestras, there may be one or two main performances per teaching semester (autumn and spring), while the community orchestras I have worked with tend to favour three programmes per year, with concerts taking place at the end of periods that parallel with secondary/high school terms.[4] The fundamental logistics are the date, venue, and potential soloists, and other possible features such as pre-concert talks or audio-visual elements associated with the event. Programming—and by extension the selection of repertoire—remains critical, presenting a challenge that any conductor should tackle wholeheartedly. The title of this chapter alludes to this practice, with the quote taken from a studio recording of music for the 1951 Tweety Pie short *Putty Tat Trouble*,[5] a cartoon from the Warner Bros stable that gave us Looney Tunes and Merry Melodies. Alongside memorable characters including Bugs Bunny and Daffy Duck, one of the real stars of Warner Bros was the composer Carl

Stalling, who provided illustrative orchestral scores for its cartoons during an incredibly prolific twenty-year period.[6] He is referred to in his IMDb entry as "the most famous unknown composer of the 20th century."[7] The cue to be recorded, 'Putty Tat Trouble, Pt. 6,' is heard four times in all, with Stalling conducting. Before the final take, he can be heard saying: "Once more—this will be the one!" Finally, he announces: "That's the one!"

This has always reminded me of the long-standing annual ritual that I engage in when contemplating repertoire for the university orchestra's upcoming season. I hear a work not previously considered for performance and Stalling's words begin to resonate: "This will be the one!" The next step is the acquisition of a score and a rapid assessment of technical suitability for the group. All too often, this simple stress test fails. There will regularly be passages that could stretch an orchestra far beyond its comfort zone, notably in the case of the university ensemble, where ability is likely to be mixed, while membership is necessarily transient on account of the constantly changing student population. This has happened so many times, I imagine a virtual pile of discarded scores that have accumulated as I have tossed them behind me growing taller with each successive rejection. The list is not endless, but it is rather substantial, and some examples are evaluated here.

There are beloved works in which exquisitely detailed orchestration might be obscured by dependence on supreme confidence among soloists or individual sections; among these are Debussy's *La Mer* (1905) and Ravel's *La Valse* (1920). Textural changes in each are like subtly shifting sands, and their reputation as masterpieces of so-called 'impressionistic' soundscapes belies the need for absolute precision in execution for them to be impactful. One section of *La Mer* in particular gives me pause for thought for a non-professional performance: when the cellos split into four melodic parts just before figure 9 in the first movement ('De l'aube sur midi de la mer'), with the composer specifying eight, then sixteen, cellos.[8] The lines are high in register, rhythmically elaborate, and explicit in dynamic outline. No matter the likelihood of even having sixteen cellos in the first place, rendering such a passage secure and convincing with students or amateurs would be a prodigious task, and your musicians may not thank you for trying. *La Valse* jettisons the conventions of waltzes past, those composed explicitly for social dancing, by being a relentless, dizzying joyride that ultimately seems to hurtle out of control, like a train coming off its tracks. Few works come as close to portraying the universal condition voiced in W.B. Yeats's contemporaneous poem "The Second Coming" with the lines: "Things fall apart; the centre cannot hold,/Mere anarchy is loosed upon the world."[9] However, Ravel's music cannot succumb to such threatening chaos, which is a perpetual danger in the non-professional realm, and to attempt it does the composer—and the performers—a disservice. So, perhaps unsurprisingly, *La Mer* and *La Valse* go on the pile.

I recall one instance when an accomplished young violinist was engaged to play with the university orchestra in the first of our series of movie-themed concerts, and we were open to suggestions. One made by the soloist was Erich Korngold's Violin Concerto (1945), which made good sense on account of Korngold's glittering career in Hollywood, being written during one of his most prolific periods as a film composer. As only so much technical information can be attained by listening alone, a score was ordered, acquired, viewed, and rapidly tossed on the pile. This is clearly a lavishly textured work requiring a rich orchestral sound, allied to heightened levels of sensitivity and flexibility that could prove challenging for even a professional ensemble. Korngold was thus forgotten about, and a viable alternative was quickly selected.

Another example relates to my involvement with a panel that was advising on selecting a new principal conductor for a community orchestra, one whose mainstay repertoire centred on works such as symphonies by Beethoven, Tchaikovsky, and Brahms. Each applicant was asked to supply a sample programme that they would propose for a first concert. This was a valuable exercise in ascertaining the suitability of each candidate, and how well they had done their homework on the orchestra's proficiency. One suggestion for such a programme was Nielsen's Symphony No. 5, another that has been consigned to 'the pile' more than once. There are exposed sections for the bassoons (at the opening of the first movement) and for clarinets (notably the wildly undulating lines from figure 77 in the second movement).[10] There are 100 bars of unison quaver movement in the strings, commencing after figure 51 in the second movement, for which even professional orchestras seem to be on the edge of their seats. Most hazardous of all is the final section of the work, especially from figure 114, featuring closely harmonized arpeggiation in the brass, with horns in particular in the upper reaches of their register. With ensemble and tuning so crucial in this passage, the risk of it not quite coming off for non-professional brass players is just too great, especially as it provides the dominant material with which the work closes; the axiom "all's well that ends well" is only too relevant to live musical performances.

## Who Benefits?

Of course, the magic words—"That's the one!"—do occasionally apply, and that ostensibly minor triumph may come as a surprise. But it is always advisable to take a step—or several steps—back before committing to a final decision. The starting point should be the question, to borrow a legal term, *cui bono*: "Who benefits?" If you are a young conductor seeking to make an impression, with ambitions to produce thrilling performances that shall live long in the memory of members of the orchestra and the public, then it is natural to conceive of ideal circumstances featuring your dream repertoire. However, this may not correspond to what is suitable for the ensemble with whom you are about to collaborate. The first step is to consider the potential beneficiaries of your decisions: the musicians, other 'stakeholders' associated with the musicians (such as committee members or sponsors), the (presumably paying) audience, and you as the conductor. These categories are not, of course, mutually exclusive, as, for example, a full auditorium with an appreciative crowd is naturally advantageous for musicians and management, benefitting player esteem and orchestral finances.

Let us take the case of the community orchestra, sometimes referred to as a voluntary or amateur orchestra, although the latter term has potentially pejorative connotations so is favoured less and less frequently. The conductor shall probably be employed in a professional capacity on behalf of the orchestra membership by a representative committee, and part of your relationship with this committee will be to determine a modus operandi for the group. You might ask about their priorities, which could be great performances, ticketing income, social bonding, community building, or any of these factors in combination. In terms of the players, you want to know how much they want to be stretched or challenged, and this will entail a method of assessing levels, since in the case of both university and community orchestras, ability will undoubtedly be mixed.[11] An initial way to inform this judgement is by examining an archive of recent performances, going back five years or so, and trying to gauge what has produced positive results according to members of the orchestra (e.g., the leader) and the committee.

To assist with repertoire selection in this process, I have contemplated the relevance of several models for strategic analysis in business.[12] The most established of these is SWOT, and to speak of a SWOT analysis is now very much part of the planning lexicon in businesses and other institutions. The acronym signifies Strengths, Weaknesses, Opportunities, Threats. While it can be useful in terms of reviewing the capabilities of your players, this method has a negative slant, being focused on risks rather than results. A more positive take would be to view weaknesses and threats as opportunities in themselves, as they may be part of the reasoning behind choosing appropriate works. I also believe that the maxim "you are only as strong as your weakest link" does not apply in the aspirational environment of community groups or education;

stronger players establish the standards and help raise the bar for ambition throughout the group.

Other comparative schemes include the following:

- NOISE (Needs, Opportunities, Improvements, Strengths, Exceptions).
- SOAR (Strengths, Opportunities, Aspirations, Results).
- SCORE (Strengths, Challenges, Options, Responsiveness, Effectiveness).

While SCORE may seem the most apt in terms of the acronym, SOAR better reflects the positive ethos that we aim to instil in non-professional orchestras. In addition, the five-step nature of NOISE and SCORE is unnecessarily overcomplicated, with arguably repetitive or superfluous elements. In a time-pressured environment, such as working with a scratch orchestra assembled to accompany a choir, the Tuckman model (Form, Storm, Norm, Perform) might be distinctly beneficial.[13] However, the types of ensemble we are examining normally have the luxury of extended rehearsal periods, usually over a number of weeks or even months.

For the express purposes of repertoire selection, I eventually turned to the adage about the three essential qualities for medical practitioners—the Three As—and adapted it to the conductor's brief. So, instead of Affability, Availability, and Ability, we contemplate Playability, Availability, Viability, and Bankability—the Four Abilities.

- *Playability*: how likely is it that the music you have chosen shall be technically achievable with the players at your disposal?
- *Availability*: are the orchestral parts in print, under copyright, or too expensive to purchase/hire within the limits of your budget?
- *Viability*: are there prohibitive elements in the scoring, such as unusual instruments, additional player requirements, or multiple soloists?
- *Bankability*: does the concert need to be a commercial success, thus do the selected works need to have popular appeal?

When a chosen piece satisfies all these criteria—it is playable, available, viable, and bankable—then it becomes a compelling option. However, there is a danger of continuously returning to the same body of music. A trawl through the catalogue of past concerts by many local community orchestras will reveal recurring works, some of which will have been scheduled with great frequency. They would likely include Dvořák's *New World Symphony*, Tchaikovsky's Symphony No. 5, Mendelssohn's *Hebrides Overture*, Grieg's Piano Concerto, and most of Beethoven's symphonies. If bankability is not a priority, then other works might get a look in, even some examples by the same composers; for example, Dvořák's *Czech Suite*,

Tchaikovsky's *Storm Overture*, or Grieg's *Symphonic Dances*, all of which I have conducted or performed with voluntary groups. If there are few financial constraints, thus partly diminishing the importance of availability and viability, then you might favour Gershwin's *Rhapsody in Blue*, a hugely popular work that will guarantee a sizeable audience. Ample ticketing income will also help to offset primary budgetary concerns, which come from hire of the orchestral parts, an expanded orchestra (including saxophones and banjo), a soloist's fee, and possible piano hire. Of course, these are all individual examples that may be central to your eventual plan, but there is still plenty to be done in creating a feasible and rewarding concert programme.

**The Goldilocks Zone**

Balance should be your objective. You need to address the factors discussed previously according to your strategic priorities and not merely as a box-ticking exercise. You are seeking to enter the Goldilocks Zone, a term utilized by astronomers to describe the position of exoplanets that are situated at just the right distance from their stars, at temperatures that are neither too hot nor too cold, but just right for the cultivation of habitable conditions.[14] A concert programme in the Goldilocks Zone will satisfy your selection criteria harmoniously, but balance can also imply contrast, as most concerts shall explore some combination of differing styles, tempi, or genres. For the purposes of non-professional musicians, technically or physically demanding pieces can be complemented by ones that are more manageable. Even within a single work, this can be relevant. Take Sibelius's Symphony No. 2, for example, in which the middle movements are more technically arduous than the first movement or finale, while the broad exultation of its ending feels like an indulgent reward for the exertion of the earlier sections. Similar situations are encountered in Stravinsky's *Firebird Suite* or Shostakovich's Symphony No. 10, in which the scherzo and finale can each be considered a 'roast,' while the first and third movements are slower and less onerous on the players. In the *Firebird Suite*, one could argue that the technical complexity of the 'Infernal Dance' is offset by how thrilling it is to perform, and your musicians will surely wish to rise to such a challenge.

A community orchestra might relish a work with which a student orchestra will struggle, since members of community groups are often music enthusiasts and regular concertgoers, so they tend to know what to listen for in mainstream repertoire. This is very much the case for a composer such as Brahms, whose symphonies exhibit the character of large-scale chamber music, often exploring rhythmic devices—hemiolas, syncopations, and other emphases on weaker beats—that have the potential to destabilize ensemble. However, we should never underestimate the fearlessness of youth. I remember discussing this with Katherine Lewis, director of the Irish National Youth Ballet until her untimely death in 2019.[15] Katherine had asked me to form an orchestra to accompany her dancers for live shows, and one of the convictions we shared was that young artists possess an openness to the new, in many ways not registering that something might be too difficult; they simply raise their game. I have witnessed this sense of adventure many times with young orchestras.

If you have your heart set on a major symphonic work that requires a great deal more rehearsal time, then it could be performed on its own, perhaps in a less conventional time slot (lunchtime or early evening) or preceded by an introductory talk.[16] Another way of addressing this is to be creative with the make-up of the group. Here are some options with examples:

- Create a chamber group that is a subset of the whole orchestra and have this reduced ensemble perform a large portion of the concert. In the university orchestra, we once presented Tchaikovsky's Symphony No. 4 in the second half of a concert, following a first half featuring baroque pieces for soloists and a reduced string orchestra.
- Divide by section, so there could be separate items by the brass (and possibly percussion), woodwinds, and strings. This effectively generates more time for rehearsal as they could all operate in parallel sessions, and this might also provide a podium opportunity for a student or trainee conductor. When I began to conduct a community orchestra several years ago, the committee had already decided upon a concerto that only required a string orchestra, and Copland's *Fanfare for the Common Man*, scored for brass and percussion. For the remainder of the programme, we decided upon a woodwind serenade plus a symphony for the full orchestra.
- Share the programme with a choir: you could potentially perform a single piece together then split the rest of the concert between the two groups. On returning to the concert hall stage following the hiatus enforced by Covid-19, our university choir and orchestra shared a programme, affording the orchestra a rehearsal schedule dedicated primarily to one large-scale composition, Saint-Saëns's *Organ Symphony*.[17]

Logistical considerations may remain. You might have to work within limitations of instrumentation and may require additional percussion, orchestral piano, or expanded wind and brass sections that are beyond standard mid-nineteenth-century dimensions, and this could apply equally to professional as well as non-professional groups. It would be a brave conductor making their debut with an orchestra that insists upon scheduling, for example, Percy Grainger's orchestration of Ravel's *La Vallée des Cloches*, which includes piano, celesta, metal and wooden marimba, harp, dulcitone, bells, and gong. You should also beware of insufficient rehearsal time for unfamiliar and problematic pieces, especially modern and contemporary scores.

### To Theme or Not to Theme?

Creating a programme is not necessarily tied to building a themed concert, and sometimes committing to a theme makes the goal of achieving balance more complicated, but it is a potentially helpful ploy. Themes can be the most straightforward of notions, such as a single composer, territory, or epoch, or a combination of the latter two, such as 'Viennese Classicism' or 'Russian Romantics.'[18] They can be explicit or implicit, titled or untitled. An explicit and titled theme will please whoever handles your promotions or designs your flyers, as it makes it easier to sell the concept and create a visual identity. Implicit or untitled topics will give the audience a chance to make connections, or they might be elucidated in concert notes or via a spoken introduction. Certain themes can be periodically recycled, such as music from films, television, opera, or ballet.

With film you have the bonus of being able to include bespoke soundtrack music with concert pieces by established composers who have been appropriated in films. So, John Williams, Hans Zimmer, and Hildur Guðnadóttir can appear alongside Beethoven, Brahms, and Johann Strauss II. The second movement of Beethoven's Symphony No. 7 adds significant weight to the climax of *The King's Speech* (Tom Hooper, 2011), Brahms's Hungarian Dance No. 5 has a memorable outing during a barbers' scene in Charlie Chaplin's *The Great Dictator* (1940), while Strauss's *Blue Danube Waltz* sets the graceful tone for a balletic space docking sequence in Stanley Kubrick's *2001: A Space Odyssey* (1968). There are also movie scores from a pantheon of twentieth-century composers, including Shostakovich, Prokofiev, Copland, and Bernstein. Vaughan Williams scored *Scott of the Antarctic* (Charles Frend, 1948), then adapted the music into his *Sinfonia Antarctica* (1952), while Stravinsky began to compose music for a film version of Frank Werfel's novel *The Song of Bernadette* (Henry King, 1943) that was ultimately not used. He subsequently incorporated the themes he had written into his *Symphony in Three Movements* (1945). Thus, the Vaughan Williams and Stravinsky symphonies could also be central to a film-themed programme.

An opera theme has unbounded possibilities, with a profusion of celebrated arias, duets, overtures, choruses, and entr'actes. This is an occasion to work with a choir or engage acclaimed singers as soloists, and, as with film music, there is huge popular appeal. Other themes that suggest a vast array of pieces include war, love, mythology, the sea, the elements, the seasons, and so on. Under the heading of love, there are several literary or mythical relationships that have been commemorated in music, including Romeo and Juliet (Tchaikovsky, Berlioz, Prokofiev), Daphnis and Chloë (Ravel), and Pelléas and Mélisande (Fauré, Debussy, Schoenberg, Sibelius). There are works invoking the four seasons by Vivaldi and Glazunov, while individual seasons have been portrayed in orchestral works by Frank Bridge (*Summer*), Prokofiev (*Autumnal Sketch*), Tchaikovsky (Symphony No. 1, 'Winter Daydreams'), Lili Boulanger (*D'un matin de printemps*), and, of course, Stravinsky, if you have the resources and courage to tackle *The Rite of Spring*.

One means of conceptualizing a concert is to incorporate another medium or performative feature: a live film screening, dance, acting or recitation, theatrical elements such as puppetry, or even working with a DJ or band. The latter category might necessitate a theme based on one popular artist. Puppetry is ideal for a family or children's concert, recitation for a literary theme, such as works based on the plays of William Shakespeare. Be as creative—and ambitious—as you dare.

## Concluding Remarks

Your priority with non-professional orchestras ultimately must be the players themselves. The subscriptions in a voluntary orchestra may be paying your wage, but do not lose sight of the amount of time you will be spending with the players in rehearsal; the journey is at least as important as the destination. Once the commitment has been made to your considered choices, there really is no turning back, although occasional thinking outside the box can come to your rescue. I once embarked on a programme that was stretching the ability of the orchestra in question, when one relatively short work in particular was causing tension in the ensemble, although the players never complained. The primary issue was that the parts were hired rather than purchased and had arrived later than had been expected. A decision was made to drop it from the programme not long before the concert, causing no end of relief among the players. An announcement was made to the audience on the night as it had been listed in the printed booklet, and this minor inconvenience was all but forgotten by the end of the evening. So, it is best not to panic since there is always an available solution. Finally, ask yourself: "What is the best possible outcome?"

Or perhaps: "What shall constitute a successful outcome?" Any success will ultimately be your success, by virtue of association. Balance is again a keyword as you will need to negotiate between collaboration and leadership. Hopefully, by making the whole process an enriching one for everyone involved, you will also be able to enjoy yourself along the way.

## Notes

1. Currently 38,417 according to "UCD by Numbers," UCD, accessed 14 September 2023, https://www.ucd.ie/about-ucd/about/ucdbynumbers. The total figure includes "overseas operations."
2. I am particularly grateful to UCD's chair of music, Professor Harry White, for his initial encouragement and steadfast advocacy in the ensuing years. An account of the founding of the orchestra is related in Ciarán Crilly, "The First Decade and Beyond: The UCD Symphony Orchestra 2002–14," in *100 Years of Music at UCD: A Centenary Festschrift*, ed. Wolfgang Marx (Dublin: UCD School of Music, 2014), 54–59. I should also acknowledge the work of the European Network of University Orchestras (https://www.enuo.eu/) and the European Student Orchestra Festival (https://esofestival.com/), which have created opportunities to observe corresponding ensembles in Europe and how they operate. Many of the orchestras we have listened to and collaborated with can boast a substantially longer history than those based in Ireland. The Royal Academic Orchestra based in Uppsala University, for example, "has existed since 1627." See "The Royal Academic Orchestra," Uppsala University, updated 11 January 2022, https://www.akademiskakapellet.uu.se/about-us/about-the-orchestra/.
3. A parallel strategy for choirs is discussed in Chapter 12 by Kari Turunen in this volume.
4. This is frequently due to such orchestras rehearsing in school halls, so the schedule would be subject to school closures.
5. "Putty Tat Trouble, Pt. 6 (1951)," The Carl Stalling Project Volume 2, YouTube, audio, published 23 January 2017, https://www.youtube.com/watch?v=qMDCtQnvWRQ. This short clip (just eighty seconds long) constitutes a model of how to run a studio recording session swiftly and efficiently. It evolves over four takes as follows: run through; the musicians are afforded an opportunity to fix initial problems in a second run; the conductor identifies issues that have persisted and communicates them to the players, then they go again; one more just to be sure—while there may be more takes, if necessary, under advisement from the control room.
6. See his list of contributions in "Carl W. Stalling (1891–1972)," IMDb, accessed 12 February 2023, https://www.imdb.com/name/nm0006298/.
7. "Carl W. Stalling (1891–1972)."
8. Claude Debussy, *La Mer: Trois Esquisses Symphoniques*, full score (Kassel: Bärenreiter, 2019).
9. W.B. Yeats, "The Second Coming," *The Collected Poems of W.B. Yeats*, ed. Richard J. Finneran (New York: Scribner, 1996), 19.
10. All figure numbers refer to Carl Nielsen, *Symphony No. 4*, full score (Copenhagen: Skandinavisk Musikforlag, 1950).
11. This will contrast with ensembles based in music conservatories, where a higher minimum level is to be expected and the conductor shall treat the musicians as professionals-in-training.

12  See, for example, Abdul Momin, "5 Alternatives to SWOT Analysis, Tackling Its Limitations," Pestle Analysis: SWOT and Business Analysis Tools, published 4 March 2023, https://pestleanalysis.com/alternatives-to-swot-analysis/.
13  This was originally outlined in Bruce Tuckman, "Developmental Sequence in Small Groups," *Psychological Bulletin* 63, no. 6 (1965): 384–99, https://doi.org/10.1037/h0022100.
14  See "Goldilocks Zone," NASA, published 15 December 2022, https://exoplanets.nasa.gov/resources/323/goldilocks-zone/.
15  "Katherine Lewis Obituary: Passionate, Driving Force in Irish Ballet," *Irish Times*, 27 April 2019, https://www.irishtimes.com/life-and-style/people/katherine-lewis-obituary-passionate-driving-force-in-irish-ballet-1.3872657. For a brief history of the Irish National Youth Ballet, including the orchestra, see "History of the Company," Irish National Youth Ballet, accessed 2 September 2023, https://www.inybco.com/history/.
16  With the UCD Symphony Orchestra, I inaugurated a series of concerts in 2019 that have presented core symphonic works (including Tchaikovsky's Symphony No. 6 and Elgar's Cello Concerto) following a critical introduction, which included excerpts from the featured work and other relevant pieces.
17  The full programmes can be viewed in online archives for the UCD Symphony Orchestra ("Past Concerts," UCD Symphony Orchestra, accessed 12 September 2023, https://www.ucd.ie/orchestra/concerts/pastconcerts/) and Dublin Orchestral Players ("Concert Diary 1998–2023," Dublin Orchestral Players, accessed 12 September 2023, https://www.dublinorchestralplayers.com/pb/wp_ceb8f51e/wp_ceb8f51e.html).
18  Two of the most commercially successful concerts given by the UCD Symphony Orchestra were celebrations of Russian music, on each occasion selling out Ireland's premier classical music venue, the National Concert Hall in Dublin, which has a maximum capacity of 1,200.

# 7
# THE ROLE OF THE CONDUCTOR IN US ORCHESTRAS
## A Concise Guide

*Peter Shannon*

On graduating with a BMus from University College Dublin in 1992, I was accepted to study orchestral conducting at the Hochschule für Musik Franz Liszt Weimar, after which I completed a second postgraduate degree in orchestral conducting at the Hochschule für Musik Karlsruhe. Following ten wonderful years as director of the Collegium Musicum at the University of Heidelberg, I was ready for a change and began applying for positions in the United States. Posts at the helm of a professional orchestra in the United States are hugely competitive, and it is common for even smaller orchestras to have hundreds of qualified applicants. Luckily, conducting skills and communication skills are high on the list of 'must haves' when auditioning for these coveted posts. However, understanding the constitutional map of these organizations, and being able to speak to issues, such as outreach and educational programmes, fundraising, and other responsibilities of the conductor, can help in the audition process.

Until relatively recently, most conductors needed to have decades of experience of personal music-making on an instrument and of conducting before being considered for a position at the helm of a symphony orchestra. When I studied conducting, for example, piano was hugely important in the audition process. Being a world-class violinist alone was not sufficient; excellent keyboard skills were also essential. This has changed dramatically, and piano proficiency is no longer a requirement in most schools. Also, as the age of conductors being appointed to even major orchestras in the United States gets younger and younger, vast experience as a conductor is not required. However, an understanding of the dynamics and workings of an orchestra may make the difference between the two or three final conducting candidates.

This chapter is a concise conductor's guide to how orchestras in the United States are set up; it aims to provide some insight into their organizational map and how the conductor fits into this map. This short guide is simply that: a short guide. It is by no means exhaustive, but rather a starting point. My hope is that it may serve to help younger conductors understand how the system works in the United States, and that it may help them to navigate the audition process to become the conductor of a professional orchestra there.

## Becoming an Orchestral Conductor in the United States

Applying for jobs in the United States can be a daunting task. When I began applying for positions there while based in Germany, I had no guidance. In fact, my story is extremely atypical, and not a path I would suggest to other would-be conductors. In my case, I was extremely fortunate to make my way through the various rounds of competition, meeting the board, executive director (ED), key orchestral players, and community leaders, and, of course, conducting rehearsals and concerts with the orchestra.

Here are a few more typical ways to apply for a job in the United States:

1. Find an agent for conductors in the United States.
2. Win a major conducting competition.
3. Apply as an assistant conductor for a professional symphony orchestra, preferably in a metropolitan city.
4. Take part in conducting courses, assist a well-known conductor, and ask for their help. Sit in on rehearsals of major orchestras and enquire how to become an assistant on a project, and so on.

Ideally, one should look to tick two or three of these boxes to set yourself up for a position in the United States. Even though it worked for me, cold call applications without agency representation will almost certainly not be considered. Getting started in conducting is a classic chicken-and-egg scenario. Without experience, it is difficult to get an agent; without an agent, it is difficult to get an orchestra. My advice is to do as much conducting while at college, organizing small ensembles, and undertaking as many concerts as possible.

Certainly, being around a music centre will help. Cities such as London, New York, Vienna, or Berlin afford rich possibilities to get to know the very best in the music industry. While I am incredibly indebted to the Franz

Liszt Weimar for my education as a conductor, my advice would be to concentrate on schools in large metropolitan areas. Studying at conservatories in these major music centres will allow access to visiting conductors and soloists. Conductors differ, of course: some may be extremely generous with their time and advice, while others may offer no help at all. But there are many stories of conductors taking younger students under their wing and mentoring them. This can lead to wonderful opportunities.

## The Organizational Map

The symphony orchestra entity in the United States is not simply the musicians and the conductor, but a multifaceted institution that combines business and accounting, public relations, branding and marketing, regulatory compliance, as well as musicianship. Understanding the structure of a symphony organization, and how the conductor fits into that organization, is essential when seeking a conducting appointment.

### The Board

Most symphony orchestras are structured as not-for-profit corporations (501(c)(3) in the Internal Revenue Service (IRS)), and a symphony board will be charged with oversight responsibilities prescribed in the federal regulations governing such an entity. The board, headed by a chairperson, will ordinarily have between ten and thirty members, depending on the organization's size and location. As a corporation, it is subject to state law; as a 501(c)(3) non-profit, the entity will also be subject to federal regulations. One should not mistake the title 'not-for-profit' to mean that a symphony is less fiscally responsible than its for-profit neighbours. Both should be fiscally responsible and avoid deficit operations. The difference between a not-for-profit symphony board and a for-profit corporation board is a simple yet important one: the mission statement. A for-profit organization is guided by its bottom-line, while a not-for-profit is guided by its mission statement. That said, a well-run not-for-profit is just as fiscally sound as a for-profit entity, even enjoying an operating surplus.

A symphony board in the United States is typically made up of philanthropists and successful members of the community (e.g., business leaders, doctors, attorneys), but these individuals are not professional board members. They are not paid for their service. Though most board members themselves have had successful careers, they should understand that their role within the organization is to offer their problem-solving and operational skills, or any other particular skill that they may have that may be of benefit. It is important that board members are identified by the board chairperson, the ED, and the governance committee according to the skill set they bring: a board of twenty people does not need five attorneys.

Key responsibilities typically vested in the board include hiring the ED, artistic director (AD), and conductor, overseeing the performance of those key individuals to ensure consistency with the goals and objectives of the organization, and evaluating performance for the purpose of continuing employment. It is important to understand that the board does not—and should not—involve itself in the day-to-day running of the orchestra; this duty lies with the ED and AD.

A well-run board is a huge asset to both the ED and the AD, enabling them, supporting them, and also guiding them where necessary. It provides constructive feedback as well as being an 'ear to the ground' in the community. Personally, I have found that listening to diverse board members' opinions can give the AD a more holistic impression of the board and has enabled me to understand issues such as programming, finance, and outreach within a much broader context. I recommend seeking out board members and asking for their advice, even—and maybe more particularly—the ones whose opinions differ from yours. During the first years of my appointment to an orchestra in the United States, I found the politics and culture to be hugely different from what I was used to in either Ireland or Germany. Having lived in the United States, for over fifteen years, I now have a much richer understanding of the issues that still perplex most Europeans. Some of my closest friends today are those who held leadership roles in the boards of my orchestras, and whose advice I sought. I encourage others to do the same.

The board usually will have an executive committee that can meet when it is impracticable to assemble the full board; for example, over the summer. The executive committee can also act in the place of the board in an emergency, subject to any limitations on committee powers set forth in the bylaws. The executive committee should always be transparent in its operation, particularly when giving its report to the full board or seeking ratification for any actions already taken. Some organizations have regular executive meetings a week or so before a full board meeting, to discuss matters to be presented to the full board. Meetings should be planned to run efficiently; this is consistent with the board's function of oversight of the organization's operations, as opposed to detailed management. For example, if a plan needs to be drawn up for the board to fulfil a particular function (e.g., participation in a fundraising event), that planning should not begin at a board meeting; instead, the plan should be designed in advance and presented to the board for discussion and approval. Efficiently planned and run meetings help to encourage busy professionals to participate in voluntary board service. I have always asked to be included in board meetings as AD, though some orchestras do not include the AD. I like to think that an AD reporting once a month—or whenever board meetings are scheduled—gives the conductor a chance to answer questions or address concerns such as repertoire choice and outreach.

*The Executive Director*

The ED is responsible for the day-to-day running of the organization. They are responsible for all business decisions, for managing the office staff, and ensuring that staff fulfil their roles. The ED is answerable to the board, so must not only understand and be fully committed to the mission of the organization, but also be scrupulously honest in all business matters. It is always a good thing when the ED and chairperson of the board work well together. In my experience, the ED will meet weekly with the chairperson to discuss finances (fundraising or other upcoming events, corporate and private donors) and how to engage the board actively in support of the organization. A successful ED must be innovative when changing circumstances dictate and cannot rigidly adhere to the ways that things have been done in the past. The ED must help the chairperson to understand how outside forces (e.g., the economy) impact the potential for success. Nothing better illustrates this principle than the recent experience of symphony orchestras during the Covid-19 crisis. Clearly, the ED is responsible for the money side of the organization, but fundamentally, the ED should have control over every aspect outside the artistic product, which should be solely the responsibility of the AD.

*The Conductor and Artistic Director*

The AD is to the artistic product what the ED is to the financial side of the business. They should have full oversight into anything that represents the artistic side of the organization. This begins with the selection and retention of musicians, the music programming, and extends to setting an overall artistic vision. The AD is also responsible, together with the ED, for monitoring the performance of production staff, including the head of artistic operations, operations manager, backstage manager, and outreach coordinator.

In smaller organizations, it is typical for the conductor to have the title 'Conductor and Artistic Director.' In larger ones, this role is often divided, with the conductor's role limited to choosing repertoire for concerts and conducting them, as well as serving as a public face (e.g., for involvement in fundraising events). The AD in a larger organization would then be responsible for choosing other repertoire, guest conductors, and soloists, and the oversight of production staff.

## The Artistic Director and the Executive Director Dynamic

The relationship between the ED and AD is arguably the most important relationship for any symphonic organization to get right. Ultimately, the board decides who will be ED and AD. When hiring an ED or AD, a good board will pay attention to the opinion and suggestion of the incumbent AD or ED in the selection of their new business partner. However, ultimately the board decides on who is the AD and ED. While the map says that the ED is the business boss and the AD is the artistic boss, there are huge crossovers in the roles. As AD, I have found it important to keep a clear line of communication open with the ED, preferably on a weekly basis. Any ED will also have an active interest in the artistic product, and it is fitting that the AD should pay attention to the artistic suggestions or recommendations of the ED. Engaging the ED in the artistic choices helps a sense of teamwork and sends a signal to the ED that their opinion and ideas are valued. At the same time, it is essential that the AD appreciates the fiscal status of the organization when designing programmes; more complex works with very large ensembles requiring more rehearsal time (e.g., a Mahler symphony) will cost far more than a smaller ensemble performing baroque repertoire. With a successful orchestra, there will be room for both, smartly positioned in the season.

## So, Who is the Boss?

Ultimately, the chairperson of the board is the boss. The ED and AD both report to the board, but a wise board will be cautious about involving itself in the day-to-day running of the business. Simply put, the ED is the business boss, and the AD is the artistic boss, with the board being responsible for the hiring/firing of ED and AD. This may seem rather one-dimensional, but nonetheless serves as a useful general guide.

## The Board Member Dynamic: Collaboration with the Artistic Director and Executive Director

Board members may have a particular interest in some area that is the remit of the AD or ED. Many board members are, or have been, successful in their respective careers, and it is important for the ED to engage these skills whenever that can be done for the efficient operation of the organization. A marketing or branding professional or former CEO of a corporation may have excellent advice for the ED, and the smart ED will leverage that expertise. Similarly, other board members may have strong ideas on programming or artistic direction. As AD, one has to be sensitive to the wishes or suggestions of board members. Listening is important, and I have often found that it is possible to acknowledge programming suggestions and incorporate them into my artistic vision.

## The Difference between Orchestras in the United States and Europe

The most important difference between orchestras in the United States and their counterparts in Europe is the manner in which financing is structured. Orchestras in the United States rely hugely on corporate and individual donations, which typically will make up 60 per cent of the annual budget. State funding is usually only a small percentage of the budget. A recent article by the Georgia Arts Council stated: "A total of 266 grants were awarded that will provide more than $2 million in funding towards arts initiatives throughout the state."[1] In 2020–21, the Atlanta Symphony Orchestra, for example—just one of a number of orchestras in the state of Georgia—had an annual operating budget of $27 million.[2] This is in contrast to European orchestras, which are mostly government funded and/or funded through state grants.

## Unions

Most orchestras in the United States are unionized: musicians who choose to belong to the union are protected by their local union, which in turn is supported by the National Union of Musicians.

## Outreach and Education

The best orchestras in the United States pay particular attention to their Outreach and Education programmes for good reason. While an orchestra's primary goal must be to produce excellent concerts, orchestras also look beyond the concert hall to improve their 'narrative' as to why they are relevant to their communities. Given that much of the funding for orchestras comes from within the community in the form of private and corporate philanthropy, organizational staff (including the AD) need to be aware of the interests of local businesses and individual or would-be donors. It is important to recognize that not all donors to a symphony orchestra are necessarily classical music fans. In the United States, businesses will often have a list of targets that must be fulfilled in order to release funding.

For example, a company that is focused on improving their employees' standard of living may be interested in buying tickets for them to attend a concert or fund a programme that allows their employees and family members to attend a dress rehearsal. Or a private donor who gives generously to a local hospital may be interested in funding smaller ensembles to visit and play in the lobby of the hospital. It is not uncommon for private donors to donate tens or even hundreds of thousands of dollars to a symphony orchestra's education or outreach programmes. Such donations, referred to as 'restricted funding,' must be used only for the purpose set out by the donor.

As orchestras prefer to receive 'unrestricted funding,' finding a connection to a donor through a particular scheme *outside the concert hall* is a significant first step in engaging their interest. Once this engagement happens, there is a strong possibility that, with careful negotiation, the donor may consider investing in the organization. As an example of this, under my direction and guidance, one of my orchestras performed three concerts a season in the most 'at-risk' neighbourhoods of the city. A small ensemble of around ten players performed an eclectic mix of music in a relaxed atmosphere in a social housing setting with a high crime rate that included weekly shootings. We invited a local street vendor to grill barbecue food and we found a private donor to underwrite free ice cream for children. We were careful to invite leaders from across the community and asked the local police and fire crews to attend. When the master of ceremonies managed to arrange a dance-off between the local police and fire crews, the day was won. On the strength of these programmes, the city council chose to increase their financial support to the orchestra considerably.

While the oversight of educational and outreach initiatives is often the shared remit of both the ED and the AD, the AD, as the 'face' of the organization, can often motivate or encourage donations. Also, as the creative force, they may have an area of expertise or interest outside the concert hall that may be utilized in either the education or outreach area for the orchestra. In my case, I have long had an interest in the power of music in a healthcare setting. Both my orchestras in the United States developed robust Music and Healing programmes at cancer centres, hospitals, hospices, and long-term memory care units. At the time of writing, my orchestra has just received a donation from an individual of over $300,000, an incredibly generous gift that was motivated largely by the Music and Healing enterprise of the symphony.

### Planning a Season

The annual operating budget will dictate how many concerts any orchestra can produce. Obviously, population and the number of businesses in a certain community are drivers of their economy, and thus the budget of their symphony, but this is not always the case. A total of 66 per cent of orchestras in the United States are community orchestras or semi-professional, having a small operating budget of up to $300,000. Some 4 per cent have a budget of between $2 and $5 million, 3 per cent have a budget of between $5 and $20 million, and 2 per cent have an annual operating budget of more than $20 million.[3] As a professional conductor, one is most likely to be successful in orchestras with an annual operating budget of between $300,000 and $2 million. These orchestras will typically have at least one concert per month, with larger cities also repeating concerts on subsequent days. Orchestras in this group in the United States typically divide their season into pops and classical concerts, so it is always beneficial when the AD feels comfortable in many genres. I do not use a baton in pops concerts and make a concerted effort to help create a more relaxed feel to the evening by chatting with the audience and having some banter with the band.

**Repertoire Choices: How to Get It Right**

Since I began conducting, the narrative that classical music audiences are dwindling has been constant. Since the Covid-19 pandemic, this narrative is even more pronounced and has led to new discussions as to how to gain and retain audiences. Every conductor of any professional orchestra in the United States will have had countless discussions regarding repertoire, with everyone from audience members to ED and board members all offering their 'solutions' to the problem. Here, I would like to offer a few insights into my approach to planning a season of a small to mid-sized professional orchestra in the United States. It is based on my own philosophy and beliefs surrounding music, and my own personal experience as a conductor of two professional symphony orchestras in the United States.

The first truism is that pops concerts are more popular (broadly speaking) and that the classical concerts are financed on the back of the pops concerts. Christmas concerts can be 'cash cows' for most orchestras, many choosing to do repeat performances of the Christmas concert and Christmas family concerts for additional revenue. EDs, orchestral managers, and ADs can expect to be inundated with agents selling and marketing their artists and shows, all of which span the gamut from pops to classical. Typical pops concerts marketed are those featuring the music of a famous band or artist arranged for full symphony orchestra, and come with singers and a small band of anywhere from three to seven or more musicians who play alongside the orchestra. These shows tend to bring in larger audiences. Unfortunately, there is not a lot of audience transfer from these concerts to the classical concerts, so, what can we do better?

One mistake a lot of American orchestras make is to separate their classical and pops concerts, and packaging or pitting one genre against the other. A way around this is to programme hybrid concerts featuring different genres. This might be in the form of a themed concert, where classical music can be presented alongside pops. A Halloween concert might include Herrmann's *Psycho Suite* alongside *A Night on Bald Mountain*, plus music from *Harry Potter* or *Ghostbusters*.

My philosophy on programming comes down to one thing: trust the music to bring the audience. For better or worse, most audiences are not coming to a concert to hear Prokofiev's Piano Concerto No. 3, Shostakovich's Cello Concerto No. 1, or Tippett's Symphony No. 4, but pieces like this have huge energy and drive. When choosing lesser-known repertoire, I look for music that I know will forge an instant connection with audience members. You do not need a sophisticated, over-educated audience to enjoy classical music like this, but you do need to present it in a creative and appealing way. Francie Ostrower and Thad Calabrese's article in *Classical Music*, entitled "Audience Building and Financial Health in the Nonprofit Performing Arts," examines trends within the orchestral world, particularly in relation to audience participation and attendance at concerts. My own experience concurs with an important point raised in the article:

> A widespread theme in the literature is that audiences do not attend solely, or even primarily, for the art presented, but for an *arts experience*, and that arts organizations are not currently responsive to this desire. Answers vary, however, as to what experiences audiences seek and how organizations could provide these.[4]

The 'experience' is the whole package offered, of course, and includes information pertinent to the concert, such as a video of the featured soloist sent to concertgoers before the concert, or a video or quotes from selected orchestral players as to why they are looking forward to the concert. Before I conduct a piece of challenging repertoire, I always speak to the audience and explain the music—what to listen for—and I am careful to allow space for audience members to be creative with their own headspace, perspective, and creativity. I also invite them to come up with their own 'meaning' to the piece they are hearing. Such inclusive talks can be hugely rewarding for attendees. Once audience members get used to this inclusivity, they enjoy it, and my experience is that they 'trust' the repertoire more and welcome the challenge of discovering previously unknown repertoire.

There have been many attempts to make classical music more attractive with additional content; for example, a film of the Milky Way for Holst's *The Planets*, or an aerial trapeze artist for Bizet's *Carmen*. I have previously heard it said that: "We need to give people what they want." While this perspective is understandable and laudable, I prefer to show audiences what they do not yet have, and to show them where we—as musicians—know they would want to be. No amount of bells and whistles can make the slow movement of Rodrigo's *Concierto de Aranjuez* more meaningful than knowing it was written for his deceased son. No video can add to the experience of humanity on hearing the last note of Beethoven's Symphony No. 9, when one recounts that Beethoven was deaf when he conducted the first performance, and with the knowledge that one of the soloists supposedly had to gesture to him to turn around and acknowledge the audience because he was still deep in thought turning over pages of the score. It is our job as conductors to find ways for this music to 'speak' to the audience. This begins with the music itself, of course, but transfers quickly into the intensity and integrity of our own compassionate connection to the musicians as conductor, and our trust in the endless humanity of all our audience members.

## Notes

1  "Georgia Council for the Arts Awards More than $2 Million in Grant Funding to Support Arts throughout Georgia," Georgia Department of Economic Development, published 7 July 2021, https://www.georgia.org/press-release/georgia-council-arts-awards-more-2-million-grant-funding-support-arts-throughout.
2  Jessica Saunders, "CFO of the Year: Susan Ambo Balanced ASO FY2020 Budget Despite Revenue Loss from Covid," *Atlanta Business Chronicle*, 21 May 2021, https://www.bizjournals.com/atlanta/news/2021/05/21/cfo-of-the-year-aso-susan-ambo-balanced-budget.html.
3  "Orchestras at a Glance," League of American Orchestras, published September 2022, https://americanorchestras.org/orchestras-at-a-glance/.
4  Francie Ostrower and Thad Calabrese, "Audience Building and Financial Health in the Nonprofit Performing Arts: Current Literature and Unanswered Questions (Executive Summary)," in *Classical Music: Contemporary Perspectives and Challenges*, ed. Michael Beckerman and Paul Boghossian (Cambridge, UK: Open Book Publishers, 2021) 66–67, https://doi.org/10.11647/OBP.0242.

# 8

## FOSTERING THE NEXT GENERATION

*Gerhard Markson*

> How do you expect to control an orchestra if you cannot control yourself? . . . If the orchestra plays without you as well as with you, you are superfluous!
>
> *Igor Markevitch*[1]

In the early 1970s, as part of my preparative training in conducting, I participated in the international conducting courses of Igor Markevitch in Monte Carlo. These courses shaped my entire perspective on conducting.

Markevitch had established a brilliant career as a composer in the late 1920s. He was famous. They called him the second Igor—Stravinsky was not amused. Then he began conducting. Today he is remembered as one of the leading conductors of the mid-twentieth century.

Markevitch's work as a conductor was prolific. Throughout his tenure as principal conductor of L'Orchestre Lamoureux, he etched his legacy on so many recordings for Philips that at one point in the 1960s and early 1970s in Germany buying a classical music record effectively meant choosing either a recording by Igor Markevitch or Herbert von Karajan. His style was also distinctly recognizable; video recordings of his concerts in Stockholm, Aix-en-Provence, Tokyo, and elsewhere show his stunning control over the score. He conducted exclusively by heart, while his minimalist movements would show the orchestra everything they need and nothing more. No dancing around, no acting—simply music.

As his students, we had the privilege of learning exactly these elements of conducting. During the course, no student was allowed to conduct the Orchestre Philharmonique de Monte Carlo until they knew the score by

DOI: 10.4324/9781003299660-11

heart. Beyond the score, Markevitch also insisted we master the physical techniques of conducting, reasoning, "We expect singers or instrumentalists to be technically perfect when they perform in public—why do we not expect the same from a conductor who is supposed to control and inspire an orchestra?" To Markevitch, technical mastery was a key element of the profession, not an added luxury. An example of this physical competency was moving and using both arms independently to guide the orchestra. We learned to control the tempo with our right arm, while cueing or demonstrating dynamic changes with the left. To further our ability to consciously use our bodies in the work of conducting, Markevitch's courses included regular sessions with Mosché Feldenkrais, the legendary founder of the Feldenkrais Method. Feldenkrais's mantra was: "You need to be able to have your body do exactly what your brain tells it to do!" This was precisely Markevitch's approach to conducting: be conscious of what you are doing.

To this day, you can recognize any conductor who has studied with Igor Markevitch. Watch his videos, and then consider Herbert Blomstedt's recordings. Blomstedt—now in his nineties and his most famous student—still refers to Igor Markevitch as The Master. I concur: Markevitch was a master of the trade, and he taught many of us what conducting is all about.

In 1974, I started my own career as a conductor, and quickly realized that the principles I had learned from Markevitch were existential. 'The Master' had not simply conveyed to me a personal arsenal of tricks that he himself used when conducting; rather he had given me a structured method that would work on principle. Realizing this made me think back to a moment during one of his courses, when Markevitch had asked a student to conduct a passage in a certain way. The student remarked he had seen Bernstein conduct the same passage in a completely different manner. Markevitch smiled mildly and said: "I am not saying that my method is the only possible way to master this passage, but I can tell you that it will work no matter *who* applies it."

Not long after I started working as a conductor, colleagues started asking me where I had studied, noting that my mental and physical approach to conducting was different from the mainstream. I offered to introduce them to the Markevitch method. Many were surprised, having experienced teachers who insisted that conducting could not be taught, that you were either born to be a conductor, or not. There may be some elements of truth to this—of course a conductor needs communication skills, an 'inner ear,' imagination, determination and so on, traits that come more naturally to some than others. However, students absolutely *can learn* how to study a score, and how to physically transport their understanding of that score to an orchestra.

As I became more experienced in my own work, I chose to pass on the Markevitch method to younger conductors through courses in Dublin and Salzburg, as well as in private sessions throughout the years. I observed how beneficial his structured method was to these young conductors.

Many of us may have aided the careers of younger conductors with an occasional letter of recommendation or a personal reference. However, to have a direct and decisive impact on a younger colleague's career is a rare gift. It requires a unique combination of personality, circumstance, and a sequence of events within which your influence can be the deciding factor. In one instance, I had the privilege of experiencing all these elements aligning.

I would like to recount the story of Georg Fritzsch.

In the early 1990s, when I was General Music Director of the Hagen Theater and Philharmonic Orchestra, I was invited to conduct a concert in Gera in the east of Germany. In the first rehearsal of Dvořák's Symphony No. 6, while we were working on the last movement, the leader of the cello section asked a question that demonstrated how exceptionally well he knew this symphony. I was flabbergasted since this symphony is not particularly popular or well known in Germany. When I asked him after rehearsal how he knew the piece so well, he answered, "I conducted it four weeks ago!" and introduced himself as Georg Fritzsch.

A few days later Georg invited me to watch the video recording of him conducting Dvořák's symphony. I generally prefer not to judge conductors based on video recordings, since observing how a conductor interacts with an orchestra in person is far more informative. That said, a video can be sufficient to see whether a conductor is technically talented. This particular one was different. Not only did it clearly show Georg's technical talent to conduct but it also clearly demonstrated that he was a great communicator.

Not long after our meeting in Gera, Georg decided to commit fully to conducting. Leaving the instrumental side of the orchestra and switching to the 'other side' is a difficult process. We agreed to stay in touch, and I offered to be of assistance whenever possible.

The following season I had invited a guest conductor to perform Liszt's *Faust Symphony* with the Hagen Philharmonic Orchestra. Six weeks before the first rehearsal, his agency informed me that they had lost contact with him and could not guarantee that he would appear in Hagen as agreed. I called Georg and asked him if he was willing to learn the symphony and be on standby. It was a big ask. To learn the *Faust Symphony*—a difficult and complex composition—in such a short amount of time, with no guarantee of performing it, would require a significant amount of dedication and willpower. Georg was up for it. His determination paid off. Georg ended up conducting the concert, which was a great success. A few years later, I retired from Hagen and recommended Georg as my successor. The orchestra voted overwhelmingly in his favour. He eventually moved on from Hagen and became *Generalmusikdirektor* in Kiel, a larger opera house. He currently holds the same position at the State Theater in Karlsruhe and conducts regularly in first-class opera houses such as Stuttgart, Cologne, Dresden, and Geneva. He just returned from his first tour in Japan. In addition to his conducting, he has also chosen to pass on his own expertise by teaching conducting at the University of Music and Performing Arts Munich.

This is what Georg's career shows us. There are a number of 'ingredients' that make for a successful conductor: you obviously need musicality, but also the dedication, willpower, and humility to learn the techniques and skills to best transport your understanding of a score to an orchestra. Finally, you need a bit of luck and a lot of patience.

If we are lucky students, we encounter a teacher such as Igor Markevitch, who is willing to pass on a wealth of unique experience and knowledge. In turn, we can show gratitude to our own teachers by passing their methods and legacy on to the next generation. And along the way, we can help younger colleagues by sharing the practical knowledge we have gained over time, to be used as they succeed on their own professional paths.

### Note

1 All quotations herein are from personal recollections and are thus unpublished.

# 9

## HOW TO HELP MUSICIANS FEEL MORE VALUED AND FULFILLED AT WORK

*Tiffany Chang*

**Something Was Wrong**

I recently left a job. I knew something was wrong: I was afraid of making mistakes. I avoided risky projects or creative endeavours. I felt like I was never good enough. I started to feel isolated and unsupported. I did not feel like I belonged to my department. I did not feel like I was welcomed. My self-worth went on a rollercoaster ride. I felt undervalued and underappreciated, that my work did not matter. I lost touch with why I was there in the first place. I felt stuck in my job and helpless in my career. I became unhappy.

Does this sound familiar?

Actually, I came to realize the majority of jobs I had were like this. I did not know that these feelings were signs of workplace disempowerment. Disempowering people means "disenfranchising them, taking away their natural sense of power and responsibility, their curiosity, and their creativity."[1] It is a definition that I find meaningful. I am also not that special. Disempowerment is so common across many industries that we have almost come to expect it as the norm—that is, until we stumble across an experience that shows us otherwise.

Luckily, I had one of those moments: I was a guest conductor for an opera company where I was making my debut. It was high stakes. I should have been overcome with fear, anxiety, and the need to prove myself. Instead, I experienced empowerment.

So what did that feel like? I felt like the company really wanted me to do my best. They were not looking over my shoulder trying to catch me

DOI: 10.4324/9781003299660-12

making mistakes. I felt trusted to try things I was not sure would work, and I felt safe knowing that it was acceptable to make some mistakes in that process—as I saw that others' mistakes met with support, not punishment. I felt free to speak up when there was a problem. I was given permission to take the initiative to do something about it. I felt seen and encouraged simply to be myself and to put effort into the things I cared about.

Most surprisingly, I did the best artistic work in my life without even trying to do so. I stopped worrying about whether I was achieving or whether I was good enough. The funny thing is that I did not think that I miraculously became a better conductor. And I did not fundamentally change who I am, my working style, or my values. I was simply empowered to be myself and to do my best work. In addition, I felt valued and fulfilled doing it, like my work truly mattered.

*How* did they do that? Why did it feel so *new*? I wanted more of it, and I could not help but think that, at the core, it is what everyone else wants too, because we are all human.

### What Do We *Really* Want?

Feeling valued and fulfilled, being allowed to be our authentic selves, and achieving our full potential at work—why do we want these things? Perhaps we should begin with our fundamental human needs. What is it that we *really* want?

More than anything else, people want to belong—to our families, organizations, and communities. We do not want to appear different because it comes with the chance of being ostracized. In our hunter-gatherer days, being excluded from a group quite literally meant more danger, as we were more likely to die without the protection and resources of the group. So, we have evolved to constantly evaluate whether we are in or out because belonging in a group ensures our survival: belonging equals safety.

When our sense of belonging is threatened, the fear-response part of the brain—the amygdala—gets triggered.[2] It is the same response that helps us fight or flee when our life is in danger. Even though our modern threats to belonging are not life-threatening, the amygdala has not caught up with the times. Our need to belong remains visceral and real. It allows us to work harder to impress and to earn our place. It can also hold us back as we tell ourselves unhelpful stories:

- We are afraid of what others might think of what we say, so we stay silent.
- If we show who we really are, maybe people will not like us.
- If we make a mistake, people will lose respect for us.

- If we fail, we will seem weak and no longer valuable to the group.
- If we do not fit in, we will be excluded from the group, and people might stop inviting us to lunch.
- If we get on our boss's bad side, we might lose a chance at a promotion, or worse, get fired.

The technical term for this is 'psychological danger,' a fear of negative repercussions and exclusion. This can drive many of our actions and thoughts, and it is perhaps more prevalent in artistic workplaces than our industry wants to admit.

Imagine what motivates us to not make a mistake in rehearsal. Of course, a portion of it is due to our desire to achieve excellence, but we also are motivated by fear. We are all afraid of embarrassment, disappointment, loss of status, and rejection. Yet, it is hard to notice just how much we are driven by fear because it has been so normalized in our education and training. For most of us, it often feels safer to fly under the radar. We stop ourselves from speaking up out of fear of retribution. We do not try things that are risky because we believe failure equals losing our status, rank, and job. Garry Ridge, CEO of WD-40, made an astute observation: "Most people only know they're doing a good job because no one yelled at them."[3]

Deep down, however, we really want to fly *above* the radar. We want to know that we belong to our group and that we contribute meaningfully to it. We want psychological safety, where we feel safe to speak up when something is wrong, to take risks to innovate, and to fail as part of iteration. We want to be seen and valued for who we are. We want to know that our work matters. Our artistic workplaces do not traditionally help empower in these ways. As musicians, we often tell ourselves that we are lucky to be doing what we love for a living. We should be so grateful. It may perhaps be bit of a social lie we tell ourselves. We may not even realize we are not as happy as we think we are. I have been haunted by a study that revealed job satisfaction rates for orchestral musicians rank below that of prison guards.[4] We can do better for our musicians. We deserve to feel more valued and fulfilled, safer, and happier at work.

As someone who interfaces with musicians, a conductor has the most crucial role in this endeavour. I was determined to find out how we can accomplish this. I followed the breadcrumbs into other fields, intrigued by discussions about topics such as improving work culture to motivate our people, how leaders are like coaches who guide employees towards job satisfaction, and why psychological safety is so crucial for high-performing teams. Everywhere I went, I found myself asking: "Why are we not doing this in music? Why are we not even talking about it?"

I will now share three compelling strategies that can improve our job satisfaction rates—and in turn, empower our musicians to feel more valued, fulfilled, and ultimately happy. These three strategies are: feed belonging, put people first, and focus on purpose.

## Strategy One: Feed Belonging

We need a lot of reminders that we belong. In *The Culture Code*, Daniel Coyle asks us to consider how many times we need to hear the words "I love you." The answer is: "Never enough."[5] We can capitalize on this understanding to feed this basic need of belonging. Coyle encourages leaders to actively signal belonging using this three-part narrative:[6]

- You are part of this group.
- This group is special; we have high standards here.
- I believe you can reach those standards.

He adds: "Alone, each of these signals would have a limited effect. But together they create a steady stream of magical feedback."[7] He cites this narrative as the winning strategy for Gregg Popovich, the coach of the San Antonio Spurs, explaining: "The Spurs don't succeed because they are good at basketball. They succeed because they are skilled at a far more important sport: building strong relationships."[8] In concept, this makes perfect sense. However, what is common sense may not always be common practice.

Given the highly competitive nature of the orchestral industry, we hold the collective illusion that we should be grateful once an orchestra has given us a coveted job. Our default premise is that the musician is lucky to be there, not that the organization is lucky to have the musician. We lead ourselves to believe that we must continually earn our place, even after we have won the job. Our standing is constantly being jeopardized. Leaders do not help dissolve this concern by assuring musicians that they belong, deserve to be there, and can expect security in their jobs. Conductors and arts leaders are used to walking into high-stakes situations where the intention is quality control. After all, if we do not, our business will suffer. We are often saying: "We are not really sure if you can reach those standards. Prove to us that you can." The default expectation is that people need 100 per cent fixing and 0 per cent encouragement. In other words, we expect things to be bad. And we end up signalling doubt instead of belonging. With this in mind, here are five ways in which we can signal belonging.

## 1. Believe they can

Believe our people are innately capable of achieving performance goals and remind them of this frequently. I once chose a piece for my orchestra that was just out of their comfort zone. I remember a colleague commented: "Can they really play that? I am not sure if your musicians are good enough." This person has never seen my musicians in action nor heard them play. The assumption is that they cannot do it. I realized that if this colleague were leading my musicians, their chance of failing would be pretty high.

I led my orchestra with the belief that they can. I never verbalized doubt, and I was also realistic about the artistic and technical challenges. Again and again, I reinforced my belief that they have the ability to overcome those challenges. I expected them to push themselves. I guided and supported them. And ultimately, they were able to reach the furthest in their growth that season. My belief made a difference. When you have a leader who believes in you, you feel like you can do anything, and you often surprise yourself.

## 2. Trust that they will figure it out

As leaders, it is easy for all of us to fall into the trap of micromanaging and prescribing every action. This could be telling musicians exactly how they should play something or offering solutions to problems we assume they are having. That sounds exactly like what conductors are taught to do, right? We may think that we are being effective as leaders and helping our people. However, if we are always watching behind their backs, that also sends the signal that we do not trust they can do it. We disempower our people and rob them of agency to think for themselves.

Trust empowers people to take ownership over the creation process and gives them the confidence to be independent. This means taking a step back and allowing space for the musicians to share their expertise and find their own solutions. This helps us show musicians that they are considered valuable contributors, not just a cog that does what they are told.

## 3. Remove blame

When our people fail to figure it out, what do we do then? We must have difficult conversations about what went wrong, but humans naturally look to blame people for things that did not work. Blame is a barrier to what Jim Collins calls "confronting the brutal facts" and having constructive conversations.[9]

There are four ways in which we can remove blame. First, focus on the facts and processes, not the people. Second, be curious rather than judging while uncovering the problems and discovering solutions. Third, focus on future actions rather than the wrongs of the past. Finally, be a collaborator rather than a supervisor. Most importantly, show that we are all on the same side as this feeds belonging more than anything else.

### 4. Treat failures differently

When we fail, we often just focus on the *results* of failure. We overlook the opportunity to examine the *causes*. Amy Edmondson reveals that causes for failure fall into two categories: they can be praiseworthy or blameworthy. Praiseworthy failure might entail experimentation and complexity, such as trying something a new way or making an adjustment for the first time. Blameworthy failure can include things such as incompetence and inattention, such as being unprepared or negligent. It is interesting to compare what percentage of failures are *caused* by blameworthy acts, and what percentage of failures are *treated* as blameworthy acts. The difference between those two percentages can be quite sobering.[10]

We overgeneralize mistakes in the music industry in this way. An error may be the result of lack of preparation (blameworthy) or it can be a result of trying something different for the first time (praiseworthy). Yet when we see a mistake in performance, we treat them both the same, with shame and punishment, shattered identity, and potential exclusion. We can do better by responding to praiseworthy failures with positive reinforcement and additional support, rather than punishment. As leaders, we can model this in ourselves by admitting when we do not know all the answers and that we are sometimes wrong. Communicate that it is acceptable to be wrong and make mistakes as a by-product of taking risks to advance our craft. Be clear that this is entirely different from careless errors, which can come with their own distinct consequences.

### 5. Use future orientation

An appropriate response to praiseworthy failure is to signal that the relationship will continue, what Coyle terms "future orientation."[11] Our people need to be reminded that their mistakes do not fundamentally jeopardize their standing in the group. This empowers people to normalize learning and to think of areas for growth as opportunities to be better, rather than defects to hide or threats to belonging. For example, I can tell a musician who did not just play their best in a concert: "When you join us again in the next concert, I look forward to hearing how your solo will have become more settled in your instrument."

## Strategy Two: Put People First

Once we help our people feel a sense of belonging, we can continue by putting them first—especially after the pandemic, when so many organizations are concerned about how to bring back audiences, incentivize ticket sales, donations, and so on. Being focused on the customer means that we neglect an important part of our organizations—the people who make the product, namely the musicians on stage. We care so much about the bottom line and marketing the product that our musicians are feeling undervalued, underappreciated, and disengaged.

The following sections provide three ways in which we can put our musicians first.

### 1. Stop disempowering

We can begin this process by looking at hidden ways in which we are disempowering. In *The Coaching Habit*, Michael Bungay Stanier observes: "Your advice is not as good as you think it is."[12] As leaders, we love to give advice: we love to fix things and to solve problems. It makes us feel great, valuable, helpful, smart. Stanier writes about three "advice-giving monsters": our desire to "tell it," "save it," and "control it."[13] All of these actions disempower our people.

- When we tell it, we stop others from contributing to a solution.
- When we save it, we automatically make people victims.
- When we control it, we encourage people to disengage because they have no more stake in it.

It helps to ask how we make people feel when we always jump in with advice. While we cannot just stop giving advice altogether, we can delay it: this will allow space for people to step up and provide value. We can ask questions instead of telling: questions empower people to seek the most appropriate answers on their own. They also help us further understand more about our people, which is my second point.

### 2. Treat people how they would like to be treated

We all know the golden rule to treat others as we would like to be treated. But are our needs the same as theirs? Do they want what we want? Do they think what we think? What I have learned is that you never know what people are really thinking. We need to find out by asking them questions. What we learn directly from our people equips us to empower through understanding. I came across these fantastic questions to ask our people from Marcus Buckingham:[14]

- Tell us where you are at your best?
- Where do you want people to rely on you?
- Where do you feel really good when people turn to you for it?
- Tell us where you need help?

We sometimes assume these things about our people. We think what works for us works for them. We think we know them so well because we have studied their resume. Buckingham explains: "The thing we are getting wrong is we have not taken seriously the fact that each individual human gets energy from different, very specific activities."[15] We are not experts on our people: they are. By individualizing and asking them about themselves, we are also encouraging them to become more self-aware. That self-awareness allows people to feel seen and to feel like they can have more control and agency over their lives. "We need to know where we can rely on you the most. We therefore need to be able to see you. We can't rely on what we can't see. In the best communities, you feel seen. You're seen as valuable because of what people see in you."[16] This is such a powerful mindset, and it again reveals the fact that feeling seen leads to feeling valued.

### 3. Use feedback with care

In the book *Thanks for the Feedback*, authors Douglas Stone and Sheila Heen stated that receiving feedback "sits at the intersection of these two needs—our drive to learn and our longing for acceptance."[17] We often consider feedback in the context of telling someone how they can be better, what they should not do again, and what they should learn more about. We neglect the equally important facet of feedback that is "longing for acceptance"—or belonging. The authors share three types of feedback we can give:[18]

- Appreciation—to see, acknowledge, thank, motivate.
- Coaching—to help receiver expand knowledge, sharpen skill.
- Evaluation—to rank or rate against a set of standards.

Stone and Heen continue, "When people complain that they do not get enough feedback at work, they often mean that they wonder whether anyone notices or cares how hard they are working. They do not want advice. They want appreciation."[19] When we give feedback, we do not pause to think which kind of feedback we are giving and if it is the sort of feedback the person is seeking at that moment. When we ask for feedback, we are equally unaware, and thus unspecific, about what we are hoping to get.

The match actually matters. We can help our people communicate the kind of feedback they want and make a point to match it appropriately. We can also be transparent and disclose the kind of feedback we are giving and share our intention behind it. Are we trying to show appreciation, coaching, or evaluation? Which one did they come looking for?

### *What do organizations get out of it?*

Putting our people first is hard work. It may feel like extra effort when organizations and leaders already have huge responsibilities to the bottom line and to serving the customers. However, putting our people first does not only have to benefit the people internally, but can also benefit the organization externally. In fact, being employee-centric is a definite way of being more customer-centric. The happier, more valued, and fulfilled people are at making the product, the better will be the product and the more successful the business.

In his book *The Heart of Business*, Hubert Joly, former CEO of Best Buy, encourages us to think about a company's three imperatives: people, business, and finance—in that order.[20] He advocates that excellence on the first—development and fulfilment of employees—leads to the next—loyal customers buying products again and again—and then the next—making money. Financial profit is an outcome; it is not the ultimate goal. Putting our people first will empower them to do better work so that the business and the finances can also flourish as a result.

My third strategy offers a way forward in which we connect the people to the business.

### Strategy Three: Focus on Purpose

Thus far, I have focused on how to help people feel valued and seen. Purpose helps our people to feel fulfilled. Purpose also goes hand-in-hand with values, and our values are what give us the agency to have a purpose. For example, one of my values is integrity, and my purpose is to help people be seen and valued for their full integrity as artists. This is because I have personally been struggling all my life to be seen for my full integrity as an artist and as a person. This purpose motivates me to do the really challenging work every day, and it convinces me that I am making a difference.

I would like to imagine that unlocking purpose in musicians will reveal how they are driven and what they care about. Joly takes it a step further, encouraging leaders to connect that individual purpose to an organization's purpose:

> We will do well by doing good. Simply put, purposeful leadership recognizes that all companies are human organizations composed of individuals working together for a collective purpose. And the magic happens if you connect what drives individual employees to the purpose of the company in an authentic fashion.[21]

So, what would happen if we were to intentionally align an orchestra's purpose and values with those of the individual musicians. We start by first uncovering what drives our people. We can ask questions like these in interviews and also regularly during employment:

- What gets you out of bed in the morning?
- What problems do you find interesting?
- What are your values? How are they connected to why you are here?
- What is a change you seek to make?
- How would you like to be remembered after you are gone?

We can use this information both in our recruitment process (when hiring, we can use it to help guide our methodology and decisions) and in the workplace (to inform how we can best curate their work profiles, how we motivate people, and how we give feedback).

Zappos is an online retail company known for being successfully driven by its purpose and values. They 'operationalized' their values in the hiring process and in the workplace in four different ways.[22] One of their values is "to create fun and a little weirdness," so in interviews they actually ask candidates how weird they are. Another value is "be humble," so they ask the shuttle bus driver afterwards how they were treated by the interviewees. A total of 50 per cent of performance reviews are based on core values: CEO and co-founder Tony Hsieh described it as "whether you're living and inspiring the Zappos culture in others." Zappos empowers employees to celebrate their core values in their colleagues. Once a month, each employee is given fifty dollars to reward as a bonus to a fellow co-worker.

Purpose can be powerful in allowing an organization to stand out from the rest of the market. More importantly, it attracts like-minded people who want to join the same fight. It helps align values that determine every employee's motivation, mindset, and actions from the top down. There is a deep commitment to work for the cause, and beyond the pay cheque.

"When we compare ourselves against our group and find ourselves aligned, we get a reward response."[23] This observation by Todd Rose in *Collective Illusions* is the awesome benefit of connecting organizational purpose with individual purpose. It is biological proof that purpose can help our people feel belonging through finding meaning and fulfilment in their work, finding connection to something larger than themselves. I wonder, therefore, how many of the challenges we face in our artistic work are caused by simply a misalignment of purpose between our people and their organizations. Without this alignment, employees become disengaged and unfulfilled. It becomes hard to answer questions such as "Why are you here?", "Who are we doing this challenging work for?", and "How do we know when the work is done?"

## No Bells and Whistles

Each of the three preceding strategies—feeding belonging, putting people first, and focusing on purpose—addresses our human needs of belonging and safety. Belonging empowers us to feel safe, without having to play it safe. When we feel belonging, we feel seen. When we feel more seen, we feel more valued. When we feel more valued, we feel more purposeful in our work. When we feel more purposeful, we feel more fulfilled. None of these strategies requires the latest technology or a new qualification. They require us to understand that we are in the people business and that feelings offer information. We may have been taught that feelings are a taboo subject in the workplace. I am learning that our feelings can lead us to answers on how we can be and do better. We must start by asking ourselves: "How do I feel now? What do I want to feel?"

These strategies are also not quick fixes. There are no bells and whistles for media campaigns. They are for the long game: they help us reconsider how we lead, serve, hire, and motivate musicians. They help reveal why we might feel unfulfilled in our work. They challenge what we believe is important for musical education and the part leadership training plays in it. They help us gain awareness of ourselves and then of others. With this expanded knowledge, we acquire the power to change for the better and empower our musicians from the inside—to feel more valued, fulfilled, and ultimately happy.

## Notes

1 Micah Solomon, "With No Power Comes No Responsibility: How A Broken Corporate Culture Disempowers Employees," Forbes, published 6 April 2017, https://www.forbes.com/sites/micahsolomon/2017/04/06/how-your-corporate-culture-dis-empowers-employees-and-what-to-do-to-turn-it-around/.

2 See Ron Carucci, "How Honesty and Purpose Are Tied to Business Success," TEDxSeattleSalon, YouTube, video, published 17 December 2020, https://youtu.be/xECYtfpz0gw.
3 Adam Markel, "Staying Relevant in a Disruptive Marketplace with Garry Ridge," The Change Proof Podcast, podcast, published 16 April 2019, https://adammarkel.com/staying-relevant-in-a-disruptive-marketplace-with-garry-ridge/.
4 Jutta Allmendinger, J. Richard Hackman, and Erin V. Lehman, "Life and Work in Symphony Orchestras," *The Musical Quarterly* 80, no. 2 (Summer 1996): 201, https://www.jstor.org/stable/742362.
5 Daniel Coyle, *The Culture Code: The Secrets of Highly Successful Groups* (New York: Bantam Books, 2018), 24.
6 Daniel Coyle, "How Gregg Popovich Uses 'Magical Feedback' to Inspire the San Antonio Spurs," *Time*, updated 31 January 2018, https://time.com/5125421/gregg-popovich-san-antonio-spurs-success/.
7 Coyle, "Gregg Popovich."
8 Coyle, "Gregg Popovich."
9 Concept from Jim Collins, *Good to Great: Why Some Companies Make the Leap and Others Don't* (New York: Harper Business, 2001).
10 Amy Edmondson, "Failure's Mixed Bag," YouTube, video, published 5 May 2019, https://youtu.be/VH9Y3-lCigM.
11 Coyle, *The Culture Code*, 11.
12 Michael Bungay Stanier, *The Coaching Habit* (Toronto: Box of Crayons Press, 2016), 59.
13 Concept from Stanier, *The Coaching Habit*, 59.
14 Marcus Buckingham, "Weirdness is the Key to Self-Improvement," *The Chase Jervis Live Show*, YouTube, video, published 3 August 2022, https://youtu.be/Pk00a36nwGo.
15 Buckingham, "Weirdness is the Key," 54:15.
16 Buckingham, "Weirdness is the Key," 45:26.
17 Douglas Stone and Sheila Heen, *Thanks for the Feedback: The Science and Art of Receiving Feedback Well, Even When It Is Off Base, Unfair, Poorly Delivered, and, Frankly, You're Not in the Mood* (London: Penguin, 2015), 8.
18 Stone and Heen, *Thanks for the Feedback*, 30.
19 Stone and Heen, *Thanks for the Feedback*, 32.
20 Hubert Joly, *The Heart of Business: Leadership Principles for the Next Era of Capitalism* (Boston: Harvard Business Review Press, 2021) audiobook, 2:00:50.
21 Ron Carucci, "Moments of Truth – Episode 1," Interview with Hubert Joly, YouTube, video, published 17 March 2021, https://youtu.be/bYJO_ijQveo, 04:22.
22 Tony Hsieh, "Delivering Happiness: A Path to Profits, Passion, and Purpose," Talks at Google, YouTube, video, published 12 July 2010, https://youtu.be/jJ5k_Byd9Fs.
23 Todd Rose, *Collective Illusions* (New York: Hachette Book Group, 2022), audiobook, 3:37:52.

# 10
# INTUITION
## The Missing Piece?

*Hannah Baxter*

### Introduction

A full and rounded understanding of anything in life cannot be obtained by purely intellectual means.[1] Although indispensable, if the intellect is revered to the exclusion of other forms of perception, something crucial is lost. Music is no exception. Almost every conductor that I have met or interviewed has spoken of analysis and intuition—alongside technique—with regard to their musical preparation, rehearsal, and performance. They will often be discussing their work with intense intellectual rigour, only in the next sentence to openly divulge their instincts and intuition about the piece in question. And there is never any embarrassment in doing so.

Conductor Mark Wigglesworth, in his book *The Silent Musician: Why Conducting Matters*, wrote that understanding the composer's intention "is always going to be a combination of musical experience and emotional intuition."[2] He continues: "I certainly think that musical instinct is as powerful as knowledge—and even more so in the most intuitive musicians. A natural conviction is more infectious than a studied one."[3] Indeed, it is common for conductors to override their analysis if their intuition about the performance of a piece is that strong. If it is so important, why is it not discussed more frequently? Perhaps this is partly because these intuitive individuals, and the phenomenon in question, would have to be studied and observed by those who are less inclined to rely on intuition in their own work. But, most importantly, intuition, by its very nature, cannot be reliably analysed as most often the evidence available is anecdotal. Yet if there is enough evidence, one must take notice.

## Questionnaire

In an attempt to address the oversight of this topic in conducting literature, I sent out a short survey in February 2022 to a number of conductors (either personally or via their representation). Intuition had been mentioned numerous times in previous interviews with some of these individuals but was never explored fully because of the focus on other topics and pieces of music on those occasions. To avoid confusion, this definition of intuition was used: *the ability to understand something without the need for analytical reasoning, bridging the gap between the conscious and unconscious/subconscious*. It could include things such as gut feelings, instincts, dreams, visions, physical sensations in response to certain thoughts, things happening automatically during rehearsals or performances that you had not previously considered, and knowing something would happen before it did.

The questionnaire comprised five simple questions:

1. Do you feel that intuition is an integral part of your work?
2. If so, how do you use it? Can you give specific examples of when it is/was most useful?
3. Can you rely on it? Do you test it out in any way?
4. Do you talk openly about any of this with your colleagues?
5. If I quote or mention your responses, are you happy with your name being included, or would you prefer to remain anonymous?

Answers were gathered from conductors including university lecturer/conductors, freelance conductors, musical directors, music directors, and knighted household names.

## Results

### 1. Was intuition integral?

The conductors who replied were unanimous in their answer to the first question. They answered "yes" without exception; intuition was certainly an integral part of their work. Sir Andrew Davis wrote: "I have always considered intuition to be a valuable resource both in preparation and performance. While objective analysis is important for interpreters in all the arts, I believe that getting to what one hopes is the core of the composer's vision is beyond the scope of such analysis."[4] Jonathan Hirsh, director of orchestral and choral activities at Smith College, Massachusetts, said: "Definitely. I don't know how you would be a conductor without it. It's whatever takes over whenever there's anything that doesn't go exactly as predicted."[5] London-based Australian conductor Scott Wilson agreed, and seconded Hirsh's view on intuition stepping in to deal with the unexpected: "It's necessary—and necessary through the whole process. There so often isn't time to be as prepared as one wishes."[6]

However, what the conductors actually believed this process to be, if they elaborated, varied a great deal. Holly Mathieson, music director of Symphony Nova Scotia and co-artistic director of the Nevis Ensemble, wrote:

> There is a degree of unconscious decision making with very familiar repertoire or idioms, aligned with instinct perhaps, rather than intuition. But I personally believe whatever of those two things we call it, it is learnt. Even if it is learnt through listening as a child, or from a teacher early on . . . I don't think intuition or instinct work separately from learned experience.[7]

Scott Wilson held a very similar sentiment. He felt that his intuition was more accurately described as informed guesses: "I am surely always refining my intuitive skills. Perhaps another way of referring to it is as 'experience.'"

Mathieson's and Wilson's thoughts and experiences echo the basic concepts of fast and slow thinking laid out by psychologist Daniel Kahnemann in his international bestseller *Thinking, Fast and Slow*.[8] The main premise of the book is the dichotomy between two modes of thought. He stated that intuition involves no magic or divine intervention, but that the brain is merely employing System 1, or 'fast' thinking. This is an automatic process which takes place with little or no effort and is driven by instinct and our experiences; System 2 thinking is slower, conscious, and more logical. In his introduction, Kahnemann explains how our expert intuition is purely recognition in much the same way as a child learns to recognize animals, people, and objects: "We are not surprised when a two-year-old looks at a dog and says 'doggie!' because we are used to the miracle of children learning to recognize and name things."[9] Therefore an expert recognizing or assessing a situation instantaneously is a more sophisticated version of the same phenomenon: "An expert chess player can understand a complex position at a glance, but it takes years to develop that level of ability."[10]

JoAnn Falletta, music director of the Buffalo Philharmonic, spoke in more poetic terms:

> As I work with the gifted and sensitive artists—the musicians in any orchestra—I am constantly using my intuition about their musical personalities, their needs, their freedom, their instincts. By doing this, I feel that I can help bring to life a performance based on who they are, rather than moulding them into an artificial shape. That is the beauty

of working with different orchestras—letting the music be 'them.' Since I don't have time to speak to them all at any length personally, I am using my intuition about them constantly to 'get to know them' as musicians. I consider this one of the most beautiful parts of my job as a conductor.[11]

'Fast' thinking may well be responsible for this advanced level of empathy and ability that Falletta demonstrates in reading musicians with whom she has had little previous contact. However, the experiences she outlines are also reminiscent of the approach and findings of Rupert Sheldrake, a biologist and researcher in the field of parapsychology. In his book *The Sense of Being Stared At*, he observes two types of telepathy: the first is a kind of thought transference that occurs between people already interacting with one another; the second (less applicable) type is between people or animals (or both) at a distance.[12]

In the same book, Sheldrake comments on the nature of non-verbal communication between performing musicians: "Musicians playing together use non-verbal communication all the time, sometimes using telepathic links between players, as well as between players and conductors."[13] This could also be what Falletta herself is describing. In her responses, she explained: "Just recently in an orchestra where I guest conducted, several people told me something that made me very happy. They said, 'it was as if you knew us, knew who we were inside.' That, to me, is what it is all about."

Sheldrake's work is also referenced by author Richard Osborne in his biography on Herbert von Karajan.[14] Karajan was very interested in the idea of conductor-as-hypnotist and believed that he could accurately read people's minds at a glance. Karajan spoke about using a kind of telepathy in his work:

> I have a tempo in my head long before I come to the passage in question. I know in advance, so to speak, what is going to happen. And the players react faultlessly, they don't need a gesture or glance from me. By contrast, I can also tell in advance when something is going to go wrong in the orchestra. I really can sense in advance if a player has problems with his breathing, and so I'll go faster for him. I sense in advance the fear that a player feels at a difficult entry, and I help him so that we get over the passage quickly together.[15]

## 2. How conductors use their intuition, and when it is most useful

This is where the responses got interesting and were far more varied than anticipated. The conductors use their intuition for everything from score study and programming through to rehearsals and performance. However, where they use it the most (or feel it is most adept) varies greatly between them. JoAnn Falletta wrote that she uses her intuition by "listening constantly to how they are playing, observing body language, facial language, comfort levels, signs of struggle or discomfort or worry." As already established, it is therefore primarily a tool that enables her to 'tune in' to the people she is working with, allowing her to boost morale and levels of cohesion within the orchestra.

Sir Mark Elder's response also focused on his interaction with others:

> I have a clear concept in my inner ear of how the music should go from the first note to the last. But when I start conducting, an orchestra will give me something back immediately. . . . My response to those sounds at the first rehearsal is intuitive, because I need to immediately assess how it compares to what I'd hope it would be. Perhaps it's better, perhaps it's weaker—I need to have an intuitive response.

He also uses his intuition when meeting soloists and performers: "If it's somebody who comes to play a concerto with me, I meet them and chat to them about what we're going to do. I answer their questions and just try and break the ice between us. That process of breaking the ice is very intuitive."[16]

In contrast, Taiwanese-American conductor Tiffany Chang feels that her intuition is strongest when used to generate programming: "I always find that I can trust my artistic programming choices. I can tell when pieces just seem to click and work well together in a program. It always seems to work out in practice."[17] Jonathan Hirsh also leans on his intuition during score study when answers to his questions are unavailable. This is most commonly the case with very early, or very contemporary music. In both cases, "you have to make decisions without a lot of evidence because there's just not a lot of background source material. That's where I think intuition is indispensable, [and when] you *realize* you're using it."[18]

Scott Wilson also referred to this stage of preparation:

> When learning a new score initially I'm on the hunt for the moment in the score that will allow me to 'dive in' to start studying the notes. This isn't often on page one. I have to find a doorway—often a problem—that I can scrutinise. And following that, I'm in! I rely on intuition to find that moment in the score which will open the door to the rest of the piece, hopefully as efficiently and effectively as possible.

Wilson was the only conductor who mentioned his use of intuition while teaching:

> You have so little time to assess a student and provide feedback: the teacher intuitively responds to what they see, giving the best advice in as short a time as possible. There isn't time to see/hear everything, or, indeed, hardly anything at all.

The majority of the conductors' answers focused on rehearsal and performance. George Jackson, music director of the Amarillo Symphony, said, "Intuition is knowing what needs to be rehearsed, and what doesn't need to be rehearsed. This can be about trusting the orchestra/singers, but also knowing where to fix things."[19] Nurhan Arman, music director of Sinfonia Toronto, wrote:

> In rehearsal, the conductor must have an intuitive ability to feel the level of electricity in the room; must intuitively feel how much to push to achieve tasks; how much information to provide at each stop; intuitively to feel the orchestra's level of patience with detailed and demanding rehearsal techniques.[20]

Here both conductors refer to an ability to read the room in relation to specific tasks, drawing on their understanding of both the music in question and the people with whom they are collaborating.

The most intuitive experiences during performance for Holly Mathieson occurred with specific composers:

> For me, something like a Tchaikovsky or Haydn score needs very little forethought in terms of phrasing and expression. The lessons/experiences I've absorbed over the years and the personal taste I've developed (not to mention my body's natural way of moving) find their way unconsciously. At the time, that certainly feels intuitive or instinctive.

She also referred to her experience conducting opera:

> Once one is used to working in opera, I think you develop a certain intuition about singers' rubato—when they will come off a pause, for instance. But I feel sure there's actually a process of listening to the timbre in micro-degrees of accuracy, and remembering how to judge that moment, even if these days it happens without effort.

A similar dynamic is present in other theatrical genres. A conductor (who wishes to remain anonymous) referring to his experience in musical theatre, wrote:

> My intuition arrives (unbidden and unexpected) whilst the music is in progress. It takes the form a sudden clear idea to do something different from the expected—a big change of dynamic, a big *rallentando* or *accelerando*, a sudden cut off into silence before starting again. I did the first in performance in *Jesus Christ Superstar*, the first and second in the *Carousel* 'Waltz' and *Cats* 'Jellicle Ball', and the third in *Superstar* and *Les Misérables*. Actually, I feel 'compelled' to go with the instinct... the music seems to demand it.[21]

At the time of partaking in the questionnaire, Sir Andrew Davis was studying Elgar's *Dream of Gerontius*. It is a piece he has conducted many times and was considered by Elgar himself (as well as many others) to be his best work. He described how his understanding of Elgar's inspiration for the piece, which he believed to be Elgar's love for Alice as well as Cardinal Newman's poem, carries him "to a point where the intensity of the music appears to have its wellspring":

> But this is also where such musings end their usefulness in the matter of how to relate the parts to the whole in performance. It is here, after a complete grasp of the text with all its nuances is achieved, that the moment-by-moment flow of the work must fall to intuition and instinct. No two performances will be exactly alike.... The whole sweep of the music becomes one enormous improvisation, which one hopes, every time one returns to this, as all great works, will be a true reflection of the composer's intentions.

Based on the responses given, it is clear that there is no single way of using one's intuition. The way it works is incredibly varied and does not seem to be a choice—rather something that is observed through self-reflection on one's own strengths, weaknesses, and natural way of working.

## 3. Can the conductors rely on it? Do they test it out?

When asked if they could rely on their intuition, the conductors answered with varying levels of "yes." George Jackson felt he could rely on it 100 per cent, the anonymous conductor answered, "yes, I can, and do. Almost by definition I can't test it. I just go with the 'inner voice.'" JoAnn Falletta wrote, "I do rely on it, always. [But] I cannot test it out." Sir Mark Elder said, "absolutely. At the age I am I'd better! As you develop as an artist your intuition is richer."

Other times the answer was slightly less emphatic. Nurhan Arman answered "usually," implying that he felt his intuition *is* reliable, but not infallible. Tiffany Chang's response was more nuanced:

> I can rely on it in an activity that doesn't involve other people (for example, deciding on programming). Once it involves interacting with other people, I find that I can't trust it as much. I'm realising that I don't always know what people are thinking and my 'intuition' about what I observe may sometimes be wrong. The way I test it is to practice empathy and just ask people how they are feeling or what was the intention behind their actions. I always find that discovering people's stories reveals so much that intuition cannot when it comes to interacting with people.

Most conductors did not make a point of 'testing out' their intuition in any deliberate way. Scott Wilson's observation was that "it is constantly being tested, but I'm only focused on how effectively I am undertaking each task in my work, each day. From that perspective, I'm not formally testing it." However, there were a small number of exceptions. Holly Mathieson wrote:

> A test of it, if you know an orchestra well enough, is to be spontaneous in performance and break from something you'd set out interpretatively in rehearsal. I suppose that becomes something akin to intuition at play, i.e., it's your intuition allowing you to explore with too many boundaries, rather than intuition guiding you to what is correct.

Mathieson's comments, again, relate to the experiences the anonymous conductor was describing in relation to his work in musical theatre, outlined earlier.

When asked if he tested out his intuition, Sir Mark Elder emphatically answered:

> Absolutely, all the time! I'm not timid about it. I try it one way and if it's not satisfactory my instinct will tell me to do it another way. And I know how to do it. A very simple example is how many beats you beat in any passage of music. If you try one way and it doesn't sound very good (or I feel it's the wrong choice) immediately I can change it. But

I also use it in more subtle ways. . . . A soloist within the orchestra might play a phrase in a way that I hadn't thought of, and I recognise instinctively that it's very beautiful and that I shouldn't change it.

Jonathan Hirsh gave an example from his teaching experience that illustrated how testing out intuition is easier in relation to frequently performed pieces. Whilst discussing the fermatas at the beginning of Beethoven's Symphony No. 5, he explains to his students that the recordings vary a great deal because Beethoven never specified exactly why he wrote what he did. Should the second fermata be longer than the first?

Who knows for sure, but why else would he have put a second bar there? You have to use those clues, but you can test it out if it's something like Beethoven 5. You can go and listen and see what other people have done over the years. If it's not something like Beethoven 5, then you just have to test it out yourself.

Sir Andrew Davis's response was rather more philosophical. Rather than 'testing out,' he assesses where his intuition led him post-performance:

Will this be perfect? No. There is really no such thing in art, but each time one attempts it there is that sense of adventure which is what must motivate us. I always perform a kind of post-mortem for myself afterwards: what happened as I hoped, what I could have done better. But this is only so that the next time I will come closer to a true fidelity to the author.

### 4. Do they talk openly about any of this with their colleagues?

Generally, no they do not. For the conductors that elaborated on their answer, this was for a variety of reasons. Holly Mathieson said: "I don't think I have, no. Although I think it's common for conductors to reflect enthusiastically with players or conducting colleagues if the 'flow state' of play happens in performance." Scott Wilson does, but not formally, and Nurhan Arman talks about it, but in his teaching rather than in rehearsals or discussions with colleagues. Sir Andrew Davis has never discussed it with any of his colleagues although he felt "quite sure that it is what every one of them must be aiming for also."

The anonymous maestro did not feel he needed to discuss it with his musicians. They "always seem to grasp instinctively what I'm doing—they seem to smell the musical/dramatic logic . . . and just embrace the change." And of course, the time to reflect with others simply is not a luxury most conductors have. Jonathan Hirsh, like many conductors working in higher education, only has one other conducting colleague (a younger graduate), so indulging in conversations of this nature is not a luxury available. "We just don't really have the opportunity that often . . . everybody is just so busy."

The only conductor to answer "yes" was Sir Mark Elder:

> I'm very lucky. I have a number of conductors who are great friends of mine. Over the years, I have discussed this in some detail, and with some sensitivity, with certain colleagues if we have a trusting, open and friendly relationship. We talk about our experiences and how our intuition leads us, and if it proves to be right.

(He mentioned that his personal belief is that conducting is "a constant balancing between your head and your heart, *led* by your intuition.")

Is this general lack of discussion also because intuition still holds some kind of stigma? This was not evident from the conductors' responses; however, some scepticism remains. Years ago, I had a meeting with a well-known conductor at Glyndebourne Opera House. The topic of intuition came up, and I commented on the scepticism that people experience. He immediately answered: "Ah yes, but you can select what you say to people. I think to myself 'he'll be ok with it, I can tell him *that*, but not *that*.'" It is important to be aware of who will take an interest and which colleagues may become uncomfortable.

Rupert Sheldrake addresses this issue himself in relation to the scepticism surrounding the subject in the scientific community:

> Is it simply a matter, then, of hostility to new ideas? This may be a partial explanation, but some areas of contemporary scientific speculation seem far more radical, and yet excite little or no opposition. Some physicists, for example, postulate that there are countless parallel universes besides our own. Few people take these ideas seriously, but no one gets angry about them.[22]

It is worth considering why intuition, a phenomenon that is so innate in most, if not all of us, could elicit such a response.

### Striking a Balance

Of course, no conductor relies on intuition alone, and there are some aspects of performance that are not as easy to take an instinctive view on (e.g., balancing the orchestra, dealing with intonation). Obviously, following your instinct is no substitute for knowing every note of the score. Jakub Hrůša, chief conductor of the Bamberg Symphony and music director of the Royal Opera House starting in 2025, consciously strives to strike a balance between his intellect and intuition: "While I'm rehearsing, I have a multitude of strong instincts, but I'm also questioning those instincts. . . . Music is not thinking about music."[23]

Indeed, some conductors can be so cerebral that, although it is enormously stimulating and inspiring to converse with them, this quality can lead to overthinking and rigidity in performance. However, as important as it is to strike a balance between the intellect and intuition, the same balance does not work for everyone, nor does the same approach work with each orchestra. Each conductor must play to their own as well as their orchestra's strengths. Hrůša elaborated:

> I have to say I have absolute respect for other types of conductors who are just different human beings, different personalities. For instance, certain personalities can enrich the world the most if they are lecturing everyone. . . . Other people are just all about heart and don't start thinking. But if the heart is really powerful and the instincts are brilliant, that can work too. For me it is a combination of both.
>
> You need to become free enough in the performance and go with your instincts, but somehow you also have to be inwardly sure that you took care of it intellectually as well. . . . You get on top of the work intellectually and then let it be. I use that approach in life generally. You gain a lot of knowledge about it to the extent that you can then forget the knowledge and simply let it be a part of you.[24]

## A Spiritual Experience?

There are isolated incidents where the intuitive experience in question falls into none of these categories. Musical theatre conductor Simon Beck, in conversation with me about *West Side Story*, personally felt that his experiences whilst conducting the musical went beyond the usual realms of intuition in the preceding discussion:

> When we did the 50th Anniversary Tour (2008), there were many performances during that year where the orchestra and I would leave the pit at the interval and we'd say to each other, "oh, Bernstein's come in for a visit tonight." As the conductor I very much felt I was not the one on the podium, there was some force and the musicians said that they

felt thoroughly taken over. That music was coming from some other dimension, and I personally think that's why *West Side* is timeless and works in any ensemble or style. We know we all sound crazy to the public at large but we don't care. . . . There's some magical Bernstein energy that comes out no matter who's performing it.[25]

Bernstein himself had a very similar experience to Simon on the day of the death of George Gershwin in 1937. That lunchtime he had to entertain on the piano while working as the music counsellor at Camp Onota, Pittsfield, Massachusetts. Humphrey Burton recalled:

> In the midst of the meal, Bernstein struck a loud chord to get his audience's attention: when the clatter of cutlery and crockery had ceased, he announced that America's greatest Jewish composer had passed away. He then played Gershwin's Prelude No. 2, requesting in advance that there should be no applause afterwards. When it was over there was a heavy silence in the hall. "As I walked off I felt I *was* Gershwin."[26]

Is it fair to reduce or restrict our perspective of experiences like this to something merely psychological?

## Final Thoughts

The responses to the questionnaire clearly demonstrated that intuition (regardless of what they actually perceive this process to be) was a crucial component in most, if not all aspects of the conductor's work. The acknowledgement and more thorough study of these intuitive processes, and how they combine with intellectual analysis, will lead us to a more comprehensive understanding of the role of the conductor. Nurhan Arman reflected on this issue:

> Our art is a strange one. Hard to teach, hard to explain, hard to understand for an outsider, hard to standardize, and hard to practice. But slowly . . . things may get pinned down. So many conducting books are out but so few of them shed light on some important aspects of what we do.

Intuition is certainly not infallible, yet at the same time it cannot be ignored. Elusive by nature, understanding it is not an exact science, which is perhaps why intuition is so often sidelined in academia. But is it wise to relegate this subject to merely an afterthought, when many conductors consider it one of the most crucial elements of their work? This was the anonymous conductor's closing comment in his questionnaire response:

> I'd expect every single conductor will say they use (even rely on) instinct. That's what makes them 'them.' It's what differentiates Bernstein, Mazur, Dudamel, Szell, Abbado, Levine, Pappano . . . their musicianship, competence, skill, technique, are beyond question . . . it's their personality, their vision, their instinct that defines them.

So perhaps it is intuition that gives the greatest in any field that *je ne sais quoi*. Whatever you believe the intuitive process occurring to be, if we are to move forward in our understanding of the conducting profession, we need to factor this in. Otherwise, if intuition is an essential as these conductors say it is, there will continue to be an integral missing piece.

## Notes

1. My thanks for all the discussions in preparing this chapter to my long-time academic collaborator and friend Dr Justin Grize.
2. Mark Wigglesworth, *The Silent Musician: Why Conducting Matters* (London: Faber & Faber, 2018), 120.
3. Wigglesworth, *The Silent Musician*, 131.
4. Sir Andrew Davis, email to author, 10 August 2022.
5. Jonathan Hirsh, telephone interview, 26 April 2022.
6. Scott Wilson, email to author, 10 March 2022.
7. Holly Mathieson, email to author, 28 February 2022.
8. Daniel Kahnemann, *Thinking, Fast and Slow* (London: Penguin, 2011).
9. Kahnemann, *Thinking Fast*, 11–12.
10. Kahnemann, *Thinking Fast*, 238.
11. JoAnn Falletta, email to author, 14 March 2022.
12. Rupert Sheldrake, *The Sense of Being Stared At: And Other Aspects of the Extended Mind* (London: Arrow Books, 2003), 20. See also, Robert Sheldrake, *Seven Experiments That Could Change the World* (London: Riverhead Books, 1994).
13. Sheldrake, *The Sense of Being Stared At*, 40.
14. Richard Osborne, *Herbert von Karajan: A Life in Music* (London: Chatto & Windus, 1998).
15. Osborne, *Herbert von Karajan*, 275.
16. Sir Mark Elder, telephone interview, 12 October 2022.
17. Tiffany Chang, email to author, 12 March 2022.
18. Jonathan Hirsh believes that you are less likely to realize you are using your intuition when rehearsing or performing.
19. George Jackson, email to author, 8 March 2022.
20. Nurhan Arman, email to author, 11 March 2022.
21. Anonymous, email to author, 26 February 2022.
22. Sheldrake, *The Sense of Being Stared At*, 7.

23 Hannah Baxter, "Jakub Hrůša on Conducting Opera (Bizet, Britten and Mozart)," *Notes from the Podium*, no. 6: Vocal Music of Germany/Austria, 1 October 2018, https://www.notesfromthepodium.co.uk/?p=375.
24 Baxter, "Jakub Hrůša."
25 Hannah Baxter, "Simon Beck on Bernstein's *West Side Story*," *Notes from the Podium*, no. 21: The All-American, 1 July 2022, https://www.notesfromthepodium.co.uk/?p=1341.
26 Humphrey Burton, *Leonard Bernstein* (London: Faber & Faber, 1994), 38.

**PART III**
# Conductors in Practice
## Choral Perspectives

# 11

# PLAYING THE LONG GAME

## Strategies for Building Consistency in the Chamber Choir

*Orla Flanagan*

The *a cappella* chamber choir is an instrument—a human, collective one—that can be developed and refined over time. This chapter is largely informed by my experience of conducting the same semi-professional ensemble for over twenty years and suggests some ways in which musical consistency can be built and maintained in an ensemble, even though membership may change. In the multifaceted role of the conductor, our work is in a constant flow of experimentation, as we often gather and absorb influences from disparate sources, incorporating them into our practice over time. What follows is an attempt to document some of these habitual activities and routines, bringing together various techniques that I have found helpful in my practice as a choral conductor. Constraints of time and space limit this text to the music-related elements of choir-building; there are many important elements relating to organizational structure and the running of the choir that could be considered elsewhere. I have identified five main areas of focus explored via my own practice, and will examine each in greater detail over the course of this chapter. These are: choral vocal production; musical style; repertoire, programming, and musical goals; the conductor's continuing professional development; and building choir community through the choral rehearsal.

### Choral Vocal Production: Body, Breath, Voice

The importance of instilling healthy vocal habits in a choral group cannot be overstated. Good basic vocal technique and breath control can be taught to any choir, regardless of the singers' backgrounds and experiences.

DOI: 10.4324/9781003299660-15

I believe that the choral warm-up is an important part of every rehearsal, as it provides a space where the singers can focus individually and collectively on the way they produce sound. Although there is no substitute for individual voice lessons that are specifically tailored to the singer's particular needs, the choral conductor can have a vital role in shaping a group of singers' vocal habits by demonstrating the fundamentals of healthy vocal production. Furthermore, the warm-up serves as a transition point from the activities of the singers' day into, ideally, the focused and calm atmosphere of the rehearsal; thus, it serves as an opportunity for the conductor to set the tone for what will follow.

A typical warm-up for my group follows a familiar pattern. We begin with a body scan, observing how the body feels, whether it is holding unnecessary tension, checking our alignment and posture so that the body is ready for singing, sometimes performing stretches or other tension-releasing exercises. This creates the optimal conditions in the body for successful, relaxed, and free voice production. When the singers are feeling more connected to their bodies, we begin to bring more awareness to our breath. Even the most experienced singers find that a reminder of the mechanism of good abdominal breathing is both useful and grounding; moreover, the practice of collective breathing is a powerful act of human connection as well as a calming ritual at the beginning of a rehearsal. This breathwork focuses on gently controlling the exhalation, followed by a release of the abdominal muscles so that the air can automatically fill the vacuum created by the exhalation. Something as simple as exhaling with a *sssss* sound—perhaps with the hand on the abdomen, then relaxing the abdomen, repeated a few times—is a helpful reminder of this process that is important when singing.

Gradually we add voice to the breath, starting with a small and comfortable vocal range (humming and other resonant sounds such as *nn* and *ng* are ideal), then moving to more open sounds combining vowels and consonants, with wider ranges of pitch, tempo, and dynamics. At this point in the warm-up, we can collectively draw attention to the unification of vowels, which is one of the most important ingredients for what is commonly referred to as choral blend. It can also be useful to introduce a musical problem or issue at this point—something that will be presented in the repertoire to be sung later, perhaps. I have found that tackling an anticipated challenge in this way without the use of scores, when everyone is focused, can be an effective means of pre-empting a difficulty and solving the problem before it has occurred.

Much can be done to build the choir's sound through these explorations; although the changes may be small over the course of a fifteen-minute warm-up, the gradual development of the choir's sound and technical ability over time will reward the effort expended. While it is important that this warm-up structure does not become automatic (it is a space for active listening at all times), the familiarity of this routine can build confidence and consistency in the group of singers. I am indebted to the many conductors whose warm-ups I have 'borrowed' over the years in various vocal rehearsals and workshops; in particular, I wholeheartedly recommend Sabine Horstmann's book *The Choral Warm-Up* for its clear descriptions of the vocal apparatus and many musical examples of suitable warm-ups.[1]

## Musical Style: Creative Journeys

It is a great privilege to lead a group of people in discovering music together. Choirs can develop a sense of musical style over time, from early music through Romantic works to contemporary and experimental music. It has been my experience that this knowledge of style can be developed gradually, by building familiarity with the repertoire, and eventually arriving at convincing interpretations of the artworks being performed. Perhaps the most obvious instance is music of the Renaissance and early Baroque periods, because this is music that needs considerable interpretative input beyond reading the score. By delving into the music of Schütz, Monteverdi, Byrd, Purcell, Lassus, and Victoria, for example, an ensemble can hone its skills in the performance of polyphony. Because every voice part has equal status in polyphony, hierarchy is embedded within the music—each line becomes prominent at a different moment in time. Thus, compromise and balance are required from the singers, in addition to careful listening. Consistency of articulation, when applied to this music, can bring it to life; for example, finding just the right emphasis to place on a particular syllable, or experimenting with *legato* and *poco marcato* in different phrases. Finally, in this style, if each singer shapes every phrase sensitively and consistently and according to the syllabic stresses of the text, the architecture of the music is clearly displayed. Time spent tending to the details of text stresses will be richly rewarded by a resultant flexibility in the musical lines; it is satisfying for the ensemble to hear these carefully shaped musical lines emerging from the texture they are creating. With my choir, I often liken this process to chiselling a sculpture, where the shape emerges gradually. I have found that singers are more energized and engaged with the interpretation if it is arrived at in a somewhat collaborative manner. It has been my experience that, by repeatedly returning to this style of music and giving it consistent, patient attention, the ensemble develops a natural affinity with it. Musical habits (of phrasing, articulation, treatment of text) are formed that grow more habitual over time and become a source of great pleasure and satisfaction.

Romantic music can be similarly rewarding to study and perform. Voice training, whether individual or collective, is one of the most helpful ways in which the choir can hone their skills in this musical style. The knowledge of vocal technique gained in the warm-up at the beginning of a choral rehearsal can equip singers with the capacity to produce and explore the diverse palette of dynamic contrasts and tonal colours required for the performance of Romantic music. Time spent working on blending vowels can reap huge dividends in this style, as can harmonic work in tuning chords and work on supporting the voice through long phrases. The texture of this style of music is often homophonic, and it is important that the conductor makes clear decisions regarding pronunciation and breathing to ensure that there is unity within the ensemble. A good understanding of the text (in terms of pronunciation, translation, and deeper emotional meaning) is required by both the conductor and the singers, and a sense of working together towards a common expressive goal leads to a more unified, committed performance. Another aspect of the Romantic style is the relative complexity of the harmonic world. Rich, complex harmonic structures provide a fertile ground for exploring intonation with the choir; one can use this music to open the ears of the singers to the chords they are forming, paying attention to small nuances of harmony and intonation. Finally, the contrasts of mood implicit in this style of music allow the choir to experiment with range of expression. The texts used in this musical style are often highly emotional, and it is a wonderful challenge to learn how to deliver these texts with integrity and authenticity in performance without any resultant loss in musical accuracy and vocal technique.

When approaching contemporary music, in heavily notated scores in particular, the technical challenge for the conductor and performers often lies more in executing the demands of the notation than in the musical decision-making itself. Aural acuity is important here, so that the conductor can identify areas of inaccuracy and help the singers gain confidence in challenging passages. Experimenting with improvisation in the choral ensemble can be an effective way of developing a more active approach to listening, and a greater sense of individual agency on the part of the singers. It has been my experience that, although singers may initially feel somewhat resistant to the idea of improvising, the practice of expanding boundaries by improvising enhances their sense of personal investment in the creative process. Gunnar Eriksson's concept of an 'improvisation toolkit' as presented in his *Kör ad lib* books has been immensely helpful here.[2] Eriksson presents a playful approach to creating sound during the choral rehearsal, and the Swedish and French songs in his book—many of them taken from the folk tradition—serve as a starting point for these explorations. The use of familiar songs can make the practice more accessible for both singers and audience. Techniques used include, but are not limited to, pedal notes, canons, cluster chords within a scale, augmentation and diminution, rhythmic ostinatos, and quodlibets. Improvisation can be a daunting prospect for singers, who may hitherto have gauged their level of success on their ability to follow instructions obediently and accurately. Indeed, a potential downside of the unified nature of choral singing is a reluctance to stray from the crowd, and a desire simply to do as the conductor asks. The concept of an improvisation toolkit provides concrete ideas with which both conductor and ensemble can experiment, thus removing the sense of fear, and perhaps creating a sort of safety net or scaffolding upon which an improvisation can be built.[3]

**Setting Goals: Artistic Programming**

Creative programming is a central part of the role of the conductor, both as it relates to researching and choosing repertoire and to the artistic planning of the choir's activities. Regarding the former, the area of repertoire is one of limitless potential for the conductor. Much time and energy can be devoted to researching repertoire; it is a source of endless fascination to discover new music and to source appropriate pieces for one's ensemble.[4] Now that such a wide range of music is so readily available, in both recorded and notated formats, this is a much easier task than it was twenty years ago. This accessibility is not the only aspect of repertoire selection that has changed dramatically during this time: our horizons have widened considerably in recent years as we hold ourselves to higher standards regarding diversity, inclusion, and representation. I trained as a conductor during a period where there was a clearly defined body of 'standard' repertoire—almost exclusively by white male composers—and this reinforcement of a selective repertoire based on a so-called 'canon' is increasingly being recognized as unacceptable. There is a wealth of lesser-known music to be discovered, and much exciting work is being done in uncovering music by forgotten composers, many of them women or representatives of other marginalized and neglected groups. While there is some distance to go in changing prevailing attitudes, I believe that conductors can play a role in this necessary shift through their choice of repertoire; for example, by researching, commissioning, and programming more music by women and by individuals from other marginalized groups. By presenting this music on a world stage (e.g., at international competitions and festivals), this diversity can be highlighted and attitudes will continue to change, creating a hopeful future for a more equal approach to balance in programming. Another example is that of commissioning local composers. In my own context of Ireland, we have a burgeoning choral scene, and choirs are enjoying perhaps their highest ever level of popularity. At the same time, more and more Irish composers are writing for choir, and more conductors and composers are collaborating artistically. It can be a symbiotic and rewarding connection, and a great privilege to work with composers. So, while conductors need to research and discover previously composed music, we are also ideally positioned to initiate the creation of new artworks by commissioning emerging composers and to use our platform as performers to champion this new music.

Another facet of programming—one that reinforces the sort of work discussed in the previous section of this chapter—concerns the vocal practicalities of the particular group. It is important to be realistic and to choose music wisely based on the singers in the ensemble. For example, if there are not enough singers to comfortably sing *divisi*, it is best to stay with SATB settings rather than SSAATTBB. The difficulty level of the repertoire is also a factor: the music should present a challenge to the group but should not be so difficult that it cannot be successfully realized, as this can be disheartening.[5] If a piece is in an unfamiliar language, more time will need to be allocated to its learning. It is also good to have some medium- to long-term planning built in; as discussed in the previous section, for a choir to become proficient in singing in different styles of music, they need to return consistently to these styles in successive seasons. Collective memory of a particular repertory of music—or even of a particular composer—can be very useful for building an embedded sense of stylistic knowledge over time.

Goals and milestones of varying magnitudes are a useful means of maintaining momentum in a choral ensemble. Regular concerts are an obvious example, in which the choir has an opportunity to perform the music they have been rehearsing. Choral competitions are another option, albeit somewhat more divisive. As musicians, many of us will agree that the very idea of competing in music is at odds with the joyful spirit of collective music-making that we strive to embody in our choral work; however, I have found the act of preparing for competitions to be a very enjoyable source of development in my choir, where we delve more deeply into musical expression than is often permitted by time in the case of a concert. Our usual practice is to memorize the music we sing in competitions. When the singers become comfortable performing the music from memory, they are afforded a deeper sense of engagement with both the music and the text. The result is a wonderful feeling of collective achievement, musical freedom, and unity of expression. Surprisingly enough, some of our most profoundly connected performances—on a musical, spiritual, and human level—have occurred on the competition stage. As Bud Beyer writes in his chapter on memorization:

> The performance of music touches all our senses. We come to the performance space to see, touch, smell, taste and, yes, hear the music. But if all we visually see is a recitation by musicians with their heads in the score, then our experience, though lovely, may be severely limited. The potential magic of a music performance, when the great circle is no longer interrupted by music stands and scores, may instead become the experience musicians desire to share with their audiences.[6]

In my experience, the goal of memorization has the effect of encouraging a deep affinity with the musical and textual material, thereby increasing the choir's confidence in its ability to communicate with an audience. While of course it may not always be possible to memorize every piece of music performed, I have found it to be profoundly useful as part of my artistic programming.

## The Continuing Development of the Conductor

Most conductor training programmes equip aspiring conductors with the necessary technical skills to convey musical intentions clearly to their ensemble, in addition to the aural acuity needed to correct mistakes and shape the music in rehearsal. These skills of clear conducting technique and good musicianship are the fundamental basis of the conductor's education. Many young conductors continue this important training throughout their early careers by attending short courses and masterclasses with expert conductors in order to assimilate a wide range of approaches. These intensive training opportunities allow the conductor to build on their knowledge and confidence; moreover, they are a wonderful opportunity for conductors to meet one another and exchange views—a very valuable experience in a field where work is often carried out in isolation.[7]

Indeed, the isolated nature of the conductor's work can present a barrier to continuing development. As they become more established and experienced, choral conductors need to find new ways to refresh and nourish their practice. Recent events have shaped my own thinking about choral conducting in new directions. The Covid-19 pandemic, a hugely difficult experience for all musicians, was particularly so for conductors, who were unable to make music without their 'instrument.' Like many other choral conductors, I set up online singing sessions for my choir, enabling us to maintain some sense of community, albeit in a musically challenging situation. Additionally, and somewhat unexpectedly, the pause in live rehearsals and concerts necessitated by the pandemic provided time and space for me to think deeply about my practice. Questions arose for me which I have been joyfully exploring since our return to live music-making. For example, how can I best support the singers in my role as musical leader of the group? What different facets of creativity can the conductor bring to the rehearsal room? How can I show the very essence of the music with my body language and demeanour? How can my preparation outside the rehearsal room inform the musical progress of the choir?

Although the answers to these questions will always be a work in progress, funding from the Arts Council of Ireland allowed me to collaborate with another musician colleague with the aim of addressing some of them. In a series of one-to-one meetings, we explored some of the creative areas of music-making that are often overlooked in the time-pressured and concert-focused environment of the rehearsal room. Allowing space for these somewhat intangible elements of creativity has been one of the most profound influences of my career to date. Although—or, perhaps, *because*—we were not working towards a particular performance or output, this experience has changed how I approach my practice. The time spent exploring things that we sometimes do not prioritize (e.g., emotional connection to music, body connection with music and text, approaches to memorization, ways of thinking about rehearsal) is extremely valuable. We also found inspiration in various readings and approaches, including the work of Bud Beyer, Kristin Linklater, and Stephen Nachmanovitch, as well as exercises borrowed from Feldenkrais's work.[8] Much of our work together has been reflective, and I feel already the profound influence of having been afforded the time to reflect on my practice as a musician—something which I had never before dedicated specific time to do.[9]

For the choral conductor as a leader of people, the fact that the people being led are making music with their own bodies and voices means that our role has further layers of both complexity and intimacy as distinct from other musicians. The link between conductor and choir is not merely transactional, as there are human relationships involved. It seems to me that there is considerable truth in the metaphor of the mirror; many of the conductor's qualities, both musical and personal, are often reflected back by the choir. I suggest that it is our responsibility as conductors to embody the physical posture we would like to see in our choir; to demonstrate the level of musical preparedness we would like our singers to have; to model the emotional connection to the music that we wish for. This is not simply about musical preparation, but also about attitude to the people we are leading and, more broadly, to life. Tone Bianca Dahl writes:

> As a conductor I act as a mirror. I see myself in the choir, and the choir sees themselves in me. This process works both ways—a fact it is important to be aware of. . . . By being conscious of my own tension, my own free-flowing energy and the signals I send to the choir, I am able over time to transform even the most tense and reluctant choir to one that sings from the heart.[10]

Dahl also discusses the importance of the conductor being in a state of balance and flow, and how the route to achieving this will be different for every individual. For me, extramusical physical and mental practices such as yoga, meditation, strength training, and running have been immensely helpful, particularly because of the ways in which these practices strengthen the connection between mind and body.[11] While there is no single 'arrival point,' as we are in a constant state of flux as people, I view it as a challenge to attempt to unify the people in front of me, bringing what we do into alignment. For me, this responsibility is more exciting than daunting.

**Maintaining Community: The Choral Rehearsal**

Membership may gradually change in a choral ensemble over time, but each group has its own distinct identity, influenced to a large extent by the conductor. One constant for most groups is weekly rehearsals and it is important that these are enjoyable experiences for the choir. It is my view that, with consistency, mutual respect, and a hard-working but light-hearted atmosphere, choirs will come to value weekly rehearsals as an end in themselves, something worth attending. Although singers may arrive at choir practice on a weeknight tired after their day's work, a choir rehearsal provides distraction from the busy timetable of daily life. After two hours spent collectively breathing, controlling exhalation, focusing on producing sound with the voice, striving for musical unity, with some laughter along the way, the singers usually leave the rehearsal feeling happy and refreshed. I believe it is important that this is consistently the case, so that rehearsals are anticipated with a degree of excitement rather than merely as a necessary means to an end.

For my group, the format for a typical two-hour rehearsal tends to follow a roughly familiar routine from week to week. As described earlier in this chapter, the first ten to fifteen minutes of the rehearsal are devoted to the warm-up—a crucial part of the transition from normal life into the choral rehearsal. After the singers are mentally and physically ready to rehearse, we turn to the repertoire we are currently preparing. It helps to plan how the rehearsal will flow; I usually find that the most focused work happens towards the beginning of the rehearsal. Somewhere between ten and twenty minutes per piece or per section of rehearsal tends to work well, as it is not so long that the singers might start to lose focus, yet it is sufficient to tackle whatever part of the music needs work. It can help to alternate between less and more familiar music, so that the singers do not get discouraged only practising music they cannot yet perform successfully. This also has the effect of varying the pace and energy levels in the rehearsal room and giving a break between intense concentration and relative relaxation. Another technique is to start near the end of a section, and gradually work back, so that the singers are then singing their way towards more familiar music. Also, I usually try to 'front-load' the rehearsal, with the break around two-thirds of the way through, given that my singers seem to do their most focused work in the first part of the rehearsal. This approach makes the second 'half' seem very short, and the singers are pleasantly surprised that time has flown and the rehearsal is already finished. Another golden rule is to aim to finish with something familiar and preferably uplifting, something that the singers enjoy singing, so that they leave the practice feeling good. I always aim to finish the rehearsal on time or a few minutes early, living in hope that this professionalism will affect the singers' punctuality at the beginning of the rehearsal.

A musically and spiritually enriching element of our choir community experience is the intensive full-day weekend rehearsal. The act of devoting a full Saturday or Sunday to the pursuit of high standards of singing will, of course, reap rich musical rewards: the group is fresher and more alert when not at the end of a long day's work; the singers are free of distractions and are able to focus more on the music. It is like working with a different instrument at the weekend, compared with a regular weekday evening. However, these long rehearsals also hold a special place in the hearts of the singers beyond the obvious musical benefits. The lack of time pressure lends a more relaxed atmosphere to the day. Time is spent not only going deeply into the music, but also going into the deeper musical expression and emotional import of the texts we are singing. I call upon the talents and expertise of individual choir members to help provide contextual background and there is a space for singers to offer their own textual interpretation. There is a sense of ease and fun. Food, drink, and laughter are shared. The merging of the musical and the social means that the weekend rehearsals are central to the community-building within the choir. These rehearsals are an end in themselves, something to be cherished.

As we have seen, many diverse factors influence the long-term development of a choir. Every choral ensemble has its own collective identity and *raison d'être*, whether musical or social; therefore, different techniques and habits will be required in rehearsals and in long-term planning depending on the specific goals of the group. The five main topics explored here—vocal production, musical style, artistic planning, conductor development, and the choral rehearsal—are of equal importance for building a stable, healthy choir. In my practice, I seek to combine and balance these areas where possible. Finally, the importance of the conductor communicating clearly and respectfully with their choir is paramount; the choral leader is ideally placed to ensure that a sense of mutual trust is built within the ensemble and between choir and conductor. This trust forms the foundation of a long, enjoyable, and fruitful shared exploration of the choral art.

## Notes

1 Sabine Horstmann, *The Choral Warm-up: Choral Vocal Technique* (Chicago: GIA Publications, 2009). I also highly recommend attending as many choral rehearsals and workshops as possible to learn from other conductors. For further discussion of the choral warm-up, see Chapter 13 by Róisín Blunnie in this volume.
2 Gunnar Eriksson, *Kör ad lib. Blå* (Gothenburg: Bo Ejeby Förlag, 1995); Gunnar Eriksson, *Kör ad lib. Grön* (Gothenburg: Bo Ejeby Förlag, 2008).
3 Other potentially helpful sources for developing this perhaps less-explored areas of choral singing include Pauline Oliveros's deep listening exercises, such as *Sonic Meditations* (Baltimore: Smith Publications, 1971), and Stephen Nachmanovitch's book *Free Play: Improvisation* (New York: Tarcher/Putnam, 1990). For more ideas on group vocal improvisation with a jazz/pop focus, see Chapter 16 by Jim Daus Hjernøe in this volume.
4 See Chapter 20 by Lynsey Callaghan in this volume for insights on programming in the context of youth choral music education; and for guidance on decision-making around the order of music within a concert programme, see Chapter 12 by Kari Turunen.
5 For similar considerations in an orchestral context, see Chapter 6 by Ciarán Crilly in this volume.
6 Bud Beyer, *Completing the Circle: Considerations for Change in the Performance of Music* (Chicago: GIA Publications, 2014), 62.
7 The European Choral Association (www.europeanchoralassociation.org) offers various short training courses throughout the year for conductors, with similar opportunities available in other parts of the world.
8 Beyer, *Completing the Circle*; Kristin Linklater, *Freeing the Natural Voice: Imagery and Art in the Practice of Voice and Language* (London: Nick Hern Books, 2006); Nachmanovitch, *Free Play*; Feldenkrais Guild of North America, "Feldenkrais Method: About," accessed 14 June 2023, https://feldenkrais.com/about-the-feldenkrais-method.
9 Xenia Pestova Bennett, *Befriending Performance Anxiety: Practical Tips for Performers of All Levels* (Bangor, Co. Down: Brompton Cove Press, 2022) has provided a practical and thought-provoking approach to the topic.
10 Tone Bianca Dahl, *The Choir: Singing, Leading, Communicating* (Stavanger: Cantando Musikkforlag, 2008), 110.
11 Dahl, *The Choir*, 115.

# 12
## THE OTHER SIDE OF PROGRAMMING
How to Shape a Choral Concert Programme

*Kari Turunen*

Most of the literature for choral conductors on programming concentrates on *what* to programme, whereas the focus of this chapter is *how to formulate* a programme. At its simplest, this can be a question of how to put in order the works chosen for a given concert, but as we will see, form and content are not always separate issues. While symphonic concerts often have a set structure to them, choral concerts generally do not.[1] This means that choral conductors must use their skills and imagination to organize the material of any given concert in an effective, sustainable, and meaningful way: effective in the sense that the concert programme forms a logical dramatic arch; sustainable in the sense that the performers are at their best throughout the programme; and meaningful in the sense that the order of the works maximizes the connotative web that connects the works and conveys the intention behind the programme. This chapter will attempt to give some suggestions for achieving these goals.

### Structural Solutions

Choral works are, on the whole, shorter than instrumental works. A six-minute choral composition often feels like a substantial work and a ten-minute, one-movement composition for *a cappella* choir is something of an exception. A choral concert can thus easily consist of ten to fifteen works, which makes organizing the musical material well even more important.

One clear way of organizing the music is placing it in *chronological* order. This simply means arranging the works chosen for a concert in the order of their inception. Considering that an article on programming

DOI: 10.4324/9781003299660-16

from 1994 claims that chronological programming is "the most common method," it is fair to say that the approach has lost quite a bit of favour in recent decades.[2] The chronological approach is often connected to a programme that contains a progression through several different historical periods. With the diversification of choral programmes during the last decades, this kind of programming seems to have become less common, even in educational settings, making chronologically ordered programmes the exception rather than the rule. That said, this approach is still a viable alternative. It is especially valuable in contexts such as a concert dedicated to a single composer or a single stylistic period. As with all solutions, adding some twists to the approach can be refreshing. For example, when presenting music of one historical period, it might be thought-provoking to begin the programme with the newest work and then proceed in chronological order from oldest to newest with an eye on asking and answering the question: "How did we get here?"

If we choose to approach our material without the aid of a mechanical apparatus, such as chronological order, we are left with a handful of works to compile somehow into a concert programme. In many cases, the selection of the works already contains assumptions about the way the programme will be organized, and, conversely, the chosen structural solution and the choice of works often go hand in hand. An example of the former could be a concert that is centred on a composition more substantial than the other works. A thirty-minute cantata or choral suite will, by necessity, entail considerations about the placement of this larger work in the programme and create a structural solution by default. In the latter case, the chosen approach will create the need and guide the search for works of a specific textual or musical character.

A good example of this idea-first programming is the *thematic* approach.[3] This can refer both to an overall theme and to the grouping of works into blocks to form subthemes. A programme called 'Seasons' could be broken up into four sections (Autumn, Winter, Spring, Summer); a Christmas programme could be divided into blocks according to the focal figure (Mary, Joseph, the shepherds, the Magi); or, as an example of a more connotative than concrete approach, a French programme could be broken down into the colours of the French flag and their symbolic content (Blue, freedom; White, equality; Red, fraternity). One strength of the thematic approach is that it almost automatically produces a clear title for a concert and gives clarity to marketing the programme to both performers and audiences.

A variant of the thematic approach is *storytelling*.[4] Here, the idea is to utilize the engagement that stories create in their audience and present the programme in the form of a story. This means designing a narrative flow through the programme with characteristics typical to storytelling: direction, clarity, variety, and surprise. Besides the benefit of eliciting an intellectual and emotional response from the audience, the storytelling approach makes room for a chronological, geographical, and stylistic diversity that might otherwise be difficult to combine into the same choral programme. Because the glue of the programme is the story, a Renaissance motet could very well flow into a pop song arrangement or folk song from Malaysia, as long as the logic of the narrative is congruous.

Perhaps a word of caution concerning thematic programming is in order: it is not a *deus ex machina* that solves all programming problems. A theme does alleviate the stress on the individual works, but it does not eliminate it. Unless the narrative is exceptional and the flow of the programme irresistible, the audience experiences the concert work by work. Both the works in themselves and their performances need to feel convincing even within a well-thought-out thematic programme. Themes simply make the whole easier to grasp and help tie together works of different characters.

**Formalistic Approaches**

Not all choral programmes are, or need to be, thematic or based on storytelling. There are other, more formalistic approaches to organizing the music within a programme. Compared with the preceding thematic approaches, here the focus is less on textual unity or narrative and more on a subliminal feeling of direction, energy, and shape. One does not rule out the other, and a formalistic approach can well go hand in hand with a narrative or textual theme. At its most basic, this approach could mean using the notion of an 'Aristotelian ideal' of a play with a beginning, a middle, and an end, where the middle follows from the beginning and the end from the middle. While this might sound a little vague, it helps us focus on three crucial questions:

1. How do we begin the programme?
2. What is the direction and culmination of the middle?
3. How do we end the programme?

Answering these questions will already be a major step towards a solid programme. Knowing which works constitute the beginning and end of the programme will often make the other pieces fall into place almost automatically. An additional aid is placing the climax of either the whole programme or the Aristotelian middle somewhere in the vicinity of the golden ratio.[5] In a programme with sixty minutes of music, this would mean that the climax would be close to the forty-minute mark. Identifying the works that form the beginning, the ending, and the climax will go a long way to structuring a programme.

Beginning a programme naturally depends on the character of the whole programme but engaging your audience when they are at their most receptive is the key aim. 'Coming out swinging' is always a good option if the programme idea allows for it: a short and energetic opener is usually a safe bet. When considering the climax of the programme, it is important to remember that the climax need not be the loudest, fastest, or most extrovert work, even if these are often a good place to look first. A work that is exceptionally strong, either emotionally or textually, could just as well form the climax. Successful endings, in turn, tend to fall into two categories: fading into the night or a twist in the tale. The former gradually relaxes the energy created towards the climax and the latter adds a little hook to the ending to elicit an energetic response.

Another very useful formal solution is a *mirror structure*, where all the works of a programme, or a part of a programme, are structured around one work with the other works forming layers on both sides of the focal point.[6] Presented concisely, the structure could look like this:

- C
- B
- A
- Central work/works
- A1
- B1
- C1

The benefit of this approach is that it automatically shines a light on the focal work of the programme on a visual, cognitive, and subliminal level. Additionally, because the other works are seldom so similar that the choices would be completely apparent, a network of connections starts appearing in the process of finding the coupled works around the centre. The similarities might well be concrete—character, key, tempo, text content, poet, composer—but they can also be more vague, more intuitive; a feeling that these two works share common ground. This part of the process often reveals connections that were not apparent when the works for the concert programme were initially chosen. The centre can naturally consist of more than one work, especially if these works are relatively short.

As these formalistic approaches show, almost any structural solution used in the arts can be applied to programming. A programme with two contrasting elements could well be set in a *sonata form* of sorts. For example, War and Peace could begin with works introducing each element in turn; then go through the 'development' of the themes through more connotative works; and, after a recapitulation of the main themes, end with a work that addresses both elements and forms a synthesis of sorts (Schoenberg's *Friede auf Erden* comes to mind). Similarly, there is no reason why a *rondo form* such as ABA¹CA²DA³ would not work as the basis for a choral programme. The works labelled A could, for example, be based on texts by the same poet, be by the same composer, or come from the same period, geographical area, or musical style; with B, C, and D being works that are juxtaposed to A.

## Practical Considerations

In addition to the considerations of form and engaging the audience, it is good to think about more practical features; some of these constitute a checklist for the programme, some are most relevant for the audience, and some primarily concern the performers. Most of the ground covered to this point has concentrated on creating unity and logic in programmes. But besides unity, variety and juxtaposed elements are central considerations of successful programming.[7] Creating a flow with contrasts to keep the audience engaged requires awareness of some central musical characteristics.

The most apparent of these characteristics is tempo. A useful method is to divide the works in the programme into three tempo categories: slow, mid-paced, and fast. The last category, in particular, is surprisingly rare in choral music, and mid- to slow-paced works tend to dominate. This means that the placement of the faster works in the programme is likely to be of considerable significance for creating variety and contrasts and thus deserves extra attention.

Other features to consider are keys and key progression, musical and textual character, and the length of the individual works. Beginning with the last of these, it is quite typical of choral concerts that the length of the individual works varies substantially. When this is the case, there are two major aspects to consider: first, the placement of the longer works; and second, the grouping of the shorter works. It most often makes sense not to place the longer works one after the other, but rather spread them away from each other. For the shorter works, bundling them together to form smaller entities within the larger framework can be an easy way to give a sense of unity to an otherwise fragmented programme. It can be tempting to group works with similar texts and musical character, but placing them symmetrically, for example in a mirror structure as described earlier, might be more effective in creating both variation and unity. This is especially true for the most demanding works, from the point of view of both the performers and the audience. These works demand most concentration from both parties and tend to work best when separated from each other.

If the music performed is mostly tonal (or modal), it is wise to consider the keys of the music when finalizing the programme. On the most basic level, it is worthwhile ensuring that all the music is not confined to one or two keys; on a more meaningful level, ensuring that the progression from one piece to another feels natural helps to create a sense of flow through the programme. As a blunt example, going from an E-flat major ending to the opening E major of the next work will demand at least a small gap in the programme. Natural-feeling progressions could include staying in the same key, a dominant–tonic transition, and naturally moving to any tonality that is characteristic in the previous key. Unless instruments are involved or the choir has a very strong sense of tonal centres, however, intricate key progression plans might not be realized as planned in concert. Despite this, a large-scale key progression throughout the whole programme or parts of it can add subtlety and intuitive unity. Three consecutive works could borrow a key structure from a classical sonata (e.g., A major, F-sharp minor, A major) or four pieces could use the key progression of the movements of a symphony (e.g., C minor, A-flat major, C minor, C major). The possibilities are virtually endless.

Structuring programmes is a skill that takes time to develop. As with many other skills, unfortunately, the only way to learn is through trial and error. Something that looks good on paper and even seems to work well throughout the rehearsal process can feel less successful in concert. On the other hand, at times a haphazardly assembled programme will feel ingenious. Being prepared to take risks and experimenting with different solutions will help find a voice of one's own as a programmer and a constructor of programmes. Innovative and fresh programmes, including how they are put together, can give an ensemble a lot of character and a competitive edge over similar groups.

## Considering the Performers

One central element of the practical considerations that shape a programme is planning it in a way that is reasonable for the performers. If several works in the programme stretch the singers' vocal and technical abilities, placing these challenges in the right places will increase the chances of pulling off the most difficult works in the best possible way. The best timing for these challenges is when the singers are settled into their work, but still in their best voice and clearest mind. This approach would place the biggest challenges reasonably early in the programme, or soon after an intermission. By overcoming the biggest hurdle early in the concert, a lot of stress is alleviated, and that energy can be directed into music-making and expressivity.

Some works are very strenuous on the voices of the singers. Placing these works just before a break will give the singers much-needed time to recover. On the whole, variation in the difficulty level of the chosen works is an important consideration for the performers and wise choices in this regard can make the programme much more comfortable for the singers. Radical changes in *tessitura* are also worth monitoring. Especially in chronologically and stylistically diverse programmes, the role of a voice part can change quite radically from one work to another. Distance between these works will make this vocal transition smoother. And from the point of view of the singers, changes in the positioning of the choir can feel stressful, especially when not rehearsed enough. Avoiding continuous changes is a worthwhile consideration.

If instruments are used, the placing of the works with instrumentalists is an important consideration, from the point of view of both the programme and the logistics. Thinking through the change of sound and dynamic between the instrumentally accompanied and unaccompanied works, the demands on the voices, as well as the sheer minimizing of the time needed for setting up and clearing the space needed for the instrumentalists, can help both the physical and the musical flow of the concert.

**Further Practical Considerations**

There are a few straightforward questions that need to be answered before the programme is finalized. First, is there an intermission in the programme? Naturally, this decision to some degree dictates the length of the concert. Most often, a programme without an intermission will run for fifty to seventy minutes, while a concert with an intermission will on average last between ninety minutes and two hours. From an artistic point of view, an intermission plays a major role in the shaping of a concert. With an intermission, the form becomes by default binary and defining the relationship of the halves becomes a part of the process. Whatever structural solution is used, the halves will be perceived as such and a flow through the programme will be interrupted. Deciding whether there is an intermission or not should thus be part of the planning process.

Second, where is applause expected or encouraged? Applause is a double-edged sword. On the one hand, it is a way for the audience to express both its satisfaction and its engagement and for the performers to receive encouragement and feedback. On the other, applause after each individual work makes a sense of flow and progress almost impossible. This means planning for applause is important, as is communicating this plan. Sometimes grouping the pieces in blocks in the programme can sufficiently guide the audience, but clearly stating the guidance in the concert programme or announcing it at the beginning of the concert will make the message clear. Audiences appreciate being informed about when to applaud, so there is no need to resort to discreet hints.

The third decision concerns whether someone will speak during the concert. Concert traditions vary from country to country and area to area, but it seems that at least welcome speeches are fairly universal occurrences in choral concerts. If someone does speak, it naturally begs the question who the speaker or speakers will be, how many speeches there will be, and how long they should be. There are many possible solutions and making choices between them should be included in the programming process.

When considering concert lengths, all these decisions need to be factored into the equation, as do entering and leaving the stage and any movements of the choir between works. A rule of thumb is that it will all take longer than estimated and it is worth taking even one's own timings of the music with a pinch of salt. If aiming for a seventy-minute concert, plan for one that lasts approximately sixty minutes.

Finally, it is good to consider an encore, preferably from the outset, but at least well before the last rehearsal. Being prepared for an encore is, in most cases, worthwhile, as a good encore stretches the feel-good phase at the end of a concert for both performers and audience. At best, the encore enhances the programme, or at least feels like an integral part of it, and leaves the audience with the desired emotional reaction, be it the twist in the tale or the slipping quietly into the night.

## Conclusion

Choosing a concert programme that is interesting and rewarding for both the audience and the performers is a daunting task. Once the selection of the works is completed, another challenge still lies ahead of the choral conductor: formulating a concert programme of the chosen works. A well-forged programme will create a musical flow and deliver the ideas behind the programme in an effective way. At times, the order of the programme and the underlying idea of the concert are inherently connected, as in the chronological approach. In the thematic approach, this tie is not as direct, but if the theme idea includes a sense of direction or progression, an order is almost implied. In the storytelling approach, it is quite likely that the order of the chosen works will be part of the selection process, and when it is not, the criterion for the placement of the works is where they best fit in the narrative.

When programmes are not based on any of the preceding solutions, the ordering of the concert programme most often comes after the selection of the works. Fortunately, there are many formal solutions that can be used in this process. Mere considerations of the central pillars of the programme—the beginning, climax, and end—will help structure the programme in a way that creates flow and unity, while allowing for variation. More intricate solutions, such as mirror structures, may also be of considerable aid in this phase, as may other musical structures.

Any concert programme will try to balance unity and variation. Factors to consider in this context are the tempo and character of the works, their keys and the progression from one work to another, and the difficulty of the works. Planning the programme with an eye on the performers will also help shape its structure. Making sure the most technically or vocally demanding works are placed economically will help the performers reach their optimal level, as will considering the *tessitura* shifts in the voice parts. If instruments are involved, the placement of the works with instruments is an important consideration artistically and logistically.

Some practical decisions that play a surprisingly important role in shaping the programme tend to fall between the cracks in the initial programme design. Whether the programme includes an intermission directly influences the length of the programme as well as its structure and should thus be a decision made early in programme planning. Smaller but important considerations are: where applause is expected, any possible speeches, and ending the programme with an encore.

The skill of choosing repertoire that is enjoyed by audiences and performers alike is perfected over time through a method of trial and error. The same applies to formulating concert programmes. Programming is often mentioned as a central characteristic of choral conducting skills, but ordering the works in an engaging and efficient manner is often less discussed, as is evident in the literature. Yet this ability can make concerts feel considerably more engaging and help the choir stand out among its peers. Initially, the process is based on rational considerations, but with time and experience it can become more intuitive. To reach this stage requires hard work, some lucky strikes, and even a few mishaps. Being courageous and inventive in experimenting with forms and themes is the best teacher in this process.

## Notes

1 The overture–concerto–symphony structure that dominated symphony concerts for over a century has of late given way to more flexible approaches. That said, the most popular alternative of new music–concerto–symphony is still built upon the same structural foundation. For insights on programming orchestral concerts, see Chapter 6 by Ciarán Crilly in this volume.

2 David L. Brunner, "Choral Program Design: Structure and Symmetry," *Music Educators Journal* 80, no. 6 (May 1994): 48, https://doi.org/10.2307/3398713. It is worth noting that this view is more descriptive of US collegiate choir programming than a universal assessment.
3 A thorough, practical introduction to this approach can be found in Gerald R. Hoekstra, "Thematic Choral Programming," *The Choral Journal* 20, no. 2 (1979): 20–24, http://www.jstor.org/stable/23545126.
4 A good introduction to programming through storytelling can be found in Emilie Bertram, "Utilizing the Principles of Storytelling to Design Engaging Concert Programs," *The Choral Journal* 62, no. 2 (2021): 8–19, https://www.jstor.org/stable/27089729; and Emily Ellsworth, "Concert Programs as Storytelling," *The Choral Journal* 59, no. 11 (2019): 8–17, https://www.jstor.org/stable/26662773.
5 Two units are said to be in golden ratio if their ratio is the same as the ratio of their sum to the larger unit ($a+b$ is to $a$ as $a$ is to $b$). For those less mathematically inclined, golden ratio calculators are available online.
6 The classic examples of using mirror structures in shaping a composition are the *St Matthew Passion* and the motet *Jesu, meine Freude* by Johann Sebastian Bach. In the *Zweiter Teil* of the former, movements 30–65 (Bärenreiter Neue Ausgabe numbering) are structured around the soprano recitative and aria, numbers 48 and 49. In the latter, the centre is the fugue 'Ihr aber seid nicht fleischlich.'
7 Both Brunner, "Choral Program Design," and Jon Washburn, "Programming: Getting Your Concerts into Good Shape!" *The Choral Journal* 24, no. 6 (1984): 7–10, http://www.jstor.org/stable/23546351, include excellent discussions about necessary variation. Richard Bjella "The Art of Successful Programming: Study, Selection and Synthesis," in *The Oxford Handbook of Choral Pedagogy*, ed. Frank Abrahams and Paul D. Head (New York: Oxford University Press, 2017), 281–302, concentrates more on finding suitable repertoire but also raises excellent practical considerations.

# 13

## TOGETHER FROM THE START

The Collective Power of the Choral Warm-Up

*Róisín Blunnie*

I recently encountered a challenge with my chamber choir. As we approached our summer break, with two end-of-semester concerts remaining in the schedule, I noticed that some choir members were tending to arrive later to rehearsal, so that fewer were present for the full duration of the warm-up. These are positive, committed singers, so I knew that their lateness was not the result of a negative attitude. Like many people, they lead busy lives, and getting to rehearsal on time requires effort; I wondered why that effort was, on the whole, waning. Reflecting on the problem, I realized that it had been a long time since I had articulated the purpose of our warm-up. In the absence of this information, it could have appeared that the warm-up was simply a time for preparing each member's own voice to sing, and therefore presence or absence would only impact themselves as individuals; whereas from my perspective as the conductor, the choral warm-up is so much more than that—it is a crucial collective activity at the very heart of the choir's sonic identity and developmental journey, and something for which I should advocate passionately. I gathered my thoughts and sent an email to the choir, encouraging the singers to arrive on time, and explaining:

> I really want to put the term 'warm-up' in the bin [trash], because what we are doing in this first section of rehearsal is **Choral Development: Collective Vocal Technique; Harmonically Informed Close Listening, Harmonic Series Overtone Alignment; Breathing, Positioning, Poise; Optimisation of Vowel Placement and Colour; Precise Ensemble Accuracy; Specific Treatment of Consonants; Awakening of Phrasing, Style, and Momentum;** basically all the things that contribute to a **Quality,**

DOI: 10.4324/9781003299660-17

Resonant, Supported Tone (QRST) that is distinctive to Laetare Vocal Ensemble based on the combined character and energy of every one of your individual voices and musical abilities. . . . Every voice matters in creating this, as it does for creating our Laetare sound throughout the full rehearsal. We are never just learning notes. We are making beautiful music, beautifully, from ourselves as individuals, together.[1]

The more I work as a choral conductor, the less satisfactory I find the term 'warm-up.' In my view, it does not adequately represent the intricate, substantial, multifaceted, and multi-purpose process with which many choirs begin their rehearsals. I wish to argue that we should acknowledge the often complex physical, scientific, musical, and artistic concepts at play in this opening phase of rehearsal and take ownership of the work that we do as choral leaders, in collaboration with the singers, to build our choir's technique and distinctive ensemble sound. To my mind, the expression 'warm-up' tends to downplay the extent of what is (or can be) achieved at this stage of rehearsal, and the impact that it has (or can have) on the effectiveness of the rehearsal as a whole, as well as on the overall development of the choir in the medium and longer terms.

This chapter seeks neither to put forward a particular approach to the choral warm-up nor to argue for its inclusion or usefulness, but rather to recognize the breadth and depth of what many conductors are already doing and to claim this for the sophisticated technical and musical endeavour that it is.

## Individual Versus Collective

Naturally, a primary purpose of a warm-up is to ready the singers to use their voices in a healthy, productive way. However, what we do with choirs in the opening phase of rehearsal often goes significantly beyond this immediate function. In a choral environment, the warm-up is a period of unparalleled focus, when singers and conductors can interact without the complications of repertoire or the need to look at scores. It is an opportunity to embed collective expectations for quality and precision in ensemble singing, in areas such as tuning, onsets, phrasing and momentum, tone, blend, articulation, and balance, and to instil a deep sense of vocal and artistic unity. Once established and refined in the controlled setting of the warm-up, these expectations can then be applied, whether subconsciously or intentionally, throughout the choir's rehearsal and performance activities.

The breadth and diversity of what occurs under the banner of the choral warm-up is evident from practical observation of various choirs and from a wide range of writings on the subject. A key distinction lies between warm-up sessions that focus principally or only on preparing the individual voices for group singing, and those that engage more directly with group-specific concerns or with a mixture of both. Norwegian conductor Tone Bianca Dahl states that any form of vocal warm-up "should start with creating physical and psychological balance," by bringing the singer into contact with "breathing, body and mind," and further outlines that warm-ups in a choral setting "prepare the singing apparatus . . . focus concentration . . . practice voice production and tone [and] create a sense of community in the group."[2] Ann Howard Jones notes both individual and group priorities, exploring the following areas in her outline of a choral warm-up:

- Readying the body.
- Establishing the unison.
- Manipulating the pitch.
- Exploring dynamics.
- Developing range.
- Defining articulations.
- Balancing the chorus.[3]

Sally Louise Glover explicitly addresses the distinction between individual and choral/group concerns in her article "How and Why Vocal Solo and Choral Warm-ups Differ," where she explains:

> There is an added dimension . . . when working with a group, rather than a single student. The choral warm-up must encourage independence of singing but also focus on ensemble, and this requires the choral warm-up to have a different focus. Besides warming up the voice, developing breath support and ease of production, extending the pitch range, and working on vocal technique in general, the choral warm-up also needs to work on balance and blend according to the preference of the director. An important skill that choristers must learn to achieve this aim is being able to listen to those around them, and the warm-up is an ideal vehicle to develop and refine this skill.[4]

In their book on vocal technique, Julia Davids and Stephen LaTour likewise point to opportunities for addressing specifically choral aspects during the warm-up, stating, for example, that, "in the choral setting, vowel exercises will help to ensure that all singers produce their vowels in the same way, which enhances choral tuning and blending," and "rehearsal expectations (e.g. vowel colors) can be established during the warm-up."[5] Davids and LaTour use the following headings in their recommendations for a choral warm-up: "stretching/body awareness," "breathing awareness," "connect breath with sound," "vowels and resonance," "range reinforcement/extension," "linking of registers," and "special techniques," the latter referring to challenges that may arise from repertoire, such as "articulation, consonant pronunciation, coloratura, leaps, part independence in ensembles, intonation, dynamics."[6] Guillermo Rosabal-Coto also points to the benefits of linking warm-ups to repertoire: "In order to make the warm-up session meaningful and purposeful, the conductor ought to prepare exercises that address specific vocal and musical challenges present in the music being studied or performed, after a careful analysis of the score."[7] Shirlee Emmons and Constance Chase point to a further advantage of anticipating repertoire: "Recognizing the technical overlap between a standard warm-up component and the specific spot in the repertoire you wish to improve is not only a time-saver; it raises singers' awareness that warming up is not to be taken for granted or treated as rote repetition."[8] The multi-purpose ideal of the rehearsal's beginning is noted by Simon Carrington, who argues that "all effective warm-ups should contain a vocal technique component, an aural challenge, a dynamic shading, and an expressive quality of some kind," adding that singers "should be listening vertically through the harmony and horizontally towards each side of the ensemble,"[9] while Hilary Apfelstadt observes succinctly but significantly that "warm-ups are prime teaching time."[10]

Considering the preceding perspectives, I would like to propose two primary arguments: first, that the great depth and variety of activities that often take place in the initial stages of a choir rehearsal exceed the boundaries of what is covered by the somewhat reductive and even flimsy term 'warm-up'; and second, that with effective leadership and guidance from the conductor, shared expectations of quality, precision, and unity across a range of technical, choral-specific aspects can be embedded from the very beginning of rehearsal, making collective choral-sound development an intrinsic feature as soon as the singers step into the room.

### Establishing Collective Expectations: Onset, Precision, Shape, and Momentum

In this section, I will outline a brief sample of approaches that I use to instil collective expectations during a rehearsal's opening phase.[11] Early in a rehearsal, like many conductors, I tend to use exercises with a narrow melodic range and relatively simple content, such as the exercise in Example 13.1 built with rising and falling whole tones.

**EXAMPLE 13.1**

The choir sings in unison—sopranos and altos at the pitch shown in Example 13.1, tenors and basses an octave lower—using a humming sound to activate airflow management and create a resonant tone. We work on achieving a precise, unified onset (the start of the sound) that is consciously 'placed' in relation to the conducting gesture, striving to ensure that the melody's characteristic major seconds are accurately tuned and that the exercise is sung with consistent, smooth tone across the choir, right through to the cut-off. Then we change to a selected vowel, aiming to do so without losing the quality achieved while humming. Once the vowel sound is unified, creating a blended unison, I ask the sopranos and tenors to sing the exercise a perfect fifth higher, while the altos and basses continue with the original (Example 13.2).

**EXAMPLE 13.2**

As we proceed through the exercise, moving upwards by semitone each time, I give only the lower 'new' note in each case, meaning that the sopranos and tenors must calculate their note a perfect fifth above,[12] using their inner hearing or audiation skills to imagine the sound before they sing it.[13] I find that this engenders a high level of concentration and precision—not least because the bare fifths that make up the texture offer nowhere to hide—and that such precision forms a collective expectation that then pervades the full rehearsal. For the melodic content of this particular exercise, I encourage the singers to tune rich, 'tall' fifths that resonate and ring, and to sing through the melody with a sense of direction and tonal vibrance.

I find that unison singing with keen attention to vowel unity and accurate tuning in the early stages of the rehearsal helps build a clean, defined choral sound that then becomes the norm for the choir—the singers expect to hear it, and therefore they intentionally create it, using a combination of vocal technique, musicianship, and sensitivity. As Glover explains, "unison warm-ups are essential . . . as singing with an exact match of blend and intonation is necessary to maximize the resonance and volume of the choir. Vowel equalization offers an approach to choral blend that can yield immediate and noticeable results."[14] Tailored unison exercises can also help in enhancing aspects of repertoire. Josef Rheinberger's sacred motet *Abendlied*, with its opening phrase "bleib bei uns" ("stay with us"), offers a useful example (Example 13.3).

The Collective Power of the Choral Warm-Up  **161**

**EXAMPLE 13.3**  Rheinberger, *Abendlied*, bb. 1–5.

In my experience, the plosive opening *bl* sound, combined with the soft dynamic level and the desire to achieve a well-balanced, in-tune F major chord, can cause vocal tension—and sometimes emotional stress—for singers. To alleviate this, it is useful to isolate the issue and address it in a simple exercise that the whole choir can focus on together (Example 13.4).

**EXAMPLE 13.4**

There are several points of guidance that can be given to encourage a relaxed but pinpointed collective onset. An expression I often use is "prepare the vowel and drop in the consonant," meaning that, during the preparatory breath, singers open the internal space needed for the initial vowel, *ah*, and then form the *bl* in a relaxed way—almost lazily—in front of it. This allows the choral voice to proceed smoothly through the consonants into the vowel and on with momentum through the line. In approaching the onset, I encourage the singers to think of 'releasing' to breathe, rather than inhaling, as the latter suggests an inward effort, while the former allows air to 'fall' into the body with minimal exertion and provides an ideal impetus for initiating the airflow and the sound in an easeful manner. I try to support this approach by using suitable conducting gestures and my own visible 'release.' To reduce tension while creating the *piano* dynamic, I encourage singers not to 'hold back,' but to 'sing forward quietly.'

It may be helpful to use imagery to assist the singers in achieving a smooth onset. I suggest that they imagine the sound is already in motion, and they just 'hop on board' as if to the gently moving vehicle of their choice. This minimizes the pressure on each singer, as they have the sense of joining something rather than bearing the pressure of creating it themselves. It may also be helpful to relate the moment of vocal onset to an Olympic diver smoothly entering the water having jumped from a high platform. As with the vocal onset, the smoothness of the diver's entry depends on the expert execution of technique. In the choral context, our priority is of course not the individual entry, but the unity of the collective onset, which in the case of my choir means imagining thirty-six Olympic divers, all entering the water in perfect synchronicity, with as little 'splash' as possible.

As we work on "bleib bei uns," I ask the singers to observe analytically and commit to memory the physical process they implement in approaching and executing an optimal onset, and we practise replicating this process so that the onset can be reproduced reliably, not least in the more pressurized environments of public performance or competition. Having worked in detail on the unison exercise, we then construct the opening chord of *Abendlied* by first adding a rich, tall fifth above the root as before, and finally placing the major third sensitively, so that it balances well and tunes according to the principles of 'just intonation.'[15] In subsequent rehearsals, I incorporate melodic exercises based on repetitions of the opening syllable *bla*, so singers can gain further experience of achieving relaxed onsets and of proceeding cleanly through the consonants into the unified vowel.

The beginning of rehearsal is also an ideal time for collective focus on shaping a particular phrase from repertoire, combining details such as stressed and unstressed syllables with overall momentum and vocal control, in addition to onset, vowel colour, and harmonically aware, scientifically informed intonation. *Selig sind die Toten* by Heinrich Schütz serves as an example here. In the opening six bars, all voice parts present a reasonably similar setting of the title text:

EXAMPLE 13.5   Schütz, *Selig sind die Toten*, bb. 1–7.

A simplified version of the phrase "Selig sind die Toten" ("Blessed are the Dead") can be used to work closely on the desired shaping in unison (Example 13.6).

EXAMPLE 13.6

Using a combination of vocal demonstration, conducting gesture, and precise verbal feedback, I encourage the singers to create a sense of energy and momentum as we proceed through the initial two bars towards the climax on the first syllable of *Toten*, to cultivate intensity and shape as we journey through that extended first syllable, and to maintain quality of vocal tone and blend on the same word's unstressed second syllable. This last point requires a combination of easing off with regard to textual emphasis, while staying engaged with regard to tone, shape, and vowel colour, so that this final syllable does not 'sit down,' potentially affecting intonation. The exercise can be enhanced by singing sometimes without text, instead using sounds such as *ng* (to help focus the tone), *mm* (for resonance and mutual listening), and either lip trills or a light 'j' sound, as in the French *je* (to help control airflow and manage tone consistently); then reinstating the text. In my experience, care for such details in unison creates an optimal collective sound which we bring through into our work on the piece itself.

A final example of a choral-focused activity that can be used to instil group expectations is outlined by Sharon Paul, Conductor of the University of Oregon Chamber Choir, in her book *Art and Science in the Choral Rehearsal*:

> In this exercise, I give the choir a chord to sing (or we select one from our repertoire) and then we take turns having a designated section sing louder than the rest of the sections. Then we stop and have silence for a few seconds after which they sing the chord again with the appropriate adjustments made for good balance. (Sometimes I will make suggestions for what to alter; other times I will encourage the singers to experiment to find their own solutions.) The chord pops into tune when sung correctly, which is very satisfying.[16]

Paul's exercise brings the singers' musicianship and fine listening skills into play in a welcoming, teamwork-based manner that activates high collective standards for harmonic quality and tuning. As Per-Gunnar Alldahl explains, when a chord is pure, "it will 'stop' and shine with a special lustre . . . like a slide picture that is correctly focused."[17]

## Leading and Responding

An effective choral warm-up relies greatly on the conductor's capacity to give high-quality demonstration and precise feedback that is helpful for singers; and this capacity in turn depends on our aural perception and analytical skills, polyphonic and harmonic awareness, knowledge of vocal technique, intonation, and choral tone; as well as on our ability to articulate musical, physical, scientific, and artistic information using well-judged, productive—perhaps even inspiring—language. Polyphonic perception skills enable us to identify when, for example, a note in a chord is too high, or too low, or has a vowel that is too bright or too dark or is otherwise disrupting the unity of the sound, or is lacking tone, or is too prominent for its harmonic role, or is fluctuating and causing instability.[18] As Dag Jansson observes, "the conductor is the only person who is dedicated to hearing the compound ensemble sound, meaning that aural awareness and error detection are crucial to the conductor's technical mastery."[19] Moreover, we must know how to respond in a meaningful way, using effective choral leadership. Jansson refers to the combination of musical-technical skills and effective leadership in real-time as "situational-relational mastery," explaining as follows:

> Musical-technical skills exist independent of their use, but the mastery of real-life situations involves a series of interventions which are relational in nature and require situational judgement. This mastery involves artistic decisions which must be made at every point during a rehearsal and in every precise moment of the flowing music.[20]

Such musical acuity, communication skills, and judgement are central to the success and broader impact of a rehearsal's opening phase. As Emmons and Chase argue, conductors may search for the perfect warm-up, but "no such warm-up regimen exists, underscoring the need for the directors to develop their ability to diagnose and prescribe, that is, to assess a situation and be equipped to address it."[21]

## Precedents for 'Rebranding' the Choral Warm-up

While the vast majority of scholars refer to a rehearsal's opening phase as the 'warm-up,' it is clear, first, that there is a degree of variance on what is meant by the term, with some regarding it principally as a time for warming up the individual voices for singing, and others regarding it additionally as a choral-focused activity as well as an opportunity to prepare elements inspired or demanded by the repertoire to be rehearsed; and second, that amidst the term's near-ubiquity, there is some small but notable evidence that it is not universally deemed satisfactory. For example, in *Prescriptions for Choral Excellence: Tone, Text, Dynamic Leadership*, Emmons and Chase refer to "the warm-up and training period," where their observation that "the warm-up becomes a training period whenever it is designed with purpose" suggests the authors did not find the term 'warm-up' sufficient by itself.[22] In his article "The Horse before the Cart: Redefining the Choral Warm-Up," Brian J. Winnie advocates strongly for the teaching of vocal technique as part of warm-ups in the context of school choral programmes in the United States, and draws on Kolb's theory of experiential learning to propose a specific nine-step sequence.[23] The warm-up, Winnie argues, has the capacity to be "a significant component of the choral rehearsal that focuses on targeted vocal exercises connected to specific anatomic movement and coordination needed for phonation, aural awareness, and the development of musicianship skills."[24] Of greatest relevance to this chapter is Winnie's observation that:

> The choral warm-up can incorporate many of the principle [sic] ideals of choral pedagogy and emphasize acquisition and eventual transference of skill and content knowledge. Nevertheless, the name 'choral warm-up' is not sufficient in describing these ideals. Instead, it is beneficial to think of this portion of the choral rehearsal as the 'choral tech-up,' which places emphasis on both the warm-up and technical skill development.[25]

Like Winnie's article, this chapter suggests that the existing nomenclature is insufficient. By contrast, however, I do not seek to set out a specific structure for a warm-up, but rather to argue that collective choral quality, unity, and precision, addressed intentionally by the full ensemble, can be foregrounded from the first moment of rehearsal, setting and raising shared expectations that permeate the choir's immediate and longer-term development.

## So, What to Call It?

When exploring this question in relation to my own choir, I came up with a range of possibilities, without settling on a particular one. I considered terms such as *choralization, choral development phase* (or *ensemblization* and *ensemble development phase*), *unified sound-building, choral-vocalization, coro-sonicization,* and *collective vocal preparation,* all of which emphasize the collective capacity and intricacy that I believe lie at the heart of an effective choral warm-up. Perhaps the right answer lies somewhere among these or indeed draws at times from all of them. What matters is not so much the title itself, but rather the idea that the warm-up's power and potential can be harnessed according to each choir's priorities and circumstances, led by an adept, committed conductor. As Tone Bianca Dahl asserts, "the point is not which exercises you do, but how you do them."[26] A shared understanding of the warm-up's impact, efficiency, and versatility can engender a deep sense of collaborative responsibility for cultivating the choir's tonal and artistic identity.

## Notes

1 Author email to the members of Laetare Vocal Ensemble, 11 June 2023. The term 'Quality, Resonant, Supported Tone' (QRST) emerged as part of research by myself and my colleague Barbara Dignam in developing digital choral

resources for the collaborative transnational ERASMUS+ project *PRESTO: Practices and Resources for Equipping Schools to Teach Music Online* (2021–23). See "PRESTO: Practices and Resources for Equipping Schools to Teach Music Online," Kodály Hub, accessed 9 September 2023, https://kodalyhub.com/presto.

2  Tone Bianca Dahl, *The Choir: Singing, Leading, Communicating*, trans. Andrew Smith (Stavanger: Cantando, 2008), 19, 32.
3  Ann Howard Jones, "A Point of Departure for Rehearsal Preparation and Planning," in *The Cambridge Companion to Choral Music*, ed. André de Quadros (Cambridge: Cambridge University Press, 2012), 272–80 (273–76).
4  Sally Louise Glover, "How and Why Vocal Solo and Choral Warm-ups Differ," *The Choral Journal* 42, no. 3 (October 2001): 17–22 (18), https://www.jstor.org/stable/23554079.
5  Julia Davids and Stephen LaTour, *Vocal Technique: A Guide for Conductors, Teachers, and Singers* (Long Grove, IL: Waveland, 2012), 247–48.
6  Davids and LaTour, *Vocal Technique*, 249–50.
7  Guillermo Rosabal-Coto, "Meaningful Vocal Development through Purposeful Choral Warm-Ups," *Canadian Music Educator / Musicien Educateur au Canada* 48, no. 2 (Winter 2006): 57–60 (58).
8  Shirlee Emmons and Constance Chase, *Prescriptions for Choral Excellence: Tone, Text, Dynamic Leadership* (New York: Oxford University Press, 2006), 202.
9  Simon Carrington, "Small Ensemble Rehearsal Techniques for Choirs of All Sizes," *Cambridge Companion to Choral Music*, 281–91 (284).
10 Hilary Apfelstadt, "Warm-ups: Building Strong Foundations for Ensemble Singing," *Canadian Music Educator / Musicien Educateur au Canada* 57, no. 4 (Summer 2016): 33–35 (34).
11 These are examples that suit my own mixed chamber choir, but I hope that the ideas and techniques explored may be easily adapted in the context of other choral ensembles.
12 A similar exercise can be employed in which the altos and basses must find their notes independently.
13 'Inner hearing' (*belső hallás* in Hungarian) is the term commonly used by those educated in Hungary and/or influenced by the Kodály approach to music education, while 'audiation' is the term more generally used in North America. The more specific term 'pre-phonatory tuning' is used primarily in scientific literature. Shirlee Emmons and Constance Chase provide the following helpful summary of this skill: "Audiation is to singing what visualization is to seeing. We visualize by seeing in the mind's eye; we audiate by hearing in the mind's ear." Emmons and Chase, *Prescriptions for Choral Excellence*, 207. See also Chapter 4 by Bernie Sherlock and Chapter 14 by László Nemes in this volume.
14 Glover, "Solo and Choral Warm-ups," 20.
15 For a thorough but accessible introduction to just intonation and choral tuning more broadly, see Per-Gunnar Alldahl, *Choral Intonation* (Stockholm: Gehrmans, 2008); and for a shorter but very helpful summary of key concepts, see Dahl, *The Choir*, 66–78.
16 Sharon J. Paul, *Art and Science in the Choral Rehearsal* (New York: Oxford University Press, 2020), 17.
17 Alldahl, *Choral Intonation*, 17.
18 For resources to develop polyphonic skills for the needs of conductors, see Róisín Blunnie, "Developing Polyphonic Skills Using Canon Exercises,"

created with colleagues Barbara Dignam and Shane Barriscale for the European Union ERASMUS+ project PRESTO (2021–23), Kodály Hub, accessed 9 September 2023, https://kodalyhub.com/presto/categories/developing-polyphonic-skills-using-canon-exercises.
19 Dag Jansson, *Leading Musically*, SEMPRE Studies in the Psychology of Music (London and New York: Routledge, 2018), 44.
20 Jansson, *Leading Musically*, 51.
21 Emmons and Chase, *Prescriptions for Choral Excellence*, 184.
22 Emmons and Chase, *Prescriptions for Choral Excellence*, 196.
23 Brian J. Winnie, "The Horse before the Cart: Redefining the Choral Warm-Up," *Choral Journal* 60, no. 9 (April 2023): 28–39.
24 Winnie, "The Horse before the Cart," 30.
25 Winnie, "The Horse before the Cart," 32.
26 Dahl, *The Choir*, 39.

# 14
# REHEARSAL TECHNIQUES FOR CONTEMPORARY CHORAL MUSIC

The Use of the Movable-*Do* System in the Teaching of Non-Tonal Repertoire

*László Nemes*

The issue of sight-reading atonal music is an ongoing matter of concern for many practitioners of the choral art. Those who oppose or misinterpret the movable-*do* system, widely used in musical training programmes inspired by Zoltán Kodály's concept of music teaching,[1] often question the usefulness of the system by voicing the opinion that if neither tonal function nor tonality itself exists in a composition, then surely a system in which syllables serve to define tonal functions cannot be usefully applied.[2] The practical experiences of proponents of the movable-*do* system, on the other hand, find that the intonation of atonal music does not usually represent any extraordinary challenge for singers who have been carefully prepared to sing all intervals with the sol-fa syllables of the movable-*do* system. Singing of an atonal melody can be made secure using a well-developed skill of intervallic hearing, particularly through 'inner hearing'—being able to imagine the sound of an interval (as well as other musical elements) before (or independently of) producing it through singing.[3] The movable-*do* system, used systematically in the training of sight-singing skills, develops precisely this ability.[4]

In the last two decades of my artistic work, some of the most challenging—and from a pedagogical point of view probably the most exciting—musical tasks concerned the teaching of contemporary choral compositions whose technical difficulties were significantly determined by atonal musical expression. In this chapter, I wish to share my experiences of teaching and rehearsing such compositions and to explain how it is possible to apply relative solmization (the movable-*do* system) as a teaching tool in the process of learning to sing atonal lines. The term 'atonal' is used here

DOI: 10.4324/9781003299660-18

in a broad sense, referring to music that is, using Allen Forte's definition, "characterized by the occurrence of pitches in novel combinations, as well as by the occurrence of familiar pitch combinations in unfamiliar environments."[5]

Both personal experience and rich scientific literature demonstrate the parallel connections between atonal musical expression and problems of musical perception.[6] For all who deal, even rarely, with this field of music in the course of their professional work, the challenge of performing atonal repertoire represents not only an artistic and performance issue but also a methodological issue. Many musicians know from experience that, in comparison with historical approaches in musical studies, courses in modern and contemporary techniques, even at college and/or university level, are indeed rare to find, not to speak of practical training courses connected to the performance of modern and contemporary music. Consequently, the matter of musical training related to the in-depth understanding and the performance of modern and contemporary choral repertoire falls mostly on the leader of the choir. Of course, this is not a problem for those conductors who, in addition to the musical and technical work in rehearsals, are interested in the methodological challenges concerning the teaching of modern and contemporary choral works.

In my work as a choir leader, I have always attached equal importance to the artistic, technical, and pedagogical work in the rehearsal room. My view is that, in an ideal situation, the teaching of the pieces, which partly aims at exploring the musical content and emotional dimensions of a given work, should at all times be connected organically to the technical aspects of, for example, creating a beautiful and clear choral sound that is stylistically suitable for the given musical compositions, and also to the pedagogical/methodological work which guides or assists the singers in learning the musical material and performing it with confidence. Young singers or amateur choristers are largely dependent on the conductor's well-planned coaching, circumspect guidance, and detailed information with regard to the learning of the material. Based on my practical experience, however, I dare to add that the technically and musically convincing acquisition of the musical material in the case of professional singers can also be successfully aided by well-chosen training methods. Singers are grateful if, during the rehearsal period, they receive support and easy-to-use guidelines that will make them excel in what they do. This is why I never start teaching a difficult composition by saying: "Hey, guys! Go and learn the notes of this piece before the first rehearsal!" Instead, each time I start teaching some new and especially challenging repertoire, which will perhaps also require diligent study outside the rehearsal room, I try to lead the singers into the musical realm of the composition through some preparatory presentations, interpretive verbal and visual explanations, and often the singing of various monophonic and polyphonic 'choral études' that I have prepared for them.

On the journey towards the performance of modern and contemporary choral works, both singers and conductors must face many technical challenges, especially in areas such as pitch structure, metre, rhythm, range, texture, polyphonic structure, harmony, timbre, musical gestures, dynamics, text, and rhetoric. Although in a composition these parameters naturally function together as an inseparable unit, in the learning process technical difficulties often need to be separated in order to cope with them in an efficient way.[7] Let's face it: technical difficulties are in abundance, especially when considering the stylistic variety of modern and contemporary repertoire. Navigating such repertoire, notwithstanding several dominant trends, presents challenges in terms of identifying general and specific stylistic aspects of the music. The oft-stated claim that it is worth approaching almost every new piece by presupposing some new, individual, and original artistic solution has been justified for me during the course of the past decades of working with choirs and continuously studying modern and contemporary choral literature. I can also say that there is no single, good analytical method that can be applied to reveal the content, or perhaps better to say the inner secrets, of all such works. One key does not fit all keyholes. The stylistic features of the repertoire not only influence the methods of analysis, the interpretation, and subsequently the performance of the works, but also influence, or better to say predetermine, the system of teaching tools and the teaching methods used during the rehearsal process.

In relation to the stylistic categories of modern and contemporary choral repertoire, Daniel Moe suggests that a fundamental basis for the 'quasi unity' within different trends lies in a similar approach to melodic, contrapuntal, and harmonic usage.[8] Moe distinguishes between works that employ chromatic dissonant counterpoint, works that employ diatonic dissonant counterpoint, and works that could be placed under either classification. Chromatic dissonant counterpoint is a direct descendant of the chromaticism of the late nineteenth and early twentieth centuries, the most revolutionary musical and technical innovation of which is the use of all twelve pitches of the chromatic scale, freed from the hierarchy of tonal functions related to a tonal centre. Atonal music acknowledges no definite structural and functional order among the twelve pitches of the chromatic scale; there are no basic chord types either in the sense that they exist in tonal harmony, unless we hear one or more vertical sonorities that dominate in a musical composition.

In his 1929 letter about *Von heute auf morgen*, the first twelve-tone opera, Arnold Schoenberg stated: "I think that only singers who can sight-read these parts and who have absolute pitch can really learn them reliably."[9] That may have been the case at the time, but according to my experience it is not the case anymore. Performing modern and contemporary music on a regular basis helps us get accustomed to non-tonal pitch structures and other melodic difficulties. Singers with perfect pitch seem to be in a more advantageous position than those without, but there are teaching techniques that can assist singers in the learning of non-tonal music. Learning how 'to speak' the atonal musical language fluently, and even more so to sing it, is nevertheless full of challenges. Why so?

Acculturation to the tonal system in the case of both musicians and non-musicians has been widely demonstrated in scientific research. According to Robert Francès, acculturation occurs throughout childhood and stabilizes in adolescence.[10] Hierarchical structures that characterize tonal music in terms of both pitch relations and harmonic organization have both perceptual and cognitive implications.[11] Unequal steps of the diatonic scales (major and minor seconds) make it easier to process intervals, whereas interval processing in relation to 'artificial' scales with either equal-space steps (such as the whole-tone scale) or alternating distances (such as the octatonic scale) create challenges especially for those acculturated to tonal music. In summary, it is easier to learn melodies with asymmetric arrangements of notes than those without.[12] All this seems to justify convincingly the view drawn from practical experience that processing tonal music, sight-singing, memory performance, and dictation related to tonal repertory is easier than that related to atonal music.

One might think that the proper 'atonal' way of hearing atonal music can be maintained only by learning a second musical language through the consistent, somewhat artificial suppression of hearing pitch relationships familiar in tonal music.[13] Writing about the 'demusicalization' and 'denaturalization' of Western art music in connection to atonal tendencies, Gerhard Albersheim claims that it is just as impossible for a person who has experienced tonal music to regress to non-harmonic hearing as it is for an adult to return to the innocent state of childhood.[14] According to some theorists, the "emancipation of dissonance" led to the creation of a second musical language after tonality (the primary language) for which we should learn new rules of grammar and syntax.[15] These theorists believe that to consider and try to understand this language as an extension of the tonal language might result in the distortion of its meaning.[16] Others strongly advocate that twelve-tone music is the extension of a single musical language that has grown out from music of the past.[17] Reading, for example, Schoenberg's thoughts in this regard, one can perceive that he identified his musical intentions as an extension of this primary musical language.[18] This is why I personally think (and my experiences as a choir leader have repeatedly borne out) that it is not a heresy to consider the utilization of the movable-*do* sol-fa syllables in relation to tonal thinking when learning to sing atonal music.

In the teaching of sight-reading in general, tonal musical material forms an important starting point. There is an age-old argument about whether it is more valuable to teach sight-reading in the tonal context using the fixed-*do* system or the movable-*do* system. In the former, the note names denote fixed pitches (e.g., *do* is always the note which in the English-speaking world is called 'C'); while in the latter, the syllables used for naming melodic notes indicate the relative distance between notes of the diatonic scale in addition to the tonal-functional relationship between them, thus efficiently helping the understanding of harmonic relations. As the movable-*do* system also emphasizes the relation of the notes to one another and to the tonic or the keynote of the scale, singers who perform a melodic (or harmonic) passage with note names of the movable-*do* system immediately recognize its tonal implications and can simultaneously analyse them. The keynote of any major key is always called *do* (while the note *la* represents the tonal centre of the minor scale) and therefore when singing the major scale with the sol-fa names (*do re mi fa so la ti*) in any key, they all sound alike concerning the order of whole tones and semitones. The different degrees of the scale are given constant names: *re* always marks the second degree of the major scale, *mi* the third, and so on. Regardless of the type of diatonic scale—for example, major, minor, or church modes—the distance between consecutive pitches of the scale marked by the sol-fa names sounds exactly the same (*do-re* is always a major second, *re-mi* is also a major second, while *mi-fa* is always a minor second or semitone). Not only are there separate sol-fa letters for each scale degree of the diatonic scale but there are also distinct sol-fa letters for the accidentals—the sharpened and flattened notes. The intervals between notes including chromatic alterations are also constant: *do-mi* can only be a major third, whereas *do-ma* (the flattened *mi*) is always a minor third.[19]

This is the reason why the regular singing of intervals with syllable names within the movable-*do* system helps singers to associate the note names with the sound of a given interval (e.g., *do-so* = a perfect fifth). Similar to the singing of intervals with sol-fa letters, in singing short melodic motifs or fragments with the help of solmization, it is possible to practise, learn, and remember characteristic melodic turns and patterns of tonal music. These patterns are stored in the musical memory and can be recalled during the process of sight-singing. The more frequently we sing melodic patterns with sol-fa, the stronger the pitch relations become in the musical brain.

For sight-reading in the atonal system, the movable-*do* system can be a useful tool because it assists in the accurate and secure intonation of all intervals by conditioning the relationship between the sol-fa names and the sound of the distance between two consecutive pitches, or the vertical sonority of two pitches. Scientific research proves that the diatonic tonal hierarchies can be successfully activated when listening to pitch structures characteristic of twelve-tone serial music as well.[20] Based on my practical experiences, I would supplement this statement with another one: familiarity with tonal melodic turns and the ability to sing them, and the ability to sing any interval with the sol-fa syllables of the movable-*do* system, can be adapted not only to the recognition of but also to the singing of pitch structures of atonal music. It is my experience that singers who were formerly trained in the movable-*do* system, and who regularly sing intervals and various sets of pitches with sol-fa, develop a strong and highly reliable intervallic hearing, with instantaneous recognition and clear intonation. Singers using the movable-*do* sol-fa syllables often in the process of sight-singing become capable of decoding with sol-fa any tonal melodic turns they hear.[21] This experience can later be utilized in the singing of various sets of pitches emerging in the atonal melodic process as well. The method is as follows.

The atonal melody is divided into shorter sections, each of which can be interpreted as being in one particular key, such that in addition to the diatonic notes, each section contains not more than one or two chromatic pitches. The tonal centres (key notes) of these consecutive pitch-sets are different from each other. The last note of a pitch-set and the first note of the one following it are to be connected by means of changing the *do*-position. The pivot notes that are given a name according to two different *do*-positions should be sung with two names at first, so that on the same pitch both names are pronounced. When the intervals are intoned with greater security, then either only the first or only the second name is sung. Gradually the sol-fa names are omitted and are replaced by the syllables of the original text of the choral compositions. The process is now presented in more detail with reference to selected repertoire.

### Arnold Schoenberg, *Von heute auf morgen*

The opening melody of Schoenberg's opera *Von heute auf morgen* (Example 14.1) can be sung with movable-*do* syllables, changing the *do*-position as necessary.

EXAMPLE 14.1  Schoenberg, *Von heute auf morgen*, opening melody.

## Benjamin Britten, *Missa Brevis*

This excerpt is taken from a choral piece, the 'Sanctus' of Britten's *Missa Brevis*. The musical material of the movement consists of a sequence of twelve different pitches. During the movement, this twelve-note sequence appears not only as an independent melody (see bass line of Example 14.5), but also in the form of a three-part counterpoint over a sustained D major triad, and in the form of an interval progression, both appearing in the organ accompaniment (Example 14.2).

EXAMPLE 14.2  Britten, excerpt from *Missa Brevis*, 'Sanctus.'

Next (Example 14.3), the three-part polytonal decoration over the simple D major chord is written out as a row of twelve different pitches.[22]

**EXAMPLE 14.3** Melodic reduction.

These twelve pitches can be broken down into three anhemitonic pentatonic melodic turns and one diatonic melodic fragment: *s-d'-l-m / d-r-s,-l,-m, / d-r-l-s / d-s-f-m-l* (Example 14.4).

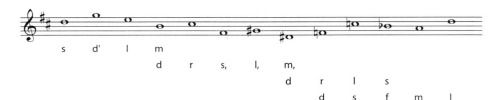

**EXAMPLE 14.4** Twelve-tone melodic reduction with sol-fa.

The first four notes are four diatonic scale degrees of the D major tonality (the first, fourth, second, and sixth degrees: *d-f-r-l,*). At the same time, they can be interpreted as a four-note fragment of the *mi*-pentatonic scale (*s-d'-l-m*). The fourth, fifth, sixth, seventh, and eighth notes of the melody (see Example 14.3) can be fitted into another *mi*-pentatonic scale (*d-r-s,-l,-m*, Example 14.4). The intonation of this second melodic fragment is quite easily achievable without the accompaniment. However, as soon as one tries to intone the notes over the D major pedal, the task becomes more challenging. While practising this melodic turn, it is strongly recommended that the singers hold the notes G-sharp and D-sharp for a longer time, and intone the semitone dissonances occurring in relation to the underlying D major triad (G-sharp against the note A, D-sharp against D). The same procedure should be followed in the case of the last five notes of the melody (nos. 8–12 of Example 14.3). The two notes closing the melodic line (A and D) can be interpreted as the third and sixth degrees of the F major scale; they can be sung together with notes 9–11 (Example 14.3) with the sol-fa names *d-s-f-m-l*. The melodic line presented in Example 14.3 and emerging from the three-part polyphonic texture appears in the bass of the organ accompaniment in the continuation of the movement, shown in Example 14.5.

**EXAMPLE 14.5** Organ accompaniment, with twelve-tone melody in the bass.

When singing the three-part counterpoint, the changes of *do*-positions shown in Example 14.6 should be applied.

**EXAMPLE 14.6** Three-part counterpoint with changing *do*-positions.

While learning is taking place, the text is replaced by the solmization syllables. The original text is only restored when the intonation of the musical material is exact and secure.

In the preceding sequence, a tailored teaching process was presented in which familiar tonal (or pentatonic) melodic patterns were utilized in the teaching and learning of a melody in which the twelve pitches occur, as Forte puts it, "in novel combination."[23] The special character of this particular theme lies in the use of pentatonic melodic turns connected together in such a way that not a single pitch is heard more than once.

A further degree of difficulty in the singing of atonal music is found in melodic turns that contain one or more large intervallic leaps, sometimes more than an octave. When dealing with such intonation challenges, it is useful to practise larger intervals by first replacing them with their smaller reciprocals (e.g., the upward leaping major seventh interval can be replaced by singing a minor second downwards); an interval larger than an octave can be replaced by singing the pitches within one octave first (e.g, instead of a major ninth, singing a major second). In the case of multiple difficulties within one specific musical passage, separating the components of music, such as melody, text, rhythm, expression, and/or accompaniment, can also work as a starting point. Focusing on the rhythmic component first or singing the melodic line to a simplified rhythmic motion in a slower tempo can be useful in the rehearsal process. The difficulties can gradually be increased (see Examples 14.7–14.10). A further piece of advice: unaccompanied singing develops independent, self-reliant singers. Let us aim to teach even music with accompaniment unaccompanied. Dependency on an instrumental 'walking stick' hinders the secure and accurate learning of challenging melodic lines, for example. When learning a single-line melody, rather than playing the notes of the melody along on the keyboard, some well-chosen pedal notes, intervals, or harmonies can support the singing effectively instead. Such supporting notes or intervals will force the singers to adjust their intonation of the pitches to the sound played (or sung) along.

### John Zorn, *Aporias: Requia for Piano and Orchestra*

Example 14.7 presents a sequence for teaching a six-part section written for six boy sopranos.

First, the notes are written out as a single melodic line, in which larger intervals are replaced by their smaller versions and with the whole passage transposed a perfect fourth lower to avoid any vocal fatigue that

The Movable-*Do* System in the Teaching of Non-Tonal Repertoire 179

EXAMPLE 14.7   Zorn: *Aporias: Requia for Piano and Orchestra* (1998), III: *Con Mistero*, bb. 6–7.

may occur during the learning process (Example 14.8). Then, the intervals are replaced by their larger versions according to the original score (Example 14.9), following which, the rhythmic progression is presented (Example 14.10).

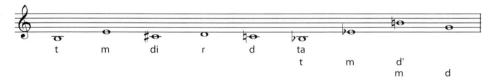

EXAMPLE 14.8   The melody transposed a fourth lower, with larger intervals adjusted.

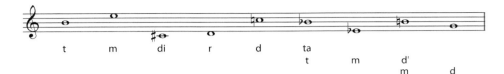

EXAMPLE 14.9  The melody including larger intervals.

EXAMPLE 14.10  The still-transposed melody with rhythm.

Finally, the material is transposed back to the original *tessitura*. In the rehearsal process, it is possible to gradually place the starting key higher and higher until reaching the original key. This way we can ensure that the singers will confidently perform the material in the original *tessitura*. The melody should be sung as a continuous line before assigning the notes to the six boy sopranos according to the score (see Example 14.7).

In addition to the singing of single atonal melodic lines, mention should also be made of the teaching and learning methods concerning polyphonic musical textures. All who regularly perform atonal polyphonic music know very well that the confident unison singing of the horizontal planes of an atonal vocal composition does not guarantee that the singing of that material with the other parts added will be free of problems. The vertical sonorities can at times be so dissonant that one is almost unsure whether one's part is sung correctly or not. Aligning one part with the other voices in an atonal setting is a task that requires a lot of concentration, as the desire to resolve dissonances instinctively can result in the slipping of the notes previously learnt when singing only in unison. It is advisable to work out the vertical sonorities carefully, perhaps starting with a pair of voices, before singing the entire polyphonic fabric. Vertical sounds could also be related to tonal harmonies. In most dissonant vertical sounds, one can often find a so-called harmonic framework to which the 'non-harmonic notes' can be attached. A few years ago, when teaching György Ligeti's *Clocks and Clouds* (1972), I led my singers in learning to sing the vertical harmonies in arpeggiation with sol-fa, so that they felt the relationship of their parts to the others more deeply. At first, the notes belonging to traditional tonal harmonies were sung, and gradually all 'non-harmonic' pitches of the clusters were added.

## Zsigmond Szathmáry, *Fukushima Requiem*

The final excerpt is taken from Zsigmond Szathmáry's 2012 composition *Fukushima Requiem*. Example 14.11 shows possible ways to sing two individual lines with movable-*do* sol-fa syllables simultaneously in two different *do*-positions (B flat-*do* and B-*do*).

**EXAMPLE 14.11**   Szathmáry, *Fukushima Requiem*, bb. 308–14.

## Conclusion

In this chapter I have presented a methodological idea for training singers in the study of atonal choral repertoire. In my work as a conductor, I gained a great deal of my practical experience of teaching atonal music in a musical environment where most choristers learned to sight-sing at a high level through the systematic use of the movable-*do* system. For these singers, their tonal experiences can be utilized effectively in non-tonal musical environments, because reliable intervallic hearing and, consequently, a secure ability for singing dissonances can be acquired with the help of solmization. To develop the skill of singing, hearing, and analysing dissonances is a matter of training. According to Schoenberg, the distinction of consonance and dissonance "simply depends on the growing ability of the analysing ear to familiarize itself with the remote overtones."[24] In Schoenberg's concept of tones, consonances are the closer and therefore more clearly audible overtones (partials) of a pitch, whereas dissonances are the more remote ones that are hardly recognizable by the ear. His conviction

182  László Nemes

that the perception of dissonance can become a reality through the development of musical abilities may be strongly felt from the preceding excerpt. Training is needed and this training can be provided by the choir leader.

To finish, I would like to draw attention to a very well-constructed textbook for the teaching of singing atonal melodies. *Modus Novus: Studies in Reading Atonal Melodies* by Lars Edlund (1922–2013) is a pioneering attempt to extend musical training in sight-reading to music written in the last century.[25] To this day, the book is unmatched in terms of its practical utility and its pedagogical purposefulness. Edlund's methodology is similar to other approaches to post-tonal ear-training that focus on the singing of various characteristic combinations of intervals.[26] His textbook contains preparatory exercises as well as musical quotations from the works of modern composers including Bartók, Schoenberg, Berg, Webern, and others. The exercises are presented in a sequential order arranged according to difficulty, and they can also be practised with sol-fa syllables using the ideas presented here in this chapter.

### Notes

1 For further reading on Kodály's concept of music teaching and its applicability to the work of conductors, see Chapter 4 by Bernie Sherlock in this volume.
2 Roger E. Foltz, "Sight-Singing: Some New Ideas on an Old Institution," *College Music Symposium* 16 (Spring 1976): 95–100.
3 See also 'audiation,' particularly in American musical literature and practice.
4 Bruce E. More, "Sight Singing and Ear Training at the University Level: A Case for the Use of Kodály's System of Relative Solmization," *The Choral Journal* 25, no. 7 (March 1985): 9–11, 13–18, 21–22.
5 Allen Forte, *The Structure of Atonal Music* (New Haven: Yale University Press, 1977), 1.
6 Gerhard Albersheim, "The Sense of Space in Tonal and Atonal Music," *The Journal of Aesthetics and Art Criticism* 19, no. 2 (Autumn 1960): 17–30; Nicola Dibben, "The Cognitive Reality of Hierarchic Structure in Tonal and Atonal Music," *Music Perception* 12, no. 1 (Autumn 1994): 1–25; Timothy J. Groulx, "The Influence of Tonal and Atonal Contexts on Error Detection Accuracy," *Journal of Research in Music Education* 61, no. 2 (Summer 2013): 233–43; Robert Sherman and Robert Hill, "Aural and Visual Perception of Melody in Tonal and Atonal Musical Environments," *Bulletin of the Council for Research in Music Education* 14 (Autumn 1968): 1–10; Cheryl L. Bruner, "The Perception of Contemporary Pitch Structures," *Music Perception* 2, no. 1 (Autumn 1984): 25–39.
7 See also Sherlock's insights on the separation of difficulties in choral pedagogy in Chapter 4 in this volume.
8 Daniel Moe, "The Choral Conductor and Twentieth-Century Choral Music," in *Choral Conducting Symposium*, ed. Harold A. Decker and Julius Herford (Englewood Cliffs, New Jersey: Prentice Hall, 1988), 153–57.
9 Martha Elliott, *Singing in Style: A Guide to Vocal Performance Practices* (New Haven: Yale University Press, 2006). Absolute pitch, also known as perfect

pitch, is the ability, possessed by a small minority of people, to identify or reproduce a specific pitch without need for a reference note.
10 Robert Francès, "Tonal Principles as Teaching Principles in Music," *Music Perception* 2, no. 3 (Spring 1985): 389–96.
11 Carol L. Krumhansl, Gregory J. Sandell, and Desmond C. Sergeant, "The Perception of Tone Hierarchies and Mirror Forms in Twelve-Tone Serial Music," *Music Perception* 5, no. 1 (Autumn 1987): 31–77.
12 Daniel Levitin, *This is Your Brain on Music: the Science of Human Obsession* (New York: A Plume Book, 2007).
13 Albersheim, "The Sense of Space in Tonal and Atonal Music," 17–30.
14 Albersheim, "The Sense of Space in Tonal and Atonal Music," 17–30.
15 Arnold Schoenberg, *Style and Idea*, ed. Leonard Stein, trans. Leo Black (New York: St Martin's Press, 1975).
16 Martha MacLean Hyde, "Schoenberg's Sketches and the Teaching of Atonal Theory," *College Music Symposium* 20, no. 2 (Autumn 1980): 130–37.
17 Graham H. Phipps, "Comprehending Twelve-Tone Music: As an Extension of the Primary Musical Language of Tonality," *College Music Symposium* 24, no. 2 (Autumn 1984): 35–54.
18 Arnold Schoenberg, *Theory of Harmony*, trans. Roy E. Carter (Berkeley: University of California Press, 1978).
19 In the practice of sight-singing using the fixed-*do* system, no syllable alterations are used for sharps and flats, which means that the syllables provide no apparent help for the singer in intoning chromatic pitches. This creates a problem when one approaches the teaching and study of correct intonation of intervals. See More, "Sight Singing and Ear Training at the University Level," 9–11, 13–18, 21–22.
20 Krumhansl, Sandell, and Sergeant, "The Perception of Tone Hierarchies and Mirror Forms in Twelve-Tone Serial Music."
21 Erzsébet Szőnyi, *Kodály's Principles in Practice* (London: Boosey & Hawkes, 1973).
22 Eric Roseberry, "A Note on Britten's *Missa Brevis*," *Tempo*, no. 53–54 (Spring–Summer 1960): 11–16.
23 Forte, *The Structure of Atonal Music*.
24 Matthew Arndt, "Schoenberg on Problems; or, Why the Six-Three Chord Is Dissonant," *Theory and Practice* 37/38 (2012–13): 1–62.
25 Lars Edlund, *Modus Novus: Studies in Reading Atonal Melodies* (Stockholm: Wilhelm Hansen, 1963).
26 See Michael Berry, "A New Approach to Post-Tonal Ear Training," *Indiana Theory Review* 27, no. 1 (Spring 2009): 23–44; Michael Friedmann, *Ear Training for Twentieth Century Music* (New Haven: Yale University, 1990); Robert Morris, *Class Notes for Atonal Music Theory* (Hanover, NH: Frog Peak Music, 1991); Edward Pearsall and John William Schaffer, "Shape/Interval Contours and Their Ordered Transformations: A Motivic Approach to Twentieth-Century Music Analysis and Aural Skills," *College Music Symposium* 45 (2005): 57–80.

# 15
## FACILITATING CONNECTIONS
Leading and Developing University Choirs

*Amy Ryan*

Tertiary education represents an exciting juncture in the choral singing infrastructure, laden with possibility for embedding music-making as an integral, rewarding part of singers' lives through the continuity of engagement it offers between adolescence and young adulthood. By participating in choral singing at the tertiary level, students may be exposed to a wide range of experiences with the potential to nourish them artistically, intellectually, and socially, broaden their aesthetic horizons, and develop their musical skills and confidence. The university choir often sits at the confluence of multiple musical experiences and cultures, and as such can present challenges to the conductor in reconciling disparate skill levels. A review of existing literature reveals a relative paucity of research in this area, and published scholarship is largely specific to the cultural context of the United States. In this chapter, I shall offer a personal perspective on the nature of these unique challenges and how they can be addressed in order to enrich a range of singers through inclusive and rewarding experiences.

### Defining the University Choir

The very term 'university choir' (or 'college choir') is not a clear-cut one; university choirs, like any choir, vary widely in their nature, according to geographical, cultural, institutional, and financial contexts, as well as in their mission and scale. Choirs vary in leadership, from the student-led model to the professionally led ensemble; in size, from small *a cappella* groups to symphonic choirs; in selectivity, from non-auditioned to auditioned; in repertoire and style; in the commitment demanded; and in their

DOI: 10.4324/9781003299660-19

function, from the choral-scholar model to the assessed module to purely recreational. Even within these subcategories, ensembles vary greatly according to the members' prior music education experience, the size and type of institution, the length of rehearsals and rehearsal periods, and the conventions of local choral culture. As a result, it is not possible to speak of a single, representative 'university choir'; one can simply identify common features which connect these ensembles:

- The current or past pursuit of higher education by its members.
- Its existence within the structures of an institution of higher education.
- Relative cultural heterogeneity among members.
- Heterogeneity of musical training and experience of members.
- The relative recency of any formal music education members may have received, when compared with other adult community choirs.
- The relatively transient nature of the ensemble's membership from year to year.
- The general association of a rehearsal period with a semester/trimester.
- The nature of the instrument, predominantly consisting of young adult voices.

I have been working with university choirs since 2013, mostly as artistic director of a cross-faculty, auditioned choral society of between 100 and 130 members, based in Ireland's largest university. During this time, the choir has performed a wide range of repertoire, spanning symphonic choral music to *a cappella* repertoire. It is open to all students, who may participate for academic credit or recreationally, as well as any interested members of staff. My view of the mission of the choir has been crystalized through my experiences and my understanding of the local music education and choral singing landscape. While this is multifaceted, I believe my mission can be distilled into a single phrase: 'facilitating connections'—the social, the artistic, the musical and the intellectual. In a more granular sense, this includes the wish to:

- Provide a platform for members to continue their engagement with music through enriching choral experiences, at the crucial transitional moment bridging secondary and tertiary level study.
- Inspire members to sustain a lifelong engagement with music, thereby nourishing their musical life outside the university as they continue their musical activities, engage as audience members or advocate for the arts in their communities.
- Facilitate students with prior musical training but with minimal or no experience in choral singing in applying their knowledge and skills to choral music.

- Facilitate members in making connections between theoretical knowledge attained in prior musical study and its practical application in new contexts.
- Provide the opportunity for those with little formal background in music to access high-quality, rewarding musical experiences and a space in which to develop their tacit musicianship into conscious knowledge, skills, and understanding.
- Acquaint singers with canonical works in a range of styles while also advocating for new music from a broad range of pens.
- Create opportunities for students to meet and learn from like-minded peers, broadening their musical, social, and intellectual horizons.
- Be a flagship for the university in contributing to the cultural life of the local and wider community.

Informed by these aims, my approach to the choir is one of inclusivity, aiming to embrace a variety of backgrounds and experience levels in order to broaden the participation in choral singing in my community, thereby sowing seeds which, I hope, will bear fruit in the wider musical culture. While the choir has an audition requirement, I generally have the resources to offer a place, where feasible, to singers of all experience levels. I have accepted members previously unfamiliar with the concept of repeating a warm-up exercise in a new key, or essentially unfamiliar with musical notation. Rather than declare prospective members unsuitable due to a lack of a particular experience I value, I am interested in their potential, and in equipping them with the skills that will allow them to access choral music beyond their university years. This inclusive approach is supported by the large size of the choir.

There are several factors that merit the conductor's consideration when approaching university choirs, but I will confine my discussion to addressing the skill-based variance, examining two aspects of the conductor's process—performance planning and rehearsal strategies—through the twin lenses of musicianship and choral singing skills. I see musicianship as a broad term encompassing elements such as aural skills, music literacy, theoretical understanding, sight-singing, and stylistic awareness. Choral singing skills, on the other hand, I will define as the technical ensemble skills required in performing choral music.

## Performance Planning and Repertoire Selection

### Identifying Goals

In planning for any choir, identifying a variety of long-term and short-term goals, both for the ensemble as an entity and for the singers, can provide a useful structure for the conductor. A helpful piece of advice given to me by an experienced colleague upon commencing my artistic director role was to consider the hypothetical 'average student' who participates in the ensemble across the span of their studies, thinking about what types of performance experience and repertoire they would engage with, and what kinds of skill they would develop in the process. Through this reflection, the conductor may establish a number of performance-based goals. For example:

- Singers will experience singing *a cappella*.
- Singers will experience singing with orchestra.
- Singers will have the opportunity to premiere a new composition.
- Singers will have the experience of singing two majors work from the choral canon, one of which features a commonly occurring text (e.g., a mass setting).

In programming, I have found it beneficial to alternate performance projects between *a cappella* and collaborative programmes featuring instrumental forces. In doing so, the ensemble's identity is established independently of a collaborating ensemble and singers develop a variety of skills and insights by engaging with a broad range of repertoire and performance contexts. Furthermore, a varied programme of events can prove helpful in motivating singers to return to the ensemble semester after semester, contributing to a more consistent instrument that reaps the benefits of more experienced members, who in turn become effective role models for their emerging peers.

Establishing performance-based goals assists in event planning and programming, which in turn provide a useful frame for planning for singers' development in choral skills and musicianship. It is similarly useful to consider the knowledge, skills, and understanding the hypothetical singer will have reliably developed after singing in the ensemble for three or four years. Having identified long-term, broad goals, I then consider the experience of a less experienced student who may sing for a single semester, to clarify achievable but impactful short-term goals that would eventually lead to the attainment of long-term goals over the span of a few years.

## Programming

The preceding parameters can also aid the conductor in identifying potential repertoire more broadly, at which point the resulting possibilities can be examined more closely. In designing a concert experience, my goal is to produce a coherent, engaging programme of aesthetic quality and appeal, broadly appropriate at all stages to the musical and vocal abilities of singers, that presents rich opportunities for student learning at varying levels of sophistication. In selecting repertoire for performance projects, aesthetic considerations, such as artistic coherence and variety, and practical considerations, such as forces, budget, and audience development, will naturally demand close attention. These factors should be considered in tandem with the musical and technical challenges presented and how these can support the development of the singers, as well as the success of the rehearsal process and performances. Well-chosen repertoire is integral to the success of the instrument, its development, and performances: my approach to repertoire selection proceeds from a belief that the value of the ensemble is not in its performances alone, but equally in the learning which occurs in the process of preparing for them. Patrick Freer summarizes this concept admirably: "The goals and purposes of choral performance and choral pedagogy are not hierarchical—they are complementary and synonymous."[1] Each piece of repertoire chosen with careful thought offers rich possibilities for nurturing singers in myriad ways and, as a result, developing the overall instrument.

Of utmost significance is the amount of rehearsal time available to the ensemble: the more limited the rehearsal time, the more acutely the conductor must be aware of the context in which they operate. Presenting a concert with a transient and inexperienced group after eight two-hour rehearsals is quite a different task to doing so after twenty equivalent rehearsals with a group of relatively stable membership. In my own context, based on the average level of music literacy and available rehearsal time, I have found that a programme of approximately thirty minutes' music per nine rehearsals is comfortably achievable. In the case of larger works, I have found it effective to spread the learning across the whole academic year, integrating appropriate movements into the first concert of the season, where possible. In considering repertoire, the conductor must balance ambition with realism, carefully examining their own situation to establish realistic aspirations, given time resources and membership. A tension exists between an appropriate, motivating challenge and an inappropriate, demotivating one. While a group can 'survive' through a highly ambitious programme and develop skills in the process, this can necessitate rehearsal processes that allow scant space for artistic subtlety or edification. Conversely, a programme that lacks attainable ambition can prove unsatisfying to those experienced singers who relish a challenge, which may prompt their withdrawal, to the detriment of the group.

## Musicianship Considerations

Variance in musicianship skills is one of the primary challenges in preparing a large university choir for performance and in offering an engaging, rewarding, and inclusive experience for all. Some members will have finely developed musicianship skills that they can deliberately apply to new music, whereas the foundational musicianship skills of others may be latent, requiring deliberate guidance to enable their conscious realization. To develop quality performances in a short time frame with a heterogeneous group of singers, the director must enable the singers to quickly realize latent and conscious musicianship skills and apply them to repertoire. To gain a sense of the appropriate balance between ambition and realism, it is a worthwhile exercise for any university choir director to familiarize themselves with their local pre-college level music education structures and curricula. These will vary widely from area to area but provide valuable information about generally appropriate expectations for both the highly experienced and the less experienced ends of the spectrum. It is also valuable for the choral director to familiarize themselves with the likely pipelines through which the singers enter: after-school music classes, local community youth choirs, church choirs, and musical theatre groups, to name but a few. This knowledge can inform selectivity in auditioning new members (if applicable), decisions about accessible repertoire and the potential to learn it within a short time frame, as well as possible approaches to rehearsal. In my experience, I have observed that although certain members may have quite significant theoretical backgrounds in music, theoretical understanding does not necessarily imply commensurate practical musicianship skills—a realization that has strongly informed my approach to rehearsals and project planning.

When choosing repertoire, it is worthwhile considering the intersection of challenges and learning opportunities contained both within the overall programme and in each item of repertoire. It can be difficult to find an accessible common entry point to music in which excessive challenges intersect. I favour repertoire and programmes in which challenges are balanced and mitigated by relative accessibility in other ways. Some particularly challenging musical features for the singer can include angular and fragmented melodic lines, remote or frequent modulations, use of an unfamiliar harmonic language, irregular phrase lengths, successive rests, use of asymmetrical metres, complex rhythms, chromaticism, and frequent tempo changes. Music that features combinations of these challenges can be rendered more accessible if simpler in other respects; for example, setting a familiar text or written in the vernacular language, short in length, diatonic, rhythmically accessible, repetitive, featuring recurring motifs, and doublings.

## Choral Skills and Vocal Challenges

Alongside musical challenges, technical challenges must be carefully assessed in order to ascertain the suitability of repertoire, with the principle of balancing challenges once again providing useful guidance. Such challenges may include regular or sustained extremes in *tessitura*, rapid changes in register, sustained singing around the *passaggio*, sustained soft singing in high registers, sustained singing at dynamic extremes, rapid text, use of an unfamiliar language, long and florid melismas, and frequent tempo changes. However, to avoid these challenges entirely is to deny singers the opportunity to develop valuable skills: technical challenges may still be broached if not excessive or sustained. This will apply not only within a single piece, but also across a full programme.

Having established the suitability of the repertoire, it is helpful to assess the practicality of a particular programme by iterating a reverse chronology across available rehearsals to establish which sections will be learned, revised, or polished in each rehearsal. Which sections are more suitable to be learned corporately and which would be most efficient in a sectional rehearsal? When will sectional rehearsals take place, and how many rehearsals will be required? In planning what is achievable, I do so on the assumption of one rehearsal fewer than available, to account for any overly optimistic planning on my own part or for unexpected circumstances.

## The Rehearsal Process

Once careful performance-planning, repertoire selection, and a semester plan have been completed, the rehearsal process begins. The success of rehearsals, and the culminating performance(s), has judicious repertoire selection at its foundation but is ultimately dependent on the thought processes that inform them. My approach to the rehearsal process is guided by a number of principles, two of which are most relevant to this discussion: 'consider every singer' and 'scaffold the learning.'[2]

### Consider Every Singer

I find it helpful to avoid assuming anything as 'common knowledge' in approaching the choir, respecting the wide variety of experiences in the group. As previously mentioned, the university choir is greatly enriched by the different backgrounds, cultures, and musical infrastructures represented among members, in which familiar languages, styles, repertoire, and approaches to learning music can vary. It can be tempting to ignore this feature as it can feel overwhelming to try to cater to all—I think the conductor does well to be aware of this variety but not to feel pressurized to micromanage every eventuality, as it can become paralysing. I tend to assume little in a spirit of inclusivity, while trusting in the great potential of singers to make connections and arrive at a more conscious understanding of concepts with deliberate guidance. This can also apply to the way in which we communicate with singers: it is useful to recognize that not all members may know what a sectional rehearsal is, what a dress rehearsal is, or what a score is. These things can be explained briefly and casually at first reference, thus serving to include emerging members without detriment to the more seasoned.

## Scaffold the Learning

Through my training and experience, I have become convinced of the importance of a deep understanding of the music in assisting the conductor in preparing singers for success. While studying and assimilating scores before rehearsals begin, it is essential for conductors to simultaneously identify opportunities within the music for developing or reinforcing particular skills, and to identify and isolate challenges, both musical and technical. Identifying challenges enables the conductor to 'anticipate the mistake,' and allows them to prepare so as to circumvent it. This leads to a feeling of success and works to avoid the repetition and memorization of mistakes, which can be difficult to correct once present, in particular for those singers more reliant on aural memory. This also demands that conductors have a clear idea of textual and interpretative detail in advance of the first rehearsal. In preparing to circumvent the mistake, I aim to distil concepts into their simplest, most immediate terms, and to scaffold accordingly. In offering this thought, I am not dismissing singers' abilities or potential, but rather recognizing that a good deal of their musicianship may be yet tacit or that their theoretical knowledge may not have been applied broadly to practical matters outside of a particular context. In discussing the rehearsal process, I will once again apply the lenses of choral skills and musicianship to examine how they can be developed to achieve successful, rewarding processes for a range of singers, informed by the preceding principles.

## Developing Choral Skills

To unify the ensemble and to create a shared understanding of the discipline of choral singing, certain fundamental skills must be developed, including:

- Following and interpreting a conductor's gesture.
- Stagger (or staggered) breathing.

- Healthy vocal production.
- Listening skills and awareness of ensemble.
- Intonation.
- Textual awareness, awareness of vowel harmony.

### *Following and Interpreting a Conductor's Gesture*

In a university choir, those with previous ensemble experience may have sung or played under experienced, trained conductors or in groups directed by someone without formal knowledge of beating patterns or conducting technique, and I am respectful of the value of all these experiences. The time imperative makes the ability to communicate with immediacy essential. To unify the new ensemble, it is important that members develop a clear, shared understanding of what exactly the conductor is doing: to insist, "Watch me!" will prove fruitless if singers do not know what it is they are watching for. To assume this as common knowledge represents a missed opportunity to develop singers as well as to improve the efficiency of rehearsals and success of performances.

### *Stagger Breathing*

Sensitive stagger breathing is a valuable skill for any choral singer, unlikely to be familiar to all members. A shared understanding of and facility with this skill can be developed through the singing of sustained chords in the warm-up, so that singers can focus on the technique independent of any other musical challenges. Once the singers have internalized the concept, the conductor can ask that they apply the technique to suitable parts of the repertoire.

### *Textual Awareness*

One of the key considerations to distinguish vocal music from instrumental is, naturally, the former's use of text: this is of particular relevance to those members from instrumental backgrounds or those without prior singing experience. There are many layers to this aspect of choral skills, of which the group must quickly develop a shared understanding, including treatment of terminal consonants, diction, elision, vowel formation, vowel harmony, and text stresses. Once again, informed by the exhortation to 'consider every singer,' these concepts can be introduced in warm-ups and/or be presented deliberately through carefully chosen examples within repertoire studied. Extending this exhortation to language, it is advisable to avoid the assumption that particular languages, such as

Latin, will be familiar, or that the meaning or relevance of standard texts of particular faith traditions will be apparent to all. It is advisable to provide literal and poetic translations for all texts and to explain their relevance.

## Developing Musicianship Skills in the Rehearsal

The conductor must be intentional in their approach to ensure successful assimilation of the music in a timely and rewarding fashion. An understanding of musicianship skills is invaluable in this endeavour. Each singer brings a particular set of skills to the ensemble, the combined effect of which benefits the collective in many ways: some singers may have strong sight-singing skills, others a keen aural memory, or others significant vocal training. In a large group, the less experienced can be carried along by the more experienced, even if they are slightly out of their depth. The larger the group, the more pronounced I have observed the effect to be, and this can create a deceptive impression of the extent to which all singers have internalized details with accuracy and confidence. Creating space for slower-paced, bespoke sectional rehearsals is an important means of balancing varying needs, gaining a clearer picture of how singers are progressing, and ensuring that sections will be able to cope if certain key personnel are not present. Also recommended is creating opportunities for smaller choirs to sing in relay, a practice that provides an opportunity for the more experienced to challenge themselves, demands greater independence, and clarifies for the conductor where issues may be arising. While the focus of the rehearsal is, on the surface, the learning of the music, connections and new learning translatable into other contexts are a subtle by-product, attained either by direct instruction or by osmosis. As mentioned previously, for many members, musical skills and experiences may be tacit, requiring deliberate assistance to make connections between the experiential and the conscious understanding of concepts that can later be deliberately applied. Assuming little, scaffolding can lead students to internalize the music while facilitating these connections. Furthermore, singers can learn a great deal from simply participating and singing side by side with more experienced peers. A 2019 study observed the phenomenon of university choir members gaining theoretical knowledge *en passant* without direct didactic instruction from the conductor, variously hypothesized as resulting from peer learning and from passive exposure to concepts during the rehearsal process.[3] This study found that students with no musical background demonstrated the greatest improvements in their theoretical knowledge. Supplementing such *en passant* approaches with carefully applied direct instruction may amplify the effect.

### Engaging with the Score

Given the often-short rehearsal periods involved, the ability of members to follow and interpret musical scores is of great benefit to the rate at which the choir can progress; it enables rehearsals to flow and maintain the interest of a wide range of singers, as well as opening vistas to a wider range of repertoire. However, music literacy may not be universal among members; even if it is, this literacy exists on a wide spectrum and does not guarantee practical skill. Although an investment of the precious resource of rehearsal time, guiding singers to engage with the score more confidently pays dividends quickly and supports future rehearsals as singers learn to navigate the score more independently. Furthermore, it equips the singer with a skill they can apply in their future choral singing. Engaging with notation can prove intimidating for those singers with little formal background in music, who may assume it is 'not for them.' To assume singers without that background are fixed in their knowledge and will find engaging with theoretical learning uninteresting or too difficult is to underestimate their potential to grow and achieve understanding. An important facet of including a wide range of singers is demystifying the score for those with less experience. Indeed, those members with more extensive training in music may not be used to reading choral scores, or indeed to sight-singing. University choirs may have access to resources such as document cameras and sound systems in their rehearsal spaces, and their use is highly recommended to this end. Displaying the score on a document camera to draw singers' attention to features, particular sections, and symbols can be of value to the less experienced and the experienced singer alike, assisting greatly with orientation on the score and ensuring that all students can follow the conductor's instructions relative to the written music. I have had success with guiding students through the displayed score while they listen to a recording, to provide an initial global sense of the music that simultaneously prepares them to read it.

### The Warm-Up

The warm-up component of the rehearsal plays an essential role in building the instrument, in terms both of vocal and choral technique and of musicianship skills.[4] An intentional, intelligent approach to the warm-up can circumvent musical and technical challenges contained within the repertoire and embed good habits which can subsequently be applied in context. For example, a particular rhythmic, melodic, harmonic, or metrical idea contained within the repertoire can be isolated to form the basis of a bespoke warm-up to prepare the singers incrementally for performing the section in question successfully and with understanding. I have found it helpful to maintain a certain number of reliable, familiar warm-ups from rehearsal to rehearsal to build confidence and provide an opportunity to reinforce technical skills they are designed to develop. That said, from semester to semester, I balance familiar exercises with new ones, to secure a general base level of familiarity in the ensemble while also providing fresh challenges for returning members.

### Theoretical Understanding and Language

As an advocate of relative sol-fa, I favour its use as a teaching tool and recommend its integration at all stages of the rehearsal: warm-ups; brief, progressive sight-reading exercises; preparatory exercises; troubleshooting; or to help singers navigate particularly tricky modulations or transitions. For directors with more frequent, longer rehearsals and longer rehearsal periods, I would encourage making use of this tool to enrich student learning and develop their aural and sight-singing skills. In my particular context, however, with shorter once-weekly rehearsals across a nine-week period, I do so in moderation and only in particular instances. I find insistence on applying relative sol-fa to entire programmes to be counterproductive in this context, and it can prove troublesome or frustrating for students without prior musical training, given the short time frame. It is also important to note that the choir membership may include a number of international students who have been trained in the fixed-*do* system.[5] I believe it is of educational value for these students to be aware of the locally preferred system and to expose them to it, but not to have their participation in the ensemble hinge upon it to a prohibitive extent. Similarly, the existence of different rhythm-value nomenclatures (e.g., quarter note or crotchet) can cause confusion in this setting. In recognition of these different systems, I would initially refer to note values in both primary nomenclatures, gradually moving towards the use of the local system only once a common vocabulary has been established.

### Movement

To explain theoretical concepts on the score with lengthy verbal explanations can be time-consuming and overwhelming for the less experienced singer. Supplementing short verbal instructions with physical gestures can be an engaging, memorable, and effective means of communicating information in an accessible, welcoming manner that favours direct experience over lengthy technical explanation. The use of gesture can support and solidify singers' assimilation and understanding of musical and technical concepts.[6] The immediacy of gesture is not only an efficient means of communicating and supporting the execution of both technical and musical challenges, but also proves instructive for the conductor in visually revealing the source of misunderstanding or confusion among singers. The use of kinaesthetic representation of concepts is particularly useful given the invisible, internal nature of the vocal apparatus and the abstract nature of musical concepts.[7]

### Developing Musicianship through the Learning Process

To help maintain singers' engagement and focus, the conductor is well served in keeping singers active to the greatest degree possible throughout the rehearsal. While the much-maligned 'note-bashing' is not a rewarding strategy for singers or conductors, to ensure the timely assimilation of the musical content some degree of rote learning will be a necessary feature of any rehearsal where the ability to sight-sing is not universal. However, a solely aural-based approach may be unsatisfying for those with more extensive levels of experience, and a solely score-based approach may be uninviting or demoralizing for those with less experience. For this reason, I have found it best to limit rote learning to sections easily learned by the full group in *tutti* rehearsals, leaving more independent textures to be worked out in devoted sectional rehearsals. Those sections I will teach by rote in *tutti* rehearsals I endeavour not to teach by rote alone, but to scaffold, so that the process has empowering pedagogical value beyond the assimilation of notes, text, and rhythm. Also worthy of time investment is the incremental integration of sight-singing instruction into rehearsals. In my experience, the subtle incorporation of musicianship training into rehearsals may be more easily accepted in the educational context, where students are present on campus to learn and are open to same. Devoting a proportion of each rehearsal to such skills can be a greater challenge for those ensembles with relatively short rehearsal periods. Owing to the time imperative, I have found it effective to derive these reading exercises from and connect them to the repertoire studied, so that the application and relevance of theoretical understanding is immediately apparent and placed in a wholly musical context. This both advances the goal of assimilating the music quickly while also making future engagement with the score less intimidating. To illustrate this idea, I will use an extract from Carl Orff's *Carmina Burana* (Example 15.1).

This movement is well suited to being taught corporately, given its homorhythmic texture, the doubling of three diatonic constituent vocal lines, and the similarity of consecutive phrases, rhythmically and melodically. The score contains some symbols and concepts which may be unfamiliar, such as the lack of a conventionally notated time signature, the use of 4/2 metre, fermatas, and the *colla parte* instruction.

**EXAMPLE 15.1** Carl Orff, 'Ave Formosissima' from *Carmina Burana*, bb. 1–2.

- Step 1: clap the opening rhythm, written in diminution (Example 15.2). 'Speak' the rhythm using words of one or two syllables.

EXAMPLE 15.2

- Step 2: introduction of a tie as preparation for the dotted rhythm (Example 15.3). A reduction of the choral parts is played to prepare the tonality and melodic material.

EXAMPLE 15.3

- Step 3: introduction of the dotted-rhythm pattern (Example 15.4). Singers speak the rhythm on a single syllable while keeping the pulse. The choral reduction is continued.

EXAMPLE 15.4

- Step 4: introduction of the fermata (Example 15.5). Singers speak the rhythm, sustaining, listening, and watching at the fermatas. Reduction continues to be played, now with the orchestral material added during the fermatas.

EXAMPLE 15.5

- Step 5: singers speak the rhythm, shown in original time signature (Example 15.6). Full reduction continues to be played.

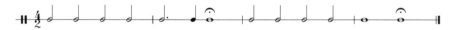

EXAMPLE 15.6

- Step 6: text is added (Example 15.7). Reduction continues to be played.

A - ve for - mo - sis - si- ma, gem - ma pre - ti - o - sa,

EXAMPLE 15.7

- Step 7: Introduction of the rhythm in the context of the complete score. Singers speak the text rhythmically from the full score, orienting themselves. The three independent vocal lines that make up this excerpt can then be taught by ear or from the score, via a more extended process. As the rhythmic content for the next phrase of the piece is similar, singers can be asked to clap the rhythm of the next phrase independently, later adding the remaining layers.

Using this process, the original rhythm is distilled to its most basic form and gradually developed to arrive at the final version. As the singers practise the rhythm, phrasing, and text, they passively experience the tonality, vocal parts, and chord progressions as played on the piano, as well as gaining familiarity with the orchestral interjections at fermatas. In this way, the rote teaching process is accelerated, the teaching of lines becomes enriching for singers and the full score less intimidating for the emerging members. Furthermore, the preparation of the rhythmic content and phrase structure serves as scaffolding to empower singers to decode the rhythm of later phrases independently, thus expediting the learning process for the remainder of the movement. In a more experienced group, the first phrase in each pair could be taught by rote, with the conductor instructing singers to then sight-read the next, almost identical, phrase, the tonality having already been prepared. There are many other 'routes into' this piece that favour the development of different skills, the preceding being but one possibility.

## Supportive Tools outside of Rehearsal

Much can be done to support a range of different learners outside of the rehearsal, to honour the different points from which singers meet with the music. The provision of good-quality line recordings can be a useful adjunct to scaffolded, critical engagement with the repertoire, in addition to recordings of pronunciation, text translations, and appropriate performance recordings. Such resources are particularly useful to those whose learning will primarily be aural and can facilitate further integration of musical concepts encountered in rehearsal. I have found the provision of an instructional session on how to use line recordings to be of benefit: demonstrating where recordings can be accessed and how to layer the difficulty of each practice session, and displaying the score while listening to a line recording sample together—returning to the axiom of 'assume little' as it is wise not to assume that all students will have learned what effective practice looks like. Modelling these steps can be effective in empowering the singer outside of rehearsals. The provision of such recordings can also support the conductor in providing more musical, meaningful, and efficient rehearsals, minimizing 'note-bashing,' and creating space for greater refinement.

In the preceding reflection I have aimed to offer my personal perspective and "wisdom of practice,"[8] by distilling same into a single phrase: 'facilitating connections.' I see the choir not only as an instrument of its own inherent artistic value, but also as a catalyst for the forging of connections: interpersonal connections, the connection between different stages of the choral singing infrastructure, and also connections between passive experience, and conscious knowledge and understanding. In supporting singers to forge these connections through enriching musical and educational experiences, conductors can equip them with knowledge, skills, and understanding that may unlock a lifetime of singing and meaningful musical engagement.

## Notes

1 Patrick K. Freer, "The Performance-Pedagogy Paradox in Choral Music Teaching," *Philosophy of Music Education Review* 19, no. 2 (Fall 2011): 164–78 (172), https://www.jstor.org/stable/10.2979/philmusieducrevi.19.2.164.
2 See David Wood, Jerome S. Bruner, and Gail Ross, "The Role of Tutoring in Problem Solving," *Journal of Child Psychiatry and Psychology* 17 (1976): 89–100, https://doi.org/10.1111/j.1469-7610.1976.tb00381.x.
3 Michael Barrett, Roy Page-Shipp, Caroline Van Niekerk, and Johan Ferreira, "Learning Music Theory *en passant*: A study in an Internationally Recognised South African University Student Choir," *British Journal of Music Education* 37, no. 2 (July 2020): 155–68, https://doi.org/10.1017/S0265051719000238.
4 For further discussion on the choral warm-up, see Chapter 13 by Róisín Blunnie in this volume.
5 For an outline of relative sol-fa and the fixed-*do* system, see Chapter 14 by László Nemes and Chapter 4 by Bernie Sherlock in this volume.
6 Ramona M. Wis, "Physical Metaphor in the Choral Rehearsal: A Gesture-Based Approach to Developing Vocal Skill and Musical Understanding," *The Choral Journal* 40, no. 3 (October 1999): 25–33.
7 Carlton E. Kilpatrick, "Movement, Gesture, and Singing: A Review of Literature," *Update: Applications of Research in Music Education* 38, no. 3 (2020): 29–37, https://doi.org/10.1177/8755123320908612.
8 Lee S. Shulman and Suzanne M. Wilson, *The Wisdom of Practice: Essays on Teaching Learning and Learning to Teach* (San Francisco: Jossey-Bass, 2004).

# 16

## INNOVATIVE CHORAL APPROACHES

'The Intelligent Choir' and the 'HyFlex' Method

*Jim Daus Hjernøe*

When I was hired in 1999 to teach jazz/pop choir directing at the North Jutland Academy of Music in Denmark, I prioritized developing an academic, pedagogical, and artistic angle on how to lead choirs within the rhythm/groove-based repertoire. At the time, there was a lack of research and literature on the subject, which led my generation to experiment, as we explored and developed the field. In 2006, I was employed full-time and started my official career as a jazz/pop choir professor at the North Jutland Academy of Music. In 2010, the North Jutland Academy of Music in Aalborg and the Royal Academy of Music in Aarhus merged into one Academy with two campuses, with a vision to establish a choir centre on a par with the best higher music education institutions in Europe and to strengthen the academy's position from an international perspective. Among other things, the merger resulted in the appointment of the American singer Bobby McFerrin as an adjunct professor from 2011 to 2016, to increase demand for our educational offerings, and in international collaborative projects.

Over the years, my colleagues and I have built a strong curriculum within the tradition of jazz/pop/improvisational choir directing at RAMA Vocal Center. We consider ourselves—with students and alumni—to be an international 'vocal family' with a joint focus on knowledge-sharing and the further development of jazz/pop choral directing methods at the highest artistic and educational level. My closest colleagues are Peder Karlsson (former singer in The Real Group and a composer and arranger in the genres of jazz, Nordic music tradition, and pop), Jesper Holm (leader of the vocal ensemble Touché and expert in vocal jazz), and Malene Rigtrup (former singer in the well-known choir Vocal Line and arranger, composer, and co-creator of the book concept *Ørehænger*, with a focus on pop/rock education for choir directors).

The starting point for developing a distinct methodology for jazz/pop choral directing is in acknowledging the limitations of classical methods for leading jazz/pop choir music. There are many similarities but also many differences between the respective styles. In my experience, the rhythmic structure of music is realized via the successful interaction of pulse, subdivisions, and accents. This is something that cannot be comprehensively encapsulated by conducting gestures. It requires that the singers' musical skills in and between these crucial parameters are well developed and balanced across bodily connection, creativity, and singing technique.

Jazz/pop vocal ensemble music, as a subgenre, originated as a 'vocalization' of the instrumental (accompanying) genres we know as jazz, gospel, rock, pop, and world music; a vocal expression for which the renowned Swedish vocal group The Real Group, in particular, was known at the start of their career.[1] In recent decades, however, the genre has become more refined and has found its expression. In Denmark, this development began especially with Jens Johansen's pioneering work with his choir Vocal Line in the 1990s and has continued through the influence of Bobby McFerrin's improvisational art form Circlesongs, which—inspired and based on African and different ethnic vocal forms—shows the way to an independent vocal genre within the rhythmic universe.[2]

### The Intelligent Choir

The Intelligent Choir (TIC) is a teaching philosophy that has arisen from my empirical research with jazz/pop choirs since the 1990s, and which forms the basis for the didactic approach and methodology I use daily when teaching at RAMA Vocal Center and abroad.[3] TIC was inspired initially by Niels Græsholm and Svend Rastrup Andersen's 1993 publication *Slå ørene ud* (Open your ears).[4] The title arises from a focus on what they call 'vigilant attention,' which, in my further development, becomes the singer's 'awareness' and 'co-responsibility' in the musical process. TIC is thus an expression of the evolution that singers and conductors undertake from the 'unreflective stage' through awareness and taking responsibility for joint musical expression towards the 'reflective stage.' Based on the individual's musicality, singers and conductors gain new musical skills and awareness of the TIC methods. These methods are designed to work with any choir at any level. To a surprisingly impressive extent, singers can unfold their musical potential greatly when the proper prerequisites and understanding of their role are present. It can feel liberating to perform in a musical context where improvisation is loved and encouraged.

So, the TIC philosophy is about unlocking our potential for making music. For inspiration, I use the Swahili term *kucheza*, meaning 'play.' When translated within the TIC philosophy, *kucheza* becomes "I am music," because to make music is to play. As TIC choir leaders, we create learning experiences that underpin creative thinking. We consider how to facilitate a comfortable learning environment, since each singer must learn how to perform with the other singers in a relaxed, uninhibited way, and also to develop as an independent musical individual. Singers must have the opportunity to improve via team building in the choir as well as fundamental training of musical skills. Taking the time to build a *kucheza* factor in a choir can be impactful in terms of processing the TIC methods over time. Play and improvisation create powerful experiences because they stimulate communication, collaboration, and exploration. TIC supports the idea of a singer-centred starting point, where the singers are regarded and respected as competent musicians who develop their skills through group interactions and a focus on the group dynamic. At the core of the curriculum is a *kucheza* element that cannot be measured but is closely related to empathy and human emotions. Through the implementation of *kucheza*, the singers' ability to interpret and express music and to master repertoire will be enhanced by the value of building a solid musical community that thinks creatively and thus *is* the music.

## Rhythm and Groove

A recurring phrase in my jazz/pop choral classes is: "The rhythm comes first!" But what makes rhythm so significant compared with other musical parameters? Every rhythm has a 'DNA code' with a unique combination of pulse (or tempo), subdivisions, and accents. When the music 'swings,' the performers have achieved a common perception of the music's rhythmic engine, where the audible subdivisions are at the centre of the overall musical expression. 'Ghost notes' (extra improvised subdivisions) often play a central role in this style. A prominent tool is 'energizing,' where we perform the music without specific pitches (like rap) and 'turn up' (and down) the extra audible subdivisions and accents until we reach the perfect blend.

We must agree on tempo, pulse, and subdivisions, and whether the music is straight, shuffle, or swing. To perform rhythm, singers need to connect the physical elements within themselves. Connections between music and movement were natural to us as children when we heard music and spontaneously started to move. Working purposefully with rhythm can also be a way to reconnect with our inner child and playground. A rediscovery of fun and play means that we experience that rhythm and pulse are present in our innate senses.

## How to Learn TIC

In my experience, the TIC methods have a particular emphasis on:

- *Kucheza*—play—I am music.
- Tactile experience with vocal music.
- Musical reflection.
- Musical creativity.
- Musical interaction.
- Co-responsibility for the musical process.
- Rhythm and groove improvement.
- Improvisation.

The methods unfold within three learning areas:

1. Development of individual skills within five main pedagogical elements.
2. Vocal Painting (VOPA).
3. *Kucheza* (liberation of voice, body, and psyche).

### 1. Developing Individual Skills within the Five Main Elements

- *Rhythm and groove* for physical ear training with basic steps, coordination, groove training, drumming/stomping, and improvised polyphonic rhythms.
- *Intonation and pitch* for theory and physical ear training. We gain in-depth knowledge of modal tones and relevant scales via sol-fa hand signs in improvised polyphonic singing.
- *Sound and blend* for basic singing technique and contrast exercises. The singers refine their voice quality, tone formation, and expressive possibilities and learn to nuance and equalize the sound of other singers.
- *Interpretation and expression* for dynamics, textual analysis, and exercises focusing on story-making elements, including scat, rap, poetry-slam, and the development of bespoke languages.
- *Stage performance* for practical and theoretical training to communicate on the auditory and visual level and with awareness of the body as a musical instrument.[5]

Each musical element is practised and used with a focus on finding musical complexity within the ostensibly simple. I call this process 'internalizing' (acquisition of skill), whereas 'externalizing' combines all five areas and represents the whole musical performance.

## 2. Vocal Painting

Vocal Painting (VOPA) is an intricate set of hand signs to enable non-verbal communication between the conductor and the vocal ensemble (and between the singers), where the smallest detail can be agreed upon and adjusted both in known material and in music created in the moment.[6] It has its roots in Soundpainting (developed in 1974 by the American composer, pianist, and arranger Walter Thompson), but has been redesigned to complement existing choir-conducting techniques and the choral tradition for jazz/pop music. There are seventy-five VOPA signs in the current curriculum for candidates in rhythmic choral directing. However, the first five signs are enough to achieve significant contrasts in musical expression for any choir.

VOPA brings an additional component to Bobby McFerrin's circlesong concert format. When developed over time, it allows for instant ensemble arranging and composing at a high artistic level. In the context of TIC, you can release the singers from choral conventions by using the VOPA technique. The aim is to perform improvised music as if it had been thoroughly composed, by adding form and complexity as well as diversity through twists and modulations, not in all circlesongs, but as a contrasting element to the evolutionary process that usually characterizes the development of circlesongs.

The five beginner VOPA signs represent: externalizing (or singing); energizing (or singing without pitch); long notes (or legato); short notes (or staccato); and filter for audible subdivisions (improvised filling-in between notes). When the choir director and choristers know the basic VOPAs, these create a direct shortcut to processing the knowledge and experience within the basic musical parameters in the repertoire. You may be surprised by the result and how quickly it works.

## 3. "Kucheza" (liberation of voice, body, and psyche)

As previously stated, in the context of TIC, the essence of *kucheza* is "I am music!" In addition to mastering the musical elements described in learning areas 1 and 2, the singers' technical skills are crucial for the choir's sound and development possibilities. It is, therefore, essential to focus simultaneously on training the voice, body, and psyche. To gain an understanding of the deeper layers in rhythm/groove-based music, everyone must master 'physical ear-training,' where the body's ability to relate to subdivisions and emphases on a physical level can control several elements or layers at the same time, as a means of supporting the vocal performance. The choir director is responsible for teaching the singers how to achieve *kucheza* and become part of TIC, and the learning process is an essential part of the overall concept. There are different tools for creating vocal improvisation sequences, and the idea is that each tool is a step on a staircase leading up to *kucheza*. In this way, one must master one tool before moving on to the next step and thus work towards the experience of feeling more and more *kucheza*.

**Instant Music**

The purpose of working with instant music, or structured improvisation, is to reach musical success every five minutes. A seven-step process is recommended for learning the TIC approach and achieving *kucheza*. Often, when you introduce improvisation, it can feel intimidating for singers. A gentler introduction goes via instant music, so everybody learns to connect to their inner *kucheza*. The following is how to do it.

*1. Framework*

You prepare the exercise by setting a tempo, time signature, and subdivisions for the choir so that there is a manageable number of opportunities to improvise your way up to a piece of music. You start with walking a basic step in tempo and time signature, as the foundation for constructing the piece. Next comes a clapping ostinato layer (bravely started by the person who dares to go first), possibly defined based on some parameters that can be instructed with VOPA, such as a maximum of notes per loop. After that, you 'energize' your clap, which means translating the clap into a vocal sound without pitches. When energizing works, you can remove the clapping ostinato to create more space to develop tones on the energizing. Finally, the VOPA director can elaborate in any desired direction, limited to the number of VOPAs the choir has implemented. At a more advanced level, the Framework progressions also develop the singers' aural and theoretical skills by introducing and working with, for example, modal keys and irregular time signatures to sharpen the inner musical 'GPS' and the general overview of the complexity of the music.

*2. Loop Songs*

These loop-based, often short, songs aim to spread knowledge of a broad repertoire within a manageable number of measures and patterns. A loop song can be a transcription of a Bobby McFerrin circlesong, a traditional African song, a canon, a self-composed song, or a starting point for improvisation with VOPA. Using loops songs, you achieve short pieces of music that sound good within a brief rehearsal time. In contrast, vocal painting can add an extra dimension to creativity and extension of the five musical parameters.

### 3. Loop Improvisation

As with the Framework progression, an overview of tempo, time signature, subdivisions, number of tracks, tonality, and possibly scale type is defined for making loop improvisation. The exercise involves the choir leader (or singers) developing loops within a defined structure for the voice groups. The structure is not the same as in the preceding Framework; here there is a direct focus on developing the loops from voice to voice. When the whole choir is singing, you can use the following basic VOPA signs: volume, tempo, break, mute, and solo. Relatively simple variations keep the improvisation straightforward, to preserve the comfort zone while extending the music. In the long term, you can develop the choir's aural and theoretical skills using modal tones and irregular time signatures, so that something that has first been addressed in the preceding Framework is then explored without the 'GPS' in Loop Improvisation.

### 4. Guide Singing

The singers stand in a circle and receive (or learn) tones, rhythms, words, sounds, or a song phrase from the singer standing next to them, as a walking story. Typically, the choir director starts by activating the entire choir through creating loops and sending them around the circle. The singers must continue reciting or singing what they have received and passed on to the next person until a new phrase comes, which again they must practise before passing it on. In this way, you can build many layers circulating in the choir in a predetermined order, where the singers develop the ability to stand alone with a specific task: to learn and pass on learning. If it turns out to be too demanding for the individual singer, you can use two circles so that the singers face each other in the two circles, and thus there are two to learn the phrase and pass it on to the following two people. You can put the flow on hold and thus have a frozen image of the music as it sounds at that moment with the many layers. You can then continue, or you can take new paths.

### 5. Circlesongs

As in its original version developed by Bobby McFerrin, circlesongs is an art form where the soloist improvises his/her way to the ideas later implemented in the vocal ensemble. It is not certain that the entire ensemble will be activated; it all depends on the singer's ideas and on the musical structure. McFerrin improvises concerts consisting exclusively of circlesongs, where it is naturally a prerequisite that you stand with a skilled vocal ensemble that can very quickly perform the musical ideas that arise, just as it requires substantial headspace and energy from the soloist to create details and variation in a ninety-minute concert that is entirely improvised. Initially, VOPA signs were not a part of the circlesongs tradition. If you miss some dimensions in your artistic circlesongs, you must go through steps 1 to 4 again with new challenges from the essential musical elements.

## 6. Group Improvisation

Here, the director facilitates the frame for time and place only before getting started. As an exercise to think outside the box, the group can agree on some milestones to aim for along the way. For example, standing with closed eyes in a circle and beginning on the same note, you could agree that at one point you will sing together very strongly or weakly, with no fixed pulse, ending on a new standard note. Anything from the five main musical elements can help the choir to expand its comfort zone. If you miss some dimensions in this phase, you must go through steps 1 to 5 again with new challenges from the essential musical elements.

## 7. TIC Music

Here, steps 1 to 6 are in free play. The choir uses vocal painting and has thoroughly mastered the processes of the previous steps. With the help of VOPA, you can navigate non-verbally between the different starting points for improvisation, and, if you like, can bring already-rehearsed palettes of music into the performance. You can use previously known arrangements and can, for example, give a signal to further develop the chorus for a while before returning to the familiar formula or going in a new direction.

### Digitally Supported Practices

In this section, I will discuss my thesis that digitally supported practices can provide added value in learning to be a choir director if you think about a design-based curriculum. In my work, I do not view digitally supported practices as a plan B (being only a digital survival kit for crises such as pandemics), but as a new plan A. The technological revolution and internationalization have led to an increased need for digital innovation and for the inclusion of online learning in teaching. My goal has been to gain a high level of knowledge about relevant technologies and methods used in higher music education, including professionalizing and harmonizing the digitally supported practices at the RAMA Vocal Center. In my twelve years of experience at the Vocal Center, I have been able to compare regular classroom teaching versus classroom teaching with supplementary online and distance learning courses. The general interest in digital multimedia tools has grown because of available technologies and because the integration of these has the capacity to enhance students' and teachers' level of reflection, interdisciplinary collaboration, and exchange of ideas.

**It Is Not Science Fiction**

Since 2010, choir rehearsals and concerts involving distantly located participants have become a reality through high-speed networks using the LoLa system.[7] The name 'LoLa' is short for 'Low Latency,' and this system allows us to sing and play together with very high technical quality up to a distance of 3,500km, with minimal delay in sound and video (below twenty milliseconds). Long before the need arose during the Covid-19 pandemic, higher education institutions such as RAMA Vocal Center have been able to use LoLa as part of a research network around Europe. LoLa was developed by the Conservatorio di Musica Giuseppe Tartini from Trieste, Italy, in collaboration with the Gruppo per l'Armonizzazione delle Reti della Ricerca (GARR), the Italian research and academic network conceived in 2005 after a demonstration of the first Intercontinental Viola Masterclass between the GARR National Conference in Pisa, Italy, and the New World Symphony Music Academy in Miami, USA.[8] LoLa technology allows students and teachers to participate in masterclasses, even when located in distant places—including performing together during the session—thus making collective performance possible without travelling. LoLa also provides the opportunity to present actual concerts for the public, where musicians at three endpoints (such as Aalborg, Tallinn, Oslo) are connected and can perform simultaneously. On several occasions, I have held choir concerts with, for example, half of the choir located in Aalborg and the other half in Aarhus, and audience members in both places listening to the same concert in real-time. Similarly, at a workshop for the European Choral Association's *Europa Cantat* Festival in 2021, I was physically present in Ljubljana in Slovenia, with eight singers who sang together with a choir situated at RAMA Vocal Center in Aalborg.

### 'HyFlex' Curriculum Design (HCD)

Students with jazz/pop directing as their major subject in many cases already have an elite choir locally rooted in their hometown. In addition, RAMA Vocal Center has an extensive international network of alumni, course participants, and guest lecturers, located at a distance from the institution. As a result of the restrictions necessitated by the Covid-19 pandemic, many people in society became adept at using online tools and platforms, but of course it is clear that an essential element is missing when we do not meet in person: being physically present in the same room. This need for in-person contact provides the starting point for effective 'HyFlex' Curriculum Design (HCD) learning. Even so, there are parts of a choral learning process that can be optimized using online tools, and I have done a development project on this in my daily work at RAMA Vocal Center. I hypothesize that digitally supported practices can provide added value in the case of a design-based choir curriculum like HCD—a holistic mindset for singer-centred learning and sustainability for students, teachers, and staff.

HCD is a model that integrates three everyday components in an individually tailored version:

- Face-to-face learning (F2F)—same time in the same room.
- Synchronous online learning—same time in different rooms.
- Asynchronous online learning—independent of time and space.

In a complete version of HCD, all three components are integrated. In recent years, from home, it has been possible to access F2F activities (e.g., choir rehearsals) synchronously online via video conference or low-latency software such as SonoBus, a free computer app that works a little like LoLa but has the great advantage of being accessible via a regular fibre connection from a standard home computer.[9] Using SonoBus, it is possible to sing together in a hybrid form, with singers physically present in the rehearsal room and online singers at a distance. A guest soloist could take part in pre-rehearsals via SonoBus if based far away, or students/singers who cancel their attendance, for one reason or another, can still interact online. HCD activities must be clearly defined, easily accessible, and offer excellent sound and image quality, as is technically possible today, within a reasonable budget. In addition, parts of the teaching activities or choir rehearsal may be recorded on video to be accessed asynchronously 24/7.

At RAMA Vocal Center, we focus on developing asynchronous online options, a priority area for us in the coming years. According to our empirical studies, here are some examples that significantly optimize the practice process and the ongoing dialogue between students and teachers:

- The teacher records short instructional videos distributed through a digital Learning Management System (LMS). The students acknowledge by uploading a short video themselves, which is briefly commented on by the instructor asynchronously before the next F2F session.
- The teacher organizes small vocal ensembles, or solo sessions, where singers sing 'with' each other by adding their voices asynchronously; for example, using an app such as Acapella.[10]
- Supplementary listening and theory lessons align with the current repertoire and subject.

I propose that we are making better use of the real potential in the information and presentation of teaching material through these innovative digital approaches than with the traditional form of teaching alone. At the same time, I realize that many teachers and music directors lack knowledge, motivation, and skills in this area. My empirical research recommends an increased focus on competence development in digital skills in my own country of Denmark and abroad. I am convinced that HyFlex can also benefit choral singing in general, and I hope that digitally supported practices in the future will not only be a plan B but a new plan A.

## Rounding Off

Choral learning requires a strong sense of community, and social interaction between the singers enhances the learning process. With the TIC and HyFlex methods, singers develop significantly through active participation in exercises and strategies implemented in the choir as a new standard. To be effective, there must be consensus on what the group's goals are in connection with the acquisition of knowledge and personal musical development. The choir director supports each singer in their experiences, helps with processing these, and guides the singer to the next level. Of course, the choir singers differ in musical abilities, personal history, and cultural and historical background. Once you have reflected on the three pedagogical areas of learning outlined earlier in this chapter, you will find it easier to decode the complexity of jazz/pop music so that the prerequisites are present to perform at a high artistic standard both as a singer with shared responsibility for the musical expression and as a choir director who facilitates the musical process. Good luck!

## Notes

1. See The Real Group, accessed 9 September 2022, https://therealgroup.se.
2. See Vocal Line, accessed 9 September 2022, https://www.vocalline.dk and Bobby McFerrin, accessed 9 September 2022, https://bobbymcferrin.com.
3. For information and support materials relating to this concept, see The Intelligent Choir, accessed 4 September 2022, https://www.theintelligentchoir.com.
4. Niels Græsholm and Svend Rastrup Andersen, *Slå ørene ud* (Egtved: Edition Egtved, 1993).
5. With inspiration from Astrid Vang-Pedersen's practical and theoretical work in the Concert Design field. See Astrid Vang-Pedersen, "Concept," Concert Design, accessed 4 September 2022, https://www.concertdesign.dk.
6. Vocal Painting app for iOS and Android, available since 2018. For more information, see "Vocal Painting App," The Intelligent Choir, accessed 4 September 2022, https://theintelligentchoir.com/vocal-painting-app.
7. "About Lola," LoLa: Low Latency AV Streaming System, accessed 4 September 2022, https://lola.conts.it.
8. Consortium GARR, accessed 4 September 2022, https://www.garr.it/en.
9. SonoBus: High Quality Network Audio Streaming, accessed 14 September 2022, https://www.sonobus.net.
10. "Acapella: Music Collab App," Mixcord, accessed 14 September 2022, https://www.mixcord.co/pages/acapella-singing-app.

# PART IV
# Changing Perspectives

# 17
# THE 'MAESTRO MYTH' REVISITED

*John Andrews*

In 1991, Norman Lebrecht surveyed the conducting profession as it entered the last decade of the twentieth century from the perspective of its height in the inter-war and immediately post-war years.[1] The image of the maestro, forged by the demanding world and authoritarian leadership models of late nineteenth- and early twentieth-century central Europe was a powerful and multifaceted one. A hero of near mythical status "artificially created for a non-musical purpose and sustained by commercial necessity," the conductor was not only the elite of his own profession, but also a hero and role-model to leaders of business, industry, and politics.[2] Virile to a degree rarely seen outside a Hollywood blockbuster, the maestro was a man of unlimited charisma, who often embraced a volatile personality bordering on brutality, combined with an almost mystical hold on those musicians under his all-powerful baton.[3] The ubiquity of the Italian usage pointed clearly to where this image had crystalized most powerfully in the public imagination: Arturo Toscanini had reached a hitherto unprecedented public in his career with the NBC Symphony Orchestra after he had settled in New York, the "living embodiment of a musical deity."[4] Although there had been plenty of irascible and short-tempered conductors in the past, it was his temper, his volatility, and his control over the orchestra that cemented these supposed characteristics in the public imagination, and in the behaviours of a generation of US-based conductors, as the essence of the maestro.

However, Lebrecht's view of the profession in the 1980s and 1990s suggested that this was not merely myth but was also frequently not far from reality. The maestro was feted in the press and in public advertising as

DOI: 10.4324/9781003299660-22

the living embodiment of musical deity, as the priest on earth taking on the persona of the composer in heaven, and this supposed musical power transferred very quickly into concrete financial and corporate power. As the public face of their orchestras and record labels, conductors were the focal points of advertising campaigns. In the United States especially, the music director was often central to fundraising from private donors. Consequently, a number of conductors amassed enormous wealth and power, in some cases even including the ability to evade the legal consequences of misbehaviour.[5] As Lebrecht was writing, this era seemed to be coming to an end. Increasingly, administrators and chief executives were taking control of the business of artistic planning; the early music boom had brought to the fore a generation of collegial 'semi-conductors' who directed from the violin and keyboard, and when on the podium sought a much less autocratic relationship with ensembles. As the record companies seemed to have satiated the market with further CDs of classic repertoire, the power of the maestro seemed to be on the wane. And yet, in the public image, the power or the conductor—charismatic, volatile, exclusively white, male, and heterosexual—remained.[6]

This is not an analysis of the accuracy of Lebrecht's portrait. Instead, it is an opportunity to ask three questions. First, what is the reality of the modern conductor's power compared with that of forty years ago? Second, how much of that change is reflected in the way in which conductors are presented to the public, and, finally, are there any vestiges of that culture that seemed to be at an end in 1991?

## Part 1: The Modern Working Environment

We can profitably examine the trends of the last few decades across four broad headings: behaviour and manner in rehearsals and performance; responsibilities and influence over programming and personnel; fees and other forms or remuneration; and finally, diversity across the profession.

### *The Conductor in Rehearsal*

Other chapters of this book examine more fully the various ways in which conductors relate to their ensembles and the ways in which they can work together. However, it is hardly surprising to note that working conditions are strongly influenced by changing both workplace cultures and the realities of employment law. With hindsight, it is perhaps worth noting that Lebrecht's book came out shortly after the fall of the Berlin Wall, and the subsequent collapse of the Soviet Union and its Eastern European satellites. The cultural models of authoritarian rule were in retreat for the next thirty years and the notion of anybody holding near-dictatorial power looked increasingly old-fashioned after the supposed "end of history."[7] This went hand in hand with the growth of employment law generally, and the increase of workers' rights across all fields of endeavour. Orchestral musicians were no exception.

The reality of the conductor's job in the twenty-first century was illuminated recently by both Mark Wigglesworth and Sir Mark Elder. Wigglesworth acknowledges that the tyrant image remains "a pervasive cliché," while pointing out that "it is the most genuine conductors who have the most authority."[8] Elder stresses that conductors must be "the best listeners on the planet."[9] While a conductor must "be happy to be the one who is going to make the decisions,"[10] it is a question of persuasion and inspiration that guides both, and both show a genuine humility not just towards the music but also towards colleagues. Both also acknowledge a cultural change in our attitudes to the printed score that curtails much of the freedom older conductors could exploit: Wigglesworth is actively happy to have grown up in an environment where reliable editions placed clear boundaries around the conductor's ego, and Elder is frequently preoccupied with getting an orchestral sound appropriate to the historical period. This is in stark contrast to the mid-twentieth century, when certain conductors and their orchestras had a recognizable sound regardless of the composer or era.[11] Although some conductors (Toscanini, Weingartner) made fidelity to the printed page part of their public image, it was often honoured more in the breach than the observance. The increasing availability of reliable urtext editions means that the interpretative excesses of conductors are treated with much more suspicion, not only by orchestras, who can now see articulation marks, dynamics and tempi that were frequently left out of their parts in older editions,[12] but also by a much more informed audience.[13]

## The Conductor's Responsibilities

Contrary to the myth, conductors had largely lost the power to hire or remove players, even in 1991.[14] Contracts of that era provided for conductors to advise management, but in Britain, Ireland, and Europe, they could not simply sack players. In mainland Europe, orchestral players and choristers have long enjoyed extremely secure tenure that is the envy of their soloist colleagues. In the United States, powerful unions have protected players since the Second World War and North American hiring practices are tightly governed by local agreements.[15] There is a considerable distinction between the standard hiring procedures in different countries, and between the British Isles and the United States in particular. In the United

States, the usual procedure is for players to be auditioned blind (i.e., behind a curtain) by a panel including the music director, and then offered a long trial period, usually one year. In Britain, it is more usual for an orchestra to give a number of players a shorter trial and see how they fit within the orchestra before offering a contract. This necessarily dilutes the power of the conductor and instead gives more influence to the orchestral musicians, who can then decide whether or not those on probation fit in both musically and in terms of personality. A music director or principal conductor may have a strong view, but they do not hold a veto.

It is perhaps surprising to note that while the content of music director and principal conductor contracts has changed comparatively little in the space of thirty years—and probably much longer—there has certainly been a shift towards appointing principal conductors rather than musical directors.[16] In both cases, contracts provide for a conductor to spend a certain number of weeks with an orchestra (usually between twelve and sixteen), and to advise and sign off on the repertoire for those concerts and the soloists contracted to appear in them.[17] While there may be an exclusivity clause relating to record contracts, it is rare for these contracts to provide for exclusivity in terms of concert or opera performances, although they may well restrict the conductor's freedom to appear with other ensembles in the same city or area.[18] The fundamental difference between a music director and a principal conductor is that the former will also advise on and sign off on the repertoire and guest artists even when they are not themselves conducting. They may also take on a much greater civic role where appropriate, and potentially engage more fully with fundraising from both private and government sources. The music director remains the default position in opera houses.[19] On the concert platform in the United Kingdom, only the Hallé, Royal Philharmonic Orchestra, and Royal Scottish National Orchestra are led by a music director; at the time of writing, all other orchestras have a principal conductor.[20]

## Fees

Artist managers generally agree that while fees did continue to rise steeply through the 1980s and 1990s, this trend has largely come to an end, with fees held at—or slightly below—inflation for the past two decades. In the heavily subsidized world of German and French orchestras and opera houses, fees have generally been supported alongside more widespread public sector settlements and with compound increases; conductors in those positions continue to be on very comfortable salaries, but not necessarily out of step with long-serving players. In the United Kingdom, there is a sharp divide between those holding salaried positions and the very large freelance community. In addition, very few conductors travel regularly by private jet, as was still a regular occurrence in the 1980s and 1990s. Such conspicuous displays of wealth have become less frequent since the financial crash of 2008. In an era of austerity for the arts, they are deemed to be in poor taste rather than glamorous.

This raises the question of international travel more generally. Jet-setting has been part of the conductor's image since Nikisch.[21] It is impossible to assess the long-term effects of the experience of Covid-19 restrictions and the increasing awareness of the environmental impacts of frequent air travel. In May 2021, the French government won the right to ban internal flights. It remains unclear how this will impact working practices for conductors, but the arrangements that existed in the 1980s—with conductors working simultaneously in two cities connected by private air travel—are increasingly unpalatable to the general public and hard to justify, particularly in those parts of the world where the arts rely on public (and, therefore, publicly accountable) funds.

## *Diversity*

One clear—and substantial—change in the conducting profession has been that of diversification. In 1991, Lebrecht could cite Sian Edwards and Simone Young as lone exceptions to a role that sustained the "myth of male potency," systematically excluding women, homosexuals, and members of ethnic minorities.[22]

Although the profession is still some way from an equal gender balance, the picture in the United Kingdom has changed beyond recognition from the partisan image of 1991. Of the fourteen largest orchestras, eight name at least one woman in their artistic team. In two cases, they also have a female assistant conductor, which points to an increasing female presence in the next generation.[23] Change has been slower in the major US orchestras where only three have a woman among their titled conductors;[24] in two of these cases it is the same person.[25] But reports of conductors having to conceal their sexuality now seem a distant memory, with Yannick Nézet-Séguin at the helm of the Metropolitan Opera in New York and the Philadelphia Orchestra, Michael Tilson Thomas in San Francisco, and Marin Alsop until recently in Baltimore.

In the United Kingdom there is an equally interesting development in progress which fundamentally changes the role of the (singular) maestro and may well prove an increasingly popular model for the future. Of the fourteen orchestras surveyed, only two list a single principal conductor as the figurehead of artistic leadership on their website. In every other case, a substantial team of conductors is listed, often supported by composers in residence and heads of community engagement. It is not possible to compare like with like, as different orchestras have different titles and roles.[26] However, if we exclude chorus master and assistant conductor posts, then the London Symphony Orchestra cites six creative leaders; the Philharmonia, Bournemouth Symphony Orchestra, Royal Scottish National Orchestra, and BBC Symphony Orchestra credit five, and the Royal Philharmonic Orchestra, the Royal Liverpool Philharmonic Orchestra, and the Hallé list four. The rest all list two or three conductors, with only two offering a single maestro.[27]

Behind the scenes, decision-making has also spread to the players to a much greater degree. Almost all orchestras now have some version of a repertoire committee or an artistic advisory group that regularly feeds into the process of programming music and perhaps even suggesting soloists. Moreover, in at least one British orchestra, all of the players are able to give anonymous feedback on guest conductors after every single concert, which means that any issues of competence or poor behaviour can be addressed immediately. Players simply do not respond to older models of authoritarian behaviour.[28] Now, they also have structures and processes whereby they can address those concerns.[29]

This acceptance that an orchestra needs a team to lead it is the most important change in the way the music business—and the professionals involved—view the role of the conductor. There is no longer a singular maestro, but a suite of *maestri*, who between them cover different repertoires. Perhaps they have different skills in terms of audience engagement, particularly with regard to the orchestra's contact with younger audiences and new audiences. It also allows orchestras to be more diverse in recruitment and to demonstrate that diversity in the breadth of their team.

The drive for diversity reflects the very particular funding structures in place. In the United Kingdom, almost all the major orchestras are reliant to a greater or lesser degree on public subsidy. Therefore, whether or not orchestras are formally required by the terms of their funding to meet diversity criteria, there is an implicit pressure to demonstrate that public money is being used to promote the public good, not merely in terms of artistic output, but also in terms of wider policy goals. The need to show that senior appointments are fair in terms of gender balance, ethnic background, sexual orientation, and disability is no less true in the music industry than in society at large and reflects the profound changes that have taken place over the last two generations. As the podium has traditionally been overwhelmingly white and male, such changes may seem comparatively slight at present. The roster of current music directors across the globe broadly reflects traditional stereotypes; however, the patterns of recent appointments suggest that this is developing rapidly. The actual business of conductor appointments (in particular guest conductors) remains highly confidential—based on negotiations with artist managers that cannot be cited without breaching confidences—but the number of managers in Europe being actively asked to propose more women and conductors from diverse ethnic backgrounds for engagements suggests that this trend is now firmly embedded. The coming decade should see an increased opening up of the role of conductor to a wider pool of talent.[30]

## Part 2: The Public Image

The survival of the single maestro image in the United States in part reflects the very different model of funding.[31] US orchestras and opera houses rely entirely on private donations. The music director, therefore, remains a central figure whose face is inextricably linked to the identity of the orchestra, having the personal power to charm donors and secure funding. The continuation of this model in the big American orchestras and houses serves to demonstrate how intertwined the reality of the conductor's role is with the image that is projected to the public. So, the next question is: To what extent has that image changed in line with the evolution of the role in the rehearsal room and on stage?

There are several conductors who are sufficiently well recognized as to be the corporate face of their ensembles. When Simon Rattle was music director of the City of Birmingham Symphony Orchestra in the 1980s and 1990s, his face was the absolute centre of the orchestra's publicity. His prestige and success reflected on the orchestra, which, in turn, was more sought after and, therefore, more marketable. At that point, the semi-religious power of the conductor's face was the selling point for orchestras across the world; the likes of Karajan and then Abbado were the very embodiment of the Berlin orchestra that they led. It was, therefore, significant that on his return to the London Symphony Orchestra, Rattle was trailed with the social media hashtag #ThisisRattle and his image remains iconic.

And iconic is an important and accurate term here. When asked about the marketing of modern conductors, a leading British artist manager answered simply "the hair." Conductors may be diversifying in terms of gender and ethnic heritage, but it is remarkable how prominent coiffuring is in the profile of many leading conductors: Gustavo Dudamel, Robin Ticciati, Nicholas Collon, Rafael Payare, Barbara Hannigan, Jonathon Heyward, and Santtu-Matias Rouvali, to name a few. This suggests that in the public's imagination at least, there is still a need for flamboyance, romanticism, and a (safe) whiff of counter-cultural danger expected on the podium, with perhaps a nod to the biblical figure of Samson.

It is important to note, though, that it was rarely the orchestras that were spending money on promoting the image of the conductor.[32] Orchestras' publicity budgets focused more heavily on the season's content, while the record industry, instead, frequently used the image of the conductor to market discs. The recording industry no longer has the purchasing power that it did in the twentieth century, and two significant trends have lessened the role of the conductor as the central focus of marketing. The first was the move, headed by Hyperion, towards the use of more abstract and artistic cover art. With some obvious exceptions, CD artwork was much more likely to reflect the character of the music rather than simply the performers. The second and more recent trend is the increase in streaming and the need for artwork to be distinctive at a size visible on a mobile device: the face of the conductor is simply not distinctive enough.

Although the physical image of the conductor—when it *is* used—may have changed comparatively little, the level of formality and approachability projected in publicity materials has changed a great deal, as might be expected from the cultural changes of the last thirty years. Herbert von Karajan was almost exclusively presented as cold, dark, scowling, brooding, and joyless in his publicity photographs, although he was occasionally caught off guard showing the hint of a smile. Images of him were prevailingly black and white and, in all cases, emphasized the distance between the viewer and the object: in most shots, he is wearing formal dress, either evening tails or a suit, or for the modern look, in a black polo neck. The same is true of the other iconic conductor of his generation, Sir Georg Solti. This shadow-heavy black and white imagery was partially an inherited style from the generation of Toscanini, Furtwängler, Klemperer, and Szell, but it continued to be used by a whole generation of conductors in the later twentieth century, as an image search for Christoph von Dohnányi, Leonard Bernstein, or the reclusive Carlos Kleiber demonstrates.

The change in iconography in the last thirty years is largely a question of approachability. Abbado was more likely than most of his contemporaries to be photographed smiling. The image of the conductor as forbidding and slightly removed from the world of mortals was already shifting as he was portrayed on CD covers in shirtsleeves or a pullover. Rattle is seemingly incapable of being portrayed without at least a twinkle in his eye. Off the podium, very few conductors are portrayed in formal wear. Robin Ticciati put on a tie to collect his OBE, but aside from that it is vanishingly rare to see a conductor portrayed in neckwear or a suit except on stage. Even when on stage, conductors tend to lead the way in less formal attire and are often more casually dressed than their orchestral colleagues who remain—the men, at least—in full nineteenth-century attire.[33] The image of the conductor as an aristocrat, or perhaps a high-ranking servant, is clearly fading.

This evolution of concert dress, of course, goes beyond the conductors themselves. The debate as to whether orchestras should continue to appear in formal evening wear is ongoing, and entirely outside the scope of this chapter, except for the additional challenge that it tends to present to women on the podium. Orchestras are now split essentially into those who wear all black, and those where the men wear full evening dress, and the women wear modern black; there are, mercifully, few orchestras that require female musicians to wear full-length evening dresses. The connection between orchestra dress becoming less codified and the rise of more women conductors means that today's orchestras must make a conscious choice about concert dress, unlike earlier generations. In 2020, Dalia Stasevska conducted the Last Night of the Proms in a colourful, silk kimino-style dress; at the same festival the previous year, Nathalie Stutzman, Elim Chan, and Mirga Gražinytė-Tyla appeared in black suits.[34] The appearance of female artists continues to be scrutinized more than that of their male counterparts, and on the podium, this is no exception. The need to make a conscious choice about how to portray the authority of the office is one that female conductors continue to face to an even greater degree than their male colleagues.

Aside from their attire, it is also notable that conductors are now generally portrayed looking straight at the camera rather than into the middle distance, inviting the viewer to appreciate their down-to-earth humanity rather than their divine otherness. This reflects a broader social change. European society, in particular, is more suspicious now of absolute authority than perhaps was the case in the middle of the twentieth century. The fall of the Berlin Wall signalled the removal of the last political models of authoritarian dictatorship in Europe and society has become increasingly less deferential to traditional models of authority. It is unsurprising then that conductors are now marketed as democratic leaders rather than monarchs.

There is also now a willingness to hold conductors' behaviour up to public scrutiny in a way that was largely unthinkable in the mid- to late twentieth century. This follows a more general trend in uncovering and seeking justice for historic abuses of power by those in the arts. The most public example was in Hollywood in 2017, when accusations were made against the producer Harvey Weinstein; he was convicted in 2020 for five felonies and subsequently extradited to Los Angeles to face further trials. In the classical music world, there have always been rumours of bullying and sexual improprieties committed by famous conductors, but these had generally never been proven or acted upon. On 2 December 2017, it was made public that the police were investigating sexual misconduct allegations against the American conductor James Levine. He was fired from all his posts, although he died without having been convicted. Rumours of Levine's behaviour went back decades—this author heard them from colleagues and teachers in the 1990s—and in 1991 Lebrecht specifically alluded to the failure of authorities to act on them as one of the strongest proofs that conductors were regarded as untouchable.[35] This is clearly no longer the case.

Similar accusations against Charles Dutoit have resulted in relations with several orchestras being severed. While accusations by female orchestral players against Daniele Gatti in 2018 were compelling enough for the Royal Concertgebouw Orchestra to terminate his appointment as chief conductor, they were not sufficient to prevent him being named chief conductor of the Orchestra Mozart and the Staatskapelle Dresden. There have been other cases where misconduct has been brought to the attention of management and dealt with quietly and without legal recourse.[36] Nevertheless, the modern conductor is expected to work within the framework of professional standards of behaviour. A conductor may be ill-tempered, cold, and ruthless, but they are not excepted from the workplace ethics that govern any other sphere of employment.

**Part 3: Survival of the Traditional Maestro**

That conductors ever had unchecked power was due, in part at least, to the historical development of the role in European courts. The *Kapellmeister* or *Maestro di Musica* was a direct employee of the monarch, answerable only to them. They, in turn, exercised a near monarchical power over their musicians because they wielded the King's (or Duke's) authority by proxy.[37] It is perhaps no coincidence that Britain, which never had a court theatre and whose orchestras were historically self-governing, has generally produced a fairly mild-mannered set of conductors, and treated visiting tyrants with open disdain—Boult calling himself rather "the chairman of a committee."[38] In Germany and France, music directors are often responsible to local politicians so can wield power in proportion to how much support they enjoy from local elites. In the United States, they are responsible only to their boards and donors. Yet, in both cases, powerful structures of employment law restrain most directorial excesses.

The only conductor in the world who still enjoys the sort of power his nineteenth-century predecessors possessed—resting on the authority of an unassailable political master—is Valery Gergiev. In 2022, this became irrevocably mixed up with the war in Ukraine, but prior to that conflict, Gergiev—when in Russia—was one of the few conductors to exercise power over players that extended to control of working hours, conditions, and personnel. This demonstrates again the very close relationship between the conductor's authority and the power structures that exist in society at large. The authority of the conductor is always, to some degree, a reflection of broader social attitudes to the legitimate exercise of authority in politics and in business.

Apart from that very specific example, the only place where conductors can act outside the considerable restraints of employment legislation is in the very ensembles that Lebrecht saw as undermining the traditional authority of the maestro: those of the early music movement. Lebrecht caustically referred to the leaders of these groups as 'semiconductors,' but this is worth examining a little further. It is undoubtedly true that many of the pioneers of early music were, and are, emollient, collegial figures; however, these ensembles remain one of the few arenas in which a conductor's authority can be reactively untrammelled. This is less a facet of individual conductors' personalities and more a product of employment structures. Like many orchestras in the United Kingdom, they employ musicians entirely on a freelance basis. Players might enjoy regular re-invitations over decades; however, each engagement is contracted individually, and nobody has a right to be re-engaged. This is the case for many orchestras, and it devolves considerable power to the fixers, under the supervision of management. Where the ensemble has been formed by a conductor, and here they are also part of the management, they will, of necessity, have a right of hire over everybody performing to a degree far beyond that of any employed ensemble.

In conclusion, the actual work of the conductor is influenced both by society's evolving expectation of how authority is exercised and by the general public's need for an authority figure who inspires and enthuses them to come and experience live music. The way in which individual conductors negotiate the tension of this paradox can be seen in other chapters of this book. Alongside soloists and composers, conductors are identifiable figures with whom audiences can relate directly, and in a room of 20 to 200 people they must exercise, in their own way, the final word where they still have the "potential to influence the life and soul of an orchestra . . . even a city."[39] The myth of the maestro continues to evolve with orchestras, choirs, and society at large, and shows little sign of redundancy just yet.

### Notes

1 Norman Lebrecht, *The Maestro Myth: Great Conductors in Pursuit of Power* (London: Simon & Schuster, 1991).
2 Lebrecht, *The Maestro Myth*, 1.
3 The classic example of a bully was Hans von Bülow. Lebrecht, *The Maestro Myth*, 23.

4 Lebrecht, *The Maestro Myth*, 67.
5 Lebrecht, *The Maestro Myth*, 216.
6 Such hegemony is addressed in Chapter 19 by Thomas Dickey and Chapter 18 by Nadya Potemkina in this volume.
7 Francis Fukuyama's influential book *The End of History and the Last Man* (New York: Free Press, 1992) argued that the collapse of the Soviet Union marked victory of democratic states over authoritarian governments, and the culture of democratic rule of dictatorship.
8 Mark Wigglesworth, *The Silent Musician: Why Conducting Matters* (London: Faber & Faber, 2018), 21.
9 Raymond Holden, *Elder on Music: Sir Mark Elder in Conversation with Raymond Holden* (London: Royal Academy of Music Press, 2019), 32.
10 Holden, *Elder on Music*, 63.
11 Most famously Herbert von Karajan and Leopold Stokowski, both of whom brought a recognizable timbre to almost all the music that they conducted which was personal to them rather than the composer.
12 It was completely standard in nineteenth-century editions (still in use throughout the twentieth century) for tempo markings to be in the full score but not the players' parts.
13 Since 1990, Bärenreiter has produced 280 new urtext editions, moving well beyond the eighteenth century into core Romantic repertoire.
14 Wigglesworth, *The Silent Musician*, 43.
15 North American orchestras are often in agreements which specify the geographical locality from which players can be drawn. Elder describes working practices in the United States as unhelpfully inflexible. Holden, *Elder on Music*, 50.
16 This information is based on interviews with artist managers and orchestral administrators.
17 In discussion with artist managers. See also Holden, *Elder on Music*, 65.
18 At one point, a British opera company's contract for its music director prevented them from appearing with any other opera company in the United Kingdom.
19 Music director contracts remain the norm in opera houses where the musical overview of programming and casting across a whole season is seen as essential to fulfilling the leadership role.
20 See Chapter 7 by Peter Shannon in this volume for comparative conventions in the United States.
21 Lebrecht, *The Maestro Myth*, 67.
22 Lebrecht, *The Maestro Myth*, 261–62. For more information on this, see Chapter 19 by Thomas Dickey and Chapter 18 by Nadya Potemkina in this volume.
23 Mirga Gražinytė-Tyla is currently principal guest conductor of the City of Birmingham Symphony Orchestra. Sofi Jeannin is chief conductor of the BBC Singers. Barbara Hannigan is associate artist of the London Symphony Orchestra. Karina Canellakis is principal guest conductor of the London Philharmonic Orchestra. Marin Alsop remains conductor emeritus of Bournemouth Symphony Orchestra, while Elim Chan was principal guest conductor of the Royal Scottish National Orchestra from 2018 to 2023.
24 There is a vast number of orchestras in the United States, so for the purposes of clarity—and because they have the largest grip on the public perception—I have confined this discussion to the fourteen largest.
25 Nathalie Stutzman is currently principal conductor of the Atlanta Symphony Orchestra, as well as principal guest conductor in Philadelphia.
26 They also differ in how they cite assistant conductors and conductors laureate.

27 John Storgårds at the BBC Philharmonic in Manchester and Jaime Martín at the National Symphony Orchestra in Dublin, but in both cases, this appears to be a temporary situation.
28 Wigglesworth, *The Silent Musician*, 43.
29 This does not address the huge and unregulated freelance sector in the United Kingdom.
30 A recent British Sociological Association study, "Social Mobility and 'Openness' in Creative Occupations since the 1970s," suggests that the arts professions as a whole are becoming less accessible to those in the lowest income groups. The question of whether the arts, and, therefore, leadership roles within arts organizations, are becoming less socially diverse is beyond the scope of this chapter. Orian Brook, Andrew Miles, Dave O'Brien, and Mark Taylor, "Social Mobility and 'Openness' in Creative Occupations since the 1970s," *Sociology* 57, no. 4 (August 2023): 789–810, https://doi.org/10.1177/00380385221129953.
31 At the time of writing, the websites of nine of the fourteen largest US orchestras display only a single principal conductor or music director. The exceptions are: the Chicago Symphony Orchestra, which lists the assistant conductor; the Philadelphia Orchestra and Atlanta Symphony Orchestra, which also list the principal guest conductor; and the Cleveland Orchestra, which lists the conductor emeritus. As discussed earlier, only the San Francisco Symphony Orchestra lists the members of its conducting academy.
32 Orchestras would, however, spend it on their fees.
33 Holden, *Elder on Music*, 24.
34 This matter is also considered in Chapter 5 by Rebecca Miller and Chapter 18 by Nadya Potemkina in this volume.
35 Lebrecht, *The Maestro Myth*, 216.
36 In discussion with artist managers.
37 Holden, *Elder on Music*, 16.
38 Lebrecht, *The Maestro Myth*, 41.
39 Holden, *Elder on Music*, 50.

# 18

## "YOU ARE NOW ONE OF THE BOYS"

Congratulations?

*Nadya Potemkina*

When in October 2021 the Atlanta Symphony Orchestra announced the appointment of Nathalie Stutzmann as its fifth music director, the social media community lit up with enthusiastic discussions of this event and soon came to realize that Stutzmann would, yet again, be the only woman leading a major North American orchestra, following Marin Alsop's departure from Baltimore just a couple of months prior.[1] In an interview for the 2020 documentary *Beyond the Grace Note*, Alsop lamented the excruciatingly slow pace of progress we have been seeing since she made her momentous career break in 2007 by being named the twelfth music director of the Baltimore Symphony Orchestra, one of the top North American ensembles. Fast-forward fifteen years, the latest diversity report presented by the League of American Orchestras—although it does indicate some progress—still confirms the suspicion that gender diversity on orchestral podiums is lacking, as evidenced by the dismally horizontal lines on a graph that spans a decade from 2014 to 2023. The percentage of male music directors has decreased, and the percentage of female music directors has increased by about 10 per cent. The 2014–19 seasons demonstrate the fastest rate of improvement, but for the past four years, the graph appears static and even shows signs of regression.[2] A survey of 130 professional orchestral musicians conducted in 2015 by Anna Edwards demonstrates the overall societal awareness of the fact that women face gender discrimination through no fault of their own: 73 per cent of respondents agreed with the statement.[3] Fanatically devoted to tradition, classical music is incredibly reluctant to embrace change, and any one woman's individual achievements, however extraordinary, will never be enough to turn the tide.

DOI: 10.4324/9781003299660-23

The change must be systemic, created by deliberate efforts of a community on a mission to promote diversity and inclusion. Even though we are going to focus here on the challenges that complicate the career progression of an average woman, it is important to remember that most of the issues we are going to touch upon pollute professional and personal experiences of any individual who does not fit into the traditional box of a 'powerful leader,' be it a person of colour, or even a white man who does not fulfil all the machismo 'requirements' of the job. In this chapter, I would like to share my musings about diversity on the podium, primarily through reflections on my subjective experiences, with occasional references to a number of sources I found helpful in trying to answer the question at hand: "Where is everybody?"

**Where is Everybody?**

I first started asking this question a few years ago, while evaluating student presentations in my class on the evolution of the symphony, a general orchestral music appreciation course created for undergraduate students who have a passion for ensemble music-making. For one of the assignments, I ask my students to look for two different video-recorded performances of a symphony of their choosing, and report on the key points of interpretation and the leadership styles of the two conductors. In nearly a decade, there have been entire cohorts that presented no female conductors. The first woman to make it onto our list was Nathalie Stutzmann; Marin Alsop joined a year later. Very recently, one person unearthed a recording of a female student at the Moscow Conservatory, but this is where our list of female conductors ends. Thinking that my students were looking in all the wrong places, I turned to YouTube myself, only to confirm that a simple search for any standard symphony brings up the names of the same dozen conductors, with a smattering of recent exceptions, such as recordings of Alondra de la Parra performing Beethoven.[4] How do we normalize the idea of a woman conductor if there are not that many of us populating the internet searches of the curious music lovers—those very people who purchase tickets and subscriptions, and keep our community orchestras afloat?

In attempts to explain women's perpetual struggle to establish unquestioned credibility in leadership roles, some people cite relatively modern manifestations of various socio-economic issues and expose stereotypical perceptions of female appearance and behaviour that often serve as mere excuses for continuous discrimination. Others, such as Mary Beard, an English scholar of Ancient History, turn to Greek mythology to show that "When it comes to silencing women, Western culture has had thousands of years of practice."[5] However, facing the age-old 'grandeur' of misogyny should not discourage or intimidate us; it should only serve as a reminder that something that took millennia to create, foster, and promote, cannot be undone overnight with a token appointment of a female assistant conductor. As a society, we must actively encourage and empower; we cannot leave it all to the women to 'fix' by publishing self-help books and sharing isolated success stories: "She has made it! Why can't you?"

Beard reminds us of some of the first recorded examples of men telling women that their voices are not to be heard in public. In Homer's *Odyssey*, Telemachus, the son of Penelope and Odysseus, explains that "speech will be the business of men," then orders his mother to go back to her room and resume weaving, after she dares to comment on qualities of entertainment during a social gathering.[6] Even women's voices themselves were subject to scrutiny: low-pitched voice indicated manly courage, while a high-pitched voice signified female cowardice. One of the orators asked his audience to imagine a terrifying hypothetical situation in which all men and boys suddenly got female voices: "Would not that be worse than a plague?"[7] Public speech was one of the "defining attributes of maleness," hence a woman speaking in public was by definition not a woman.[8] Speaking in public implies that one has knowledge to have something to speak about, expertise to believe that this knowledge is worth sharing with others, and authority to believe that others should listen.[9] These are integral components of power and leadership, which are consistently and persistently acknowledged only when presented by a man.

In spring 2022, one of my conducting students, a soft-spoken person, took the orchestra podium for his end-of-term conducting examination. After his performance, I asked the students in the orchestra for feedback. One young man in the brass section said: "You need to be more assertive!" Nothing is wrong with the comment, but the way it was delivered left me feeling uncomfortable, even though it took me some time to understand what exactly struck the nerve. The student who was offering this feedback lowered the pitch of his voice when he was saying "more assertive." He also may or may not had formed a fist in front of his chest—I did not have a good view angle to be certain—but he definitely tried for his comment to sound as 'strong' as possible: you need to be more of a man to be assertive. My concern with the conducting student's performance was that he seemed to have nothing to assert, because he struggled to actively listen to the orchestra (quite common with beginners), but competence becomes secondary to confidence once you find yourself in the position of power.

To illustrate that our cultural template for a leader remains male, Mary Beard conducted an amusing experiment of googling the term 'cartoon professor.'[10] As one would expect, out of the first hundred images that popped up, only one turned out to be that of a woman. Regrettably, she was a fictional character, but nonetheless, a female.[11] I must report that googling 'cartoon conductor' yields comparable results. If we disregard occasional railroad conductors, we get images of white (often angry and red-faced) men in tuxedos, or those of Bugs Bunny from Looney Tunes. In the first hundred images, I counted five cartoons of conducting women or girls, and was also excited to discover a Google Doodle from 5 December 2017 that celebrated the 101st birthday of the pioneer Soviet conductor Veronika Dudarova.[12] Unsurprisingly, we have no historically established template for such a female leader. Beard continues her examination of ancient Greek idioms, and it becomes clear that even though there is an impressive array of seemingly powerful women in Greek myths, they are not presented as role models. They are portrayed as abusers of power, monstrous hybrid creatures, often with masculine features, who must be tamed and put back in their place.[13] It was the duty of men to save civilization from the rule of Amazon women,[14] and the beheading of Medusa turned into a cultural symbol of opposition to women's power.[15]

Are women actually this terrifying in their assumed 'inability' to execute effective managerial strategies? Jack Zenger and Joseph Folkman, in a 2019 Harvard Business Review piece on leadership skills across genders, report that despite broad cultural biases and stereotypes against women, research shows that women in leadership are just as effective as men. Women score higher in 84 per cent of the competencies that are most frequently measured in leadership evaluations: they take initiative, act with resilience, practice self-development, and display high integrity and honesty.[16] However, when women are asked to assess themselves, they are much less generous: there is a considerable difference in levels of confidence in men and women under the age of twenty-five. Confidence levels merge by the time they turn forty, and in their sixties, men see their confidence levels decline, while women feel increasingly more assured. In other words, young, overconfident—but not necessarily more competent—men skip steps up that career ladder, only learning about their apparent limitations as they collect bumps and bruises on the way, and often arrive at retirement with a much humbler view of themselves.[17] On the other hand, women spend their youth suspecting themselves to be 'not as good' at anything, only to find out later in life that there is little they cannot do. If women statistically make better leaders by the age of sixty, imagine where they will end up if they would start out being confident in their knowledge, expertise, and ability to exercise the power to share it all with the world.

Not only are women perfectly capable, but they also naturally embody the contemporary trends in approach to leadership. Most people would agree that leadership expectations of today are quite different from those of even the most recent past. Subordinates in any professional industry seem to be less and less enamoured with tyrannical bosses who are given a pass to unleash temper tantrums because of their status as creative geniuses.

JoAnn Falletta, in an interview with Anna Edwards, draws parallels with corporate leadership:

> I think in the past, a leader was . . . someone who forced things to happen. This is probably true in the business world. The head of the company was all-knowing, all-powerful, and he told everyone what to do. Now, the corporate world has started to change . . . people are valued, [organizations] are doing team-building exercises, people are calling each other by their first names and . . . there is more interchange of information. . . . That has affected the orchestra world as well. [Musicians] do not come into the rehearsal afraid of the conductor. . . . You have to have the environment of respect, collegiality, cooperation.[18]

Another poll of professional musicians shows that competitiveness, forcefulness, an authoritative approach, or a dramatic flair stand low on the list of desired characteristics in a conductor. On the contrary, the overwhelming majority of musicians want to see a conductor who is dedicated (89 per cent), confident (96 per cent), prepared (97 per cent), and respectful (98 per cent).[19] These are exactly the qualities that women tend to possess more naturally, being praised for their warm, nurturing, participative approach to building relationships, but blamed for these exact same qualities a minute later, described as being 'too soft' to lead. Why do we remain so influenced by the unconscious bias that makes us automatically choose a man, even when there is an equally competent woman in the room?

Psychologist Tomas Chamorro-Premuzic argues that women are underrepresented in leadership because of our collective failure to let go of incompetent men. In his controversial TEDx talk "Why Do So Many Incompetent Men Become Leaders?" he suggests raising the bar for men instead of lowering standards for women. He believes that we often are unable to distinguish between confidence and competence, and our love for charismatic (i.e., charming and entertaining) individuals obscures the view of the fact that the best leaders in this world are quite humble.[20] Once we learn to manage our fascination with narcissism and place greater value on competence, humility, and integrity, the diversity and quality of leadership will improve tremendously. If we "expect the women to 'out-male the males' in order to advance in an inherently flawed system where bad guys win," the number of women leaders may increase, but the overall quality of leadership will continue to suffer.[21] I have been told by some of my teachers to never say to the orchestra "I do not know" and to never admit my mistakes, because it would not read as honesty and accountability but as weakness and lack of expertise. I was being taught to cultivate the exact same qualities that some men are being criticized for in leadership studies: self-promotion, taking credit for other people's achievements, and blaming others for your own mistakes. I needed to act more like an average autocrat to earn the respect of the orchestra, as absurd as it sounds.

An interesting approach to cultivating a self-image that is not powerful over others but brings power to a relationship through genuine interest in and connectedness to others is promoted by social psychologist Amy Cuddy, who also argues against the popular concept of 'charisma' and instead advocates for discovery of one's sense of presence. As opposed to charisma, which is "an intoxicating quality one has over other people," presence is less about how others see us, but more about how we see ourselves.[22] Cuddy demystifies the idea of presence, as it is not a "magical concept reached at the end of your life through a pilgrimage around the world," but instead "a state of being attuned to and able to comfortably express your true self, your values, beliefs, your skills, your passions."[23] This concept of presence closely relates to the previously described idea of a better leader who embodies competence, humility, and integrity, while also offering a more practical method of turning towards self, as a flip side of Chamorro-Premuzic's attempt to educate the general public that leadership qualities actually bring the best results and not just great entertainment. The number of studies that demonstrate women's not only equal but, in many ways, also superior talents and abilities in leadership is truly inspiring. Jack Zender, the CEO of a leadership development consultancy, reports that in a study of thousands of professional performance reviews, women outscored men on seventeen of the nineteen capabilities that were assigned to differentiate excellent leaders from average ones.[24] Janet Shibley Hyde works to discourage perpetuation of the "women are from Venus, men are from Mars" myth, which continues to cause considerable damage in the workplace and relationships, by presenting studies that show that men and women are quite similar in most psychological variables.[25] Nonetheless, the society, especially in some of the most conservative industries, continues to scrutinize a woman's every step with a magnifying glass, as if in a deliberate attempt to detect her shortcomings and discredit her efforts.

Women always had to be overqualified and perform far better than average just to be considered equal, because the desire to disqualify them from taking up a leadership role is sometimes so powerful that they are not allowed to make any mistakes. There is criticism that some of the women-only professional development programmes and events tend to focus on accusations of reverse discrimination, women's implied inability to compete in 'real' contests, or the isolation of women as an exotic species. However, I am convinced that whatever faults may be assigned to the Taki Alsop Conducting Fellowship, La Maestra Competition in France, or the Dallas Opera Hart Institute, they all provide their female participants with one of the most cherished of all learning experiences: the opportunity to try and fail while being yourself and to learn from it in a judgement-free zone, because in real life, women leaders rarely get a second chance.

## Women in Leadership

A conversation with a colleague at Carnegie Mellon University, which was prompted by an observation of a significant gender imbalance among graduate assistants who were allowed to teach their own classes, inspired Linda Babcock, a professor of economics, to conduct a study of starting salaries of Carnegie Mellon's recent graduates.[26] The study echoed the colleague's explanation of the lack of independent female teaching assistants. Nearly eight times more men than women had attempted to negotiate their starting salaries, even though all graduating students at the university are strongly encouraged to negotiate their job offers.[27] Babcock suggests that, with an inexplicable naivety, many women still expect life to be fair and patiently wait to be recognized for their arduous work. The causes for such a seemingly disengaged worldview are hidden in plain sight: the childhood memories and experiences of any traditionally raised girl will supply plenty of illustrations. Children observe and absorb even the tiniest, subconscious manifestations of gender rules and roles with staggering efficiency: daddy drives the car, has all the money, and fixes things.[28] Women have been able to vote and receive higher education for just a little over a century, while economic and political decision-making processes are still largely controlled by men. Women do not make life happen, life happens to them, so the concept of a woman being in charge may seem quite foreign, in some cultures more than others.[29] Women are taught to prioritize the needs and comforts of others over their own, so when it comes to asking people to do something for us, we often feel the need to apologize for being 'so demanding.' I strive to ban from my rehearsal lexicon the pleading "just one more time" in the apologetic tone that JoAnn Falletta often talks about in her interviews:

> You don't really know if it's going to be one more time. You might have to take it ten more times to achieve the result you envisioned. But if you . . . give the orchestra 'one more time' . . . that subtle kind of pleading on their goodwill [will make you feel better about requesting yet another repetition].[30]

It is even more difficult to 'inconvenience' others with your 'demands' when you are young: ageism is widespread and often spoils some of the most important early career-building experiences. Comments on one's youthful looks often imply expectations of promise and potential for a man, but sometimes brings suspicion of lack of experience or qualifications for a woman. Men get wiser as they age; women just get, well, old.[31] As I was editing this paragraph, CNN ran a story about a female news anchor who was fired for letting her hair go grey, while John Berman commented on once being told to dye his hair grey because it would make him look more distinguished.[32] Ageism goes hand in hand with objectification: women are much more likely to be judged on their physical appearance, and, especially on the podium, could be ridiculed for being not feminine enough, or chastised for being too attractive and therefore a distraction for the men in the orchestra and in the audience.

The next statement has been a punchline of many jokes, but in this case, it is a question of preserving dignity and the sense of personal identity in the workplace: "I have nothing to wear!" Everyone agrees that a woman should look 'professional' on the podium, but no one knows exactly what it would look like. The world of business and politics seems to have it figured out by adopting, with varying degrees of fashionability and appropriateness, a trouser suit for the female form. This is illustrated by Beard with a picture of two prominent women politicians as they greet each other while wearing nearly identical box-like dark suits and modest heels, and a witty caption underneath: "Angela Merkel and Hillary Clinton spotted together in their female politicians' uniform."[33] Many women attempt to treat a tuxedo as a uniform and have their suits custom-made. Some people try to neutralize their gender, so the orchestra and the audience only focus on the music. Other women insist on remaining unapologetically feminine, make a point to never wear trousers on the podium, and risk not being taken seriously. Another survey shows that 47 per cent of musicians believe that a woman's dress affects the orchestra's perception of the leadership she provides, as opposed to 26 per cent for a male conductor's attire, as if for women, sexuality and attractiveness will be primary and talent will always be secondary in the viewer's minds.[34] Everything matters: the hair must not be too big, footwear should keep you balanced, lower-pitched tone of voice is preferred, as it appears more trustworthy and inspires confidence, and a woman must converse in a way that will make her sound polite and considerate but not apologetic, strong but not overbearing.[35]

It is difficult to strike the perfect balance, and women in leadership often find themselves in a double bind. In a recent study, interviews with sixty-four senior women leaders uncovered a number of paradoxes that these women confront while navigating day-to-day work situations: they are expected to be demanding yet caring, authoritative yet participative, maintaining distance yet being approachable.[36] The article offers strategies for managing these tensions, but concludes that in the long run, what must change is the societal expectations for what it means to be a woman and what it takes to lead. The issue of women receiving unexplained negative or conflicting feedback is another catch-22. Reports from a large study of performance evaluations conducted in the military show that while objective measurements, such as academic grades or fitness records, show no signs of gender discrimination, the subjective evaluations clearly assign the women significantly more negative attributes.[37] The nearly identical length of the lists of the negative qualities for women and the positive for men is quite striking: we seem to be on a mission to discredit women with the same level of passion for which we are eager to give men a second chance. Women, on the other hand, have a tough time trying to figure out how to be more assertive without appearing aggressive, or to remain warm and likeable without losing their professional credibility.

One summer, while visiting family in Saint Petersburg, I met up with a friend from the university and we went to a concert of choral music. One choir, two conductors: a man and a woman, both professionals, both equally capable. After the performance, as we were sharing our impressions, my companion said, "Any ensemble just sounds better with a guy, don't you think?" and followed it up with a power pose, both arms in the air. I could not agree and was so struck by her comment that this brief conversation keeps resurfacing in my memory year after year. She did not say what exactly she liked about that male conductor, or what piece she found particularly effective. She did not have any specific criticism on the woman conductor's performance either. What baffled me was not the fact that she liked the male conductor more, that would be perfectly fine, but that it was a blanket statement, with no constructive feedback or criticism.

My friend's illustrative power-posing could suggest that the male conductor must have mastered some technique that would be inaccessible for a woman. However, no textbook has ever described conducting gestures as gendered tools of creative communication, though social conventions have attached permanent labels of feminine or masculine to nearly everything we do, and there appear to be no guidelines on how to be strong and powerful in a feminine way. Edwards mentions a compelling study that looked at trained movement gender recognition of female and male orchestra conductors.[38] Each conducting participant was equipped with seventeen full-body markers and asked to perform an array of conducting gestures, in addition to walking and standing. The movements were recorded with a motion capture system and presented to the viewers as black dots on a white screen. While the viewers were generally able to determine the gender of the conductor in the walking and static images, with the active conducting images gender recognition dropped to chance level.[39] It is clear that our attachment to traditional norms of gender expression is so powerful that even while most people agree that women are perfectly capable of conveying strength through gestures, we still see it as something inappropriate, unbecoming for a woman.[40] Vasily Petrenko's statement on how "a cute girl on the podium means that musicians think about other things," which he later tried to attribute to mistranslation and misunderstanding, only confirms that no matter how effective a woman's technique is, it must not interfere with her attractiveness.[41] In attempts to do some damage control, Petrenko tried to explain that he was only talking about the situation in Russia, though this does not make his original statement any less appalling. Obviously, he is not wrong, and Russia is not the only country whose culture objectifies women, but we must not accept such behaviour as a norm, let alone use it as a legitimate reason for denying a woman any form of personal, professional, or creative expression.

**Perception of Women**

One of my colleagues has a small daughter, who has been watching him conduct since she was a baby, and at the age of three was watching live-streamed opera productions from the Met with genuine fascination. Once a family friend asked her: "Aren't you looking forward to one day conducting opera yourself, like your daddy?" The child replied, without a hint of disappointment, as if stating the obvious: "Oh no, girls don't do that." No one has ever told her so, but since not a single opera production that she watched featured a female conductor, the child assumed that this is how things stand and there is nothing to be done about it. My colleague was so saddened by this incident that he shared this story on a professional forum, as a lesson to all of us that even in the most progressive and encouraging environments the lack of representation and mentorship is obvious.

Recently, I was invited to conduct at a regional high school orchestra festival. The festival director was excited when I happily accepted the invitation and said: "We just recently noticed that we have not had a woman conductor in a very, very long time." A participant in an academic study talks about being extremely annoyed by tokenism at the beginning of her career and would even refuse invitations that were focused solely on her gender that would make no mention of her artistic or pedagogical accomplishments, but with time she came to realize that we must do it for the students.[42] Otherwise, some of them will have zero representation. We must remember that when we step on the podium in front of young ensembles, we may not only empower and inspire the girls, but also demonstrate to the entire group that leaders come in all shapes, sizes, and genders, hoping with time to normalize the still novel idea of a woman in charge.

The concept of fluidity of gender expression may still require time to gain acceptance in some cultures, but even from the viewpoint of duality of gender we must strive to enrich our descriptions of a man and a woman. 'Strong versus weak' just does not cut it in the twenty-first century. The autocratic style of leadership is a thing of the past. As Chamorro-Premuzic reminds us, we are not living in medieval times: if we are encouraging our male leaders to empathize, why do we keep insisting that the women are too nice, too warm, too caring to lead?[43] There should not be feminine and masculine conducting gestures, because every gesture must serve a creative purpose and not be implemented only to 'appear' a certain way. A woman can make a fist gesture, or stand with her feet apart, and none of these gestures will make her any less of a woman if they are true to her own nature, however delicate or exuberant it may be. Yuri Temirkanov's infamous statement "The essence of the conductor's profession is strength; the essence of a woman is weakness"[44] just does not hold water: there is more to leadership than strength, and the essence of a woman—or of a man, for that matter—is whatever they discover it to be. There also were Jorma Panula's demeaning comments on how female conductors are "making faces, sweating and fussing, but it is not getting any better—only worse!" followed by a puzzling invitation to come to his masterclass and 'try,' but only with more 'feminine' repertoire, such as Debussy.[45] This obsession with archaic gender roles discriminates not only the women who are 'not feminine enough' or 'too pushy' and 'bossy,' but also the men who do not demonstrate enough 'strength.'

## Conclusion

This chapter does not aim to break any new ground, and some of the issues raised may seem no longer relevant because we have come a long way, but I am convinced that the conversation must continue until announcements of appointments of female (black, queer) conductors (airline pilots, cruise ship captains) will no longer focus solely on the gender of the winning candidate but highlight their professional accomplishments. Many of us may feel perfectly safe and free from bias in our progressive mini-habitats of an empowering workplace or a supportive family, but the subtle—and not so subtle—echoes of deep-rooted misogyny keep ringing out of centuries-deep wells of gender discrimination. In 2022, in my safe haven of a small liberal arts university, I never expect to hear the claim that Marianna Martines's music "is not as good as Mozart's, so we should not spend time studying it in class," but I do.

We all must continue to work on improving our definitions and methods of evaluation of power, manifestations of authority, and measures of leadership success; learn to accept a wide variety of gender expressions and approaches to partnership and collaboration. We all must take responsibility for our actions, give second and third chances, and offer feedback that aims to strengthen, not to discredit. Without a deliberate social effort, the success stories will continue to be just that: individual breakthroughs without any systemic progress, a convenient cover-up that allows us to say, "it is possible!" while maintaining control over who gets to climb to the top and preventing too many minorities from 'making it.' Let us focus our energy on increasing minority representation, and figuring out our true genuine selves, with a billion different gestures for *forte*, instead of trying to fit into a traditionally male mould of expression and presentation. For inspiration, I encourage everyone to subscribe to Israeli conductor Talia Ilan's #OneConductorADay posts on Facebook or Twitter (X) that feature a different female conductor every day. An astounding collage that answers the question "Where is everybody?" with undeniable clarity: we are right here. The world only needs to make an effort to notice.

## Notes

1 "Announcing Nathalie Stutzmann," Atlanta Symphony Orchestra, October 2021, https://www.aso.org/announcements/announcing-nathalie-stutzmann. The title phrase "You are now one of the boys" is part of an infamous statement made by composer George Chadwick to Amy Cheney Beach. Cited in "Women Composers: Let's Talk About Amy Beach," Dear Miss Purdy, published 31 December 2019, https://dearmisspurdy.wordpress.com/2019/12/31/women-composers-lets-talk-about-amy-beach/.
2 Antonio C. Cuyler, Evan Linett, and Kare Yair, "Racial/Ethnic and Gender Diversity in the Orchestra Field in 2023," League of American Orchestras, June 2023, https://americanorchestras.org/racial-ethnic-and-gender-diversity-in-the-orchestra-field-in-2023/.
3 Anna Edwards, "Gender and the Symphonic Conductor" (PhD diss., University of Washington, 2015), 122.
4 A Mexican conductor most recently appointed the principal guest conductor of Milan Symphony Orchestra.
5 Mary Beard, *Women & Power: A Manifesto* (New York: Liveright Publishing Corporation, 2017), xi.
6 Beard, *Women & Power*, 4.
7 Beard, *Women & Power*, 19.
8 Beard, *Women & Power*, 17.
9 Beard, *Women & Power*, 52.
10 In the United Kingdom only, looking only for cartoons to avoid polluting the findings with images of personalities who may currently be on the news.
11 Beard, *Women & Power*, 53.
12 Veronika Dudarova (1916–2009) led the Moscow State Symphony Orchestra for sixty years.
13 Beard, *Women & Power*, 59.
14 Beard, *Women & Power*, 62.
15 Beard, *Women & Power*, 75.
16 Jack Zenger and Joseph Folkman, "Women Score Higher Than Men in Most Leadership Skills," *Harvard Business Review*, 25 June 2019, https://hbr.org/2019/06/research-women-score-higher-than-men-in-most-leadership-skills.
17 Zenger and Folkman, "Leadership Skills."
18 Edwards, "Gender and the Symphonic Conductor," 104–05.
19 Edwards, "Gender and the Symphonic Conductor," 107.

20 Tomas Chamorro-Premuzic, "Why Do So Many Incompetent Men Become Leaders?" TEDx University of Nevada, published 26 March 2019, YouTube, video, https://youtu.be/zeAEFEXvcBg.
21 Chamorro-Premuzic, "Incompetent Men."
22 "Amy Cuddy and Susan Cain on Presence," The 92nd Street Y, New York, YouTube, video, published 22 January 2016, https://youtu.be/AFllLB6yQrU.
23 "Amy Cuddy and Susan Cain on Presence."
24 Zenger and Folkman, "Leadership Skills."
25 Janet Shibley Hyde, "The Gender Similarities Hypothesis," *American Phycologist* 60, no. 6 (September 2005): 581–92, doi:10.1037/0003–066X.60.6.581.
26 Linda Babcock and Sara Laschever, *Women Don't Ask: Negotiation and the Gender Divide* (Princeton: Princeton University Press, 2021).
27 Babcock and Laschever, *Women Don't Ask*, 2.
28 Babcock and Laschever, *Women Don't Ask*, 28.
29 Babcock and Laschever, *Women Don't Ask*, 24–25.
30 Edwards, "Gender and the Symphonic Conductor," 78.
31 Stephanie Deluca, "The Socio-Cultural Reproduction Experiences of Women College Band Directors" (PhD diss., Florida State University, 2021), 38.
32 "CNN Anchors and Reporters React to TV Anchor's Apparent Firing over Hair," CNN Business, video, accessed 16 September 2022, https://www.cnn.com/videos/media/2022/08/30/canada-tv-anchor-lisa-laflamme-firing-gray-hair-newday-vpx.cnn/video/playlists/business-media/.
33 Beard, *Women & Power*, 54–55.
34 Edwards, "Gender and the Symphonic Conductor," 68, 70.
35 Casey A. Klofstad, Rindy C. Anderson, and Susan Peters, "Sounds Like a Winner: Voice Pitch Influences Perception of Leadership Capacity in Both Men and Women," *Proceedings of the Royal Society B: Biological Sciences* 269, no. 1738 (7 July 2012): 2698–704, https://doi: 10.1098/rspb.2012.0311.
36 Wei Zheng, Ronit Kark, and Alyson Meister, "How Women Manage the Gendered Norms of Leadership," *Harvard Business Review*, 28 November 2018, https://hbr.org/2018/11/how-women-manage-the-gendered-norms-of-leadership.
37 David G. Smith, Judith E. Rosenstein, and Margaret C. Nikolov, "The Different Words We Use to Describe Male and Female Leaders," Harvard Business Review, 25 May 2018, https://hbr.org/2018/05/the-different-words-we-use-to-describe-male-and-female-leaders.
38 Edwards, "Gender and the Symphonic Conductor," 83.
39 Edwards, "Gender and the Symphonic Conductor," 83.
40 Ninety-one per cent of professional musicians surveyed by Anna Edwards agree or strongly agree with this statement. Edwards, "Gender and the Symphonic Conductor," 90.
41 Jamie Wetherbe, "Orchestras react better to men, conductor Vasily Petrenko says," in *Los Angeles Times*, 3 September 2013, https://www.latimes.com/entertainment/arts/culture/la-et-cm-orchestras-vasily-petrenko-20130902-story.html.
42 Deluca, "Women College Band Directors," 45.
43 Chamorro-Premuzic, "Incompetent Men."
44 Quoted in Alex Ross, "Women, Gays, and Classical Music," *The New Yorker*, 3 October 2013, https://www.newyorker.com/culture/culture-desk/women-gays-and-classical-music.
45 Norman Lebrecht, "Women conductors? It's not getting any better, only worse," *Slipped Disk*, 31 March 2014, https://slippedisc.com/2014/03/women-conductors-its-not-getting-any-better-only-worse/.

# 19

## CRACKING OPEN THE CONDUCTING CLOSET

Shared Experiences among Queer Conductors

*Thomas Dickey*

When asked about the struggles of being an openly queer conductor, Michael Morgan lamented that "you get accustomed to constructing your own world because there are not a lot of clear paths to follow and not a lot of people that are just like you."[1] To date, to my knowledge, there are no conducting workshops, masterclasses, fellowships, or competitions available only to queer conductors, nor has it been 'hip and trendy' for orchestras to purposefully hire queer conductors who live their lives openly. As this chapter will show, however, there have been many gay and lesbian conductors going as far back as the Baroque era. Well through the twentieth century, when being queer was against the law in many countries around the world, these conductors were encouraged, if not pressured, to 'hide their lifestyles,' due in large part to pressure from politically right-leaning, socially conservative arts organizations, the mainstream music press, and the music recording industry, whose consumers tended to be straight, cisgender, middle-class, middle-aged men.[2]

From the first known queer conductors in music history to openly queer conductors in the twentieth and twenty-first centuries, this chapter will consider the difficulties that queer conductors face when it comes to leadership and authority, drawing upon my own lived experiences as one of very few openly gay conductors leading graduate-level orchestral conducting programmes in North America in the process. I have participated in over twenty orchestral conducting competitions, masterclasses, and workshops through the United States, Europe, and Asia, none of which was led by an openly queer conducting teacher. With this chapter, I hope to shed light on and draw attention to the LGBTQ+ conductors

DOI: 10.4324/9781003299660-24

who have helped to crack open the closet door for the next generations of queer conductors.

## Queer

The word 'queer' entered the English language as early as 1508 and was used to describe someone who was strange, odd, peculiar, or eccentric in appearance or character.[3] By the late 1800s, the word had acquired a connotation of sexual deviance, specifically linked to men who were engaged in same-sex relationships. One hundred years later, some members of the lesbian, gay, bisexual, and transgender (LGBT) community—particularly political activists—had started to reclaim the word. By the twenty-first century, 'queer' has come to refer to a wide spectrum of gender identities and sexual orientations that are counter to the heteronormative mainstream. This catch-all term includes many people, including those who do not identify as being exclusively straight, as well as gender non-binary and gender-expansive identities. Note well: not all members of the LGBT community approve of this reclaiming of the word 'queer,' primarily because of the social and political radicalism with which the word has become associated, and perceived divisions along the lines of politics, age, race, and class within the LGBT community.[4]

A word must be said about nomenclature. The initialism LGBT has been in use since the late 1980s. In more recent years, 'Q' has been added to be more inclusive of those who identify as queer or are questioning their sexual orientation, gender identity, and expression. Another common variant is LGBTQIA, with the 'I' standing for 'intersex' and the 'A' standing for 'asexual.' In addition, '2S' is sometimes added to refer to 'two-spirit' individuals, a term that is used by some Indigenous people who identify as a third gender. To avoid the 'alphabet soup' problem, while also being as inclusive as possible, LGBTQ+ is the most popular version, with the '+' sign being used to encompass the myriad sexual orientations and gender identities.[5]

## Early Queer Conductors

The Italian-born French musician and dancer Jean-Baptiste Lully (1632–87) spent most of his career working as the royal composer of instrumental music for King Louis XIV of France. He married Madeleine Lambert (1643–1720), the daughter of the French singer, composer, and theorbist Michel Lambert, in 1662, and would go on to father six children with her. Despite all this, he had many extramarital affairs with both women and men. The king almost always forgave Lully because of their decades-long friendship, even though he was offended by these encounters. In 1685, however, just two years before his death, Lully was involved in a scandal with a young man who was being trained as a music page in the royal service. After a police raid, the young boy was sent away to a monastery and Lully fell out of favour with the king. Oddly enough, it was Lully's occupation as a conductor that led to his death, having succumbed to a fatal gangrene infection in his foot that had been inflicted by his own conducting stick.[6]

In recent years, new light has been shed concerning the possibility of other queer conductors and composers of the Baroque. For example, scholars such as Gary C. Thomas and Ellen T. Harris have posited that George Frideric Handel (1685–1759) might have been a homosexual and/or was a member of social circles whose patrons were themselves homosexuals.[7] Moving in some of the same circles as Handel, Italian violinist, composer, and conductor Arcangelo Corelli (1653–1713) is now believed to have been a discreet homosexual, seeing as he never married, lived closely with male friends, and even once served Queen Christina Alexandra of Sweden, a lesbian royal, to whom his first publication, the Twelve Trio Sonatas, Op. 1, is dedicated.[8]

A Russian national treasure and a composer known for writing soaring melodies and colourful orchestrations in some of the greatest symphonies, concertos, operas, and ballets of all time, Pyotr Ilyich Tchaikovsky (1840–93) was also a queer conductor. On his first European tour in December 1888, Tchaikovsky conducted orchestras in Germany, the Czech Republic, France, and England. At the inauguration of Carnegie Hall on 5 May 1891, Tchaikovsky was invited to conduct his *Marche Solennelle* as part of the five-day Opening Week Festival. On 16 October 1893, he conducted the premiere of his sixth symphony in St Petersburg, Russia. Despite his international celebrity status, the queer composer–conductor felt great pressure from both society and the Russian government to keep his sexual orientation a secret. In letters to his brother Modest, Tchaikovsky wrote about his sexuality that brought him both joy and despair.[9] Social conventions in nineteenth-century Russia prevented him from living openly with a male partner. The closest that Tchaikovsky came to revealing his sexual orientation with the public was the *Symphonie Pathétique*, which he dedicated to his lover Vladimir Davydov. Sadly, only nine days after the premiere of this symphonic masterpiece, Tchaikovsky died at the age of fifty-three. Although the official cause of death at the time was reported as cholera, many questions and theories about the queer conductor and composer's death remain.

## Queer Conductors in the Early Twentieth Century

The early twentieth century saw several queer conductors whose sexual orientation and gender identity jeopardized their careers and forced them to exercise great caution both on and off the podium. Benjamin Britten (1913–76) was one of the great English composers of the twentieth century and would also go on to conduct some of the United Kingdom's foremost orchestras. He made several recordings of his own music, as well as music by Walton, Grainger, and Elgar, conducting either from the piano or the podium. Britten stands out among his queer contemporaries because he lived openly for thirty-five years with his partner Peter Pears (1910–86), an English tenor for whom Britten wrote several operatic roles and song cycles. That homosexuality was illegal in England until 1967 makes his appointment to the Order of Merit by Queen Elizabeth II in 1965, and the letter of condolence that she wrote to Pears when Britten died, even more significant.[10]

A contemporary of Benjamin Britten and a fellow queer composer–conductor who lived his life openly, Aaron Copland (1900–90) earned the nickname 'the Dean of American Composers.' While in Paris at the Fontainebleau School of Music, he briefly studied conducting in 1921, but for the most part, Copland was a self-taught conductor. After receiving some words of encouragement from Igor Stravinsky, Copland began conducting major orchestras in the United States and abroad in performances of his own works in the 1940s and the works of other composers in the 1950s. Regarding his sexuality, he refrained from making public comments and was a very private person. According to the composer's biographer Howard Pollack, Copland understood and accepted his sexuality at an early age.[11] In his letters, postcards, and telegrams, one gets a glimpse of the intimate relationships that Copland had with talented, younger men who were in the arts, such as photographer Victor Kraft, artist Alvin Ross, and pianist Paul Moor.[12] Even after the romance ended, most of them remained close friends of Copland.

Greek conductor, pianist, and composer Dimitri Mitropoulos (1896–1960) is an example of a queer conductor in the early part of the twentieth century whose personal life and professional conducting career were negatively affected by his sexuality. In 1930, he conducted the Berlin Philharmonic from the keyboard in a performance of Sergei Prokofiev's Piano Concerto No. 3, making him one of the first modern conductors to do so. Shortly after making his North American debut with the Boston Symphony Orchestra in 1936, he became music director and conductor of the Minneapolis Symphony Orchestra (now the Minnesota Orchestra), a post he would go on to hold for twelve years before beginning his relationship with the New York Philharmonic in 1949. A talented conductor, often conducting from memory and with no baton, Mitropoulos was frequently criticized for his musical interpretations and his being gay. In the classical music world at the time, his sexual orientation was an open secret, and he never felt the need for a 'cosmetic marriage.'[13] In

1958, Mitropoulos was replaced by a young conductor who was thought to fit the more proper, masculine, heteronormative image that audiences at the time expected. Ironically, that conductor was Leonard Bernstein, who also was queer and, according to rumours, had a relationship with Mitropoulos.[14]

Arguably the most successful American conductor and composer of the twentieth century, Bernstein (1918–90) became music director of the New York Philharmonic in 1958 and would go on to help transform classical music by creating a distinctly American idiom in a tradition that had been dominated by European composers. However, considering the conservative nature of most boards of directors and advice he had received from his mentors and friends, Bernstein thought that marrying a woman would help him secure a conducting position with a major American orchestra. In 1951, Bernstein married Felicia Montealegre, a beautiful stage and television actor from Chile who was working in New York. That they had three children together led many to assume that Bernstein was bisexual. Felicia, however, was aware of Bernstein's same-sex desires, indicating in a letter to him that:

> *First*: We are not committed to a life sentence—nothing is really irrevocable, not even marriage (though I used to think so).
> *Second*: You are a homosexual and may never change—you don't admit to the possibility of a double life, but if your peace of mind, your health, your whole nervous system depends on a certain sexual pattern what can you do?
> *Third*: I am willing to accept you as you are, without being a martyr or sacrificing myself on the L.B. altar. (I happen to love you very much—this may be a disease and if it is, what better cure?) Let's try and see what happens if you are free to do as you like, but without guilt and confession, please![15]

Bernstein would go on to have relationships with men both during his marriage and after his wife's death in 1978, thus making him the first openly queer conductor in the twentieth century whose career did not suffer because of his sexuality. Described in his *New York Times* obituary as "one of the most prodigiously talented and successful musicians in American history," Bernstein received countless awards, including Emmy, Grammy, Tony, and lifetime achievement awards, and a Kennedy Center Honor.[16]

## Notable Lesbian Conductors

Ethel Smyth (1858–1944) was the most prominent lesbian composer-conductor in Britain in the late nineteenth and early twentieth centuries. She was also actively involved in the women's suffrage movement. As a composer of orchestral music, choral works, operas, chamber music, works for piano, and vocal works, Smyth often received mixed (and sexist) reviews. Either her music was too masculine for a "lady composer" or it lacked feminine charm.[17] In spite of all this, she would go on to become the first woman composer to be awarded a damehood. Like Britten, Smyth lived her life openly and had several relationships with very famous women. Unlike her queer contemporary, however, Smyth was not given many opportunities to conduct either her own music or works by other composers.

Frieda Belinfante (1904–95) was a Dutch Jewish lesbian conductor and cellist. Born into a musical family, she studied at the Amsterdam Conservatory and then began her conducting career directing chamber ensembles. In 1937, she was invited by the Concertgebouw management to form and conduct a chamber orchestra, a post she held until 1941, thus making her the first woman in Europe to be the conductor of a professional orchestra. Active in the Dutch Resistance, she helped other Jews escape the Netherlands before she emigrated to the United States after the war. Belinfante settled in Orange County, California, where she founded and conducted the Orange County Philharmonic Orchestra, in addition to joining the music faculty at the University of California, Los Angeles (UCLA), where she taught cello and conducting. In 1962, however, her contract with the Philharmonic was not renewed. In an oral history interview for the United States Holocaust Memorial Museum in 1994, Belinfante notes that rumours about her sexuality and gender led to her dismissal from the orchestra.[18] Fifteen years later, however, Orange County recognized her accomplishments and musical contributions to the region by declaring 19 February Frieda Belinfante Day.

Kay Gardner (1941–2002) was a queer American conductor, composer, flautist, recording artist, and sound healer, who once famously said: "Conducting, especially orchestral conducting, is the last stronghold of the musical patriarchy."[19] A celebrated advocate of women's music, she was also one of the first musicians to sue a professional orchestra. In the 1980s, Gardner sued the Bangor Symphony Orchestra for sex discrimination after she applied for their music director position and learned that members of the orchestra had been asked how they felt about playing under the baton of a woman conductor. Although the lawsuit was unsuccessful, she would go on to help produce the first openly lesbian classical recording called *Lavender Jane Loves Women* and to co-found the New England Women's Symphony.

## Twenty-First-Century Queer Conductors

Overcoming great physical difficulties while living openly as a gay man, Sir Jeffrey Tate (1943–2017) enjoyed a distinguished international conducting career. He was born with spina bifida and suffered from spinal curvature, breathing problems, and compressed internal organs, among other illnesses. He studied medicine at the University of Cambridge and worked at St Thomas's Hospital in London in the 1960s before studying music at the London Opera Centre and joining the staff of Covent Garden Opera in 1971. Over the next six years, he worked with Carlos Kleiber, Sir Colin Davis, and Sir Georg Solti, and assisted Pierre Boulez, Herbert von Karajan, and James Levine, among others. Tate would go on to conduct some of the finest orchestras and opera companies in the United Kingdom and Europe, and to make recordings of Haydn's later symphonies and Mozart's symphonies and piano concertos. While assisting John Pritchard at the Cologne Opera in 1977, he met his partner, geomorphologist Klaus Kuhlemann, and they were legally married in 2010.[20] As a queer, disabled musician, Tate saw himself as an outsider, noting in a 1998 interview that "the gay world is immensely hung up with physical perfection for some curious reason.... Therefore, being disabled in that world is harder."[21] He was appointed a Commander of the Most Excellent Order of the British Empire (CBE) in 1990 and knighted in 2017.

An openly gay conductor, pianist, and composer, Michael Tilson Thomas (b. 1944) won the Koussevitzky Prize at Tanglewood in 1968 and was soon appointed assistant conductor of the Boston Symphony Orchestra when he was just twenty-five years old. In addition to conducting positions with the Buffalo Philharmonic Orchestra, Los Angeles Philharmonic, and London Symphony Orchestra, he was the music director of the San Francisco Symphony Orchestra (SFSO) from 1995 to 2020, thus making him "the first gay conductor to achieve such prominence without masking or hiding his sexuality."[22] With the SFSO, Tilson Thomas pushed his audiences by celebrating openly queer composers and performers, and commissioning works by openly queer composers. David Del Tredici's *Gay Life* for Baritone and Orchestra (2001), a six-movement song cycle that was commissioned by Tilson Thomas, is a setting of texts that address gay lives and gay issues—particularly the AIDS epidemic—written by gay writers Allen Ginsberg, Paul Monette, Thom Gunn, W.H. Kidde, and Michael D. Calhoun. Tilson Thomas is a highly decorated conductor, earning many honours and awards, such as being named an Officer in the French Order of Arts and Letters, a member of the American Academy of Arts and Sciences, Musician of the Year and Conductor of the Year in Musical America, *Gramophone* magazine's Artist of the Year, the National Medal of Arts, induction into the American Academy of Arts and Letters, the Kennedy Center Honors, and eleven Grammy Awards.[23]

Marin Alsop (b. 1956) is a trailblazer for both women and queer conductors around the globe. In 2007, she made history as the first woman—and the first queer woman, by extension—to lead a major American orchestra, when she became the music director of the Baltimore Symphony Orchestra, a post that she held until 2021. She is also the first (queer) woman to be the principal conductor of the Bournemouth Symphony Orchestra in England, São Paulo State Symphony Orchestra in Brazil, and the Vienna Radio Symphony Orchestra. Originally trained as a classical violinist, Alsop attended the Tanglewood Music Center in 1989, where she won the Koussevitzky Prize and met Leonard Bernstein, her hero and mentor. Since 1990, Alsop has been with her long-term partner Kristin Jurkscheit, a former professional horn player and now the executive director of the Taki Alsop Conducting Fellowship. When asked about her sexual orientation and the challenges she faced early in her career, Alsop said in a recent interview:

> Well, I think I had so many—what would I call them?—strikes against me. I mean, of course, I was young. I was a woman. And I was American. That was already, like, you know, three strikes and you're out. And then, you know, being gay and, you know, feeling that I didn't really fit in anywhere, you know, I think I had so many things to carry that I just put a backpack on and said, OK, just fill it up, and let's go.[24]

Another trailblazing conductor and protégé of Leonard Bernstein, Michael Morgan (1957–2021) was an openly gay Black conductor. After serving as assistant conductor to Leonard Slatkin with the St Louis Symphony Orchestra, and Georg Solti and Daniel Barenboim with the Chicago Symphony Orchestra, Morgan held conducting positions with the Oakland East Bay Symphony Orchestra, Oakland Youth Orchestra, Sacramento Philharmonic, Bear Valley Music Festival, Gateways Music Festival, and the Festival Opera in Walnut Creek, California. He taught at the San Francisco Conservatory of Music and the Tanglewood Music Center and guest conducted many major orchestras throughout the United States, Canada, and South America. In an interview with the *Georgia Voice*, Morgan was asked about the classical music industry, the profession of orchestral conducting, and the intersections of race and sexual orientation. His thoughts, though several years before Alsop's interview, have much in common with hers: "Being a classical musician, being a conductor, being black, being gay—all of these things put you on the outside, and each one puts you a little further out than the last one . . . you get accustomed to constructing your own world because there are not a lot of clear paths to follow and not a lot of people that are just like you."[25]

Without question, Yannick Nézet-Séguin (b. 1975) is one of the most visible and most popular conductors today. The Canadian conductor and pianist is the music director of the Metropolitan Opera and the Philadelphia

Orchestra, in addition to being the honorary conductor of the Rotterdam Philharmonic Orchestra and an honorary member of the Chamber Orchestra of Europe. Nézet-Séguin is the first openly gay conductor of the Met, succeeding James Levine (1943–2021), a closeted conductor, whom the press claimed had no personal life and whose career was eventually ended by allegations of sexual misconduct.[26] Nézet-Séguin's position with the Philadelphia Orchestra also makes him the first openly gay conductor of one of the Big Five orchestras in America.[27] Living openly with his partner Pierre Tourville—a violist, singer, and administrator—when asked by the *New York Times* about being an openly gay conductor, Nézet-Séguin said: "We can be examples, in a way, to inspire young musicians who fear that this is going to be a problem in their profession and career advancement. . . . I want to embrace that role more and more."[28] Nézet-Séguin continues to break preconceived notions of what it means to be an effective artistic leader in the twenty-first century, most recently in June 2022, when he and the Philadelphia Orchestra performed a first-ever Pride concert that celebrated the region's LGBTQ+ community. The concert featured the openly queer violinist Blake Pouliot, the Philadelphia Gay Men's Chorus, and Martha Graham Cracker (Philadelphia's own Drag Queen King).

**Final Thoughts**

Despite the trailblazing efforts of several queer pioneers, orchestral conducting remains dominated by straight white men. The classical music industry continues to struggle with finding, nurturing, and celebrating artistic leaders who do not fit the traditional heteronormative mould. The life of a conductor is inherently lonely, with countless hours spent studying scores and preparing for rehearsals. At a time when so many people live their lives openly for all the world to see, quite literally, on social media platforms such as Instagram, Facebook, and TikTok, it has been my experience that queer conductors are often reserved when it comes to sharing their stories, be it in rehearsal with an orchestra, with the audience at a concert, or on social media. Always being mindful of their word choices, posture, and mannerisms, many queer conductors are hyper-sensitive in interviews, auditions, rehearsals, and pre-concert talks. From what they choose to share in concert programme biographies to the photos they post online, and the successes and anniversaries they choose to celebrate, I regularly encounter queer conductors who want to appear confident and inspiring for the musicians, all the while not acting or sounding either too masculine or too feminine.

Leading a major orchestra while living their lives openly and honestly was pie in the sky for most queer conductors until only recently. Well into the twentieth century, many queer conductors worked tirelessly to conceal their true identities for the sake of their own professional ambitions. Yet at a time when being outed would have meant career suicide, and worse, there have been queer conductors who managed to achieve success in the form of prestigious conducting positions, awards, and honours. Historically, major performing arts organizations, the press, and the recording industry tried to whitewash the sexual orientations of its own celebrated leaders. For some conductors, their queerness was a strike against them in an already hyper-competitive field. Thanks to openly queer conductors, such as Michael Tilson Thomas, the proverbial closet burst open and, for the first time in classical music, queer voices were thrust into the limelight and their stories were told. Under the baton of leaders such as Yannick Nézet-Séguin, queer pride has been celebrated in the concert hall and professional orchestras have become vehicles for social justice, diversity, equity, and inclusion. As batons are passed onto the next generation of queer conductors, one can only hope that the outdated concept of leadership will be forever changed by the queer icons who have paved the way and changed the world of classical music.

## Notes

1 Eric Politzer, "Black Gay Conductor Heads to Atlanta Symphony," Georgia Voice, published 15 March 2013, https://thegavoice.com/news/atlanta/starting-from-outside-michael-morgan-thrives-in-symphony-2.
2 Geoffrey W. Bateman, "Conductors," in *The Queer Encyclopedia of Music, Dance, & Musical Theater*, ed. Claude J. Summers (San Francisco: Cleis Press, 2004), 55.
3 *Oxford English Dictionary*, online, s.v. "queer, adj.[1]", accessed 1 July 2023, https://www.oed.com/search/dictionary/?scope=Entries&q=queer.
4 Phillip M. Ayoub and David Paternotte, *LGBT Activism and the Making of Europe: A Rainbow Europe?* (London: Palgrave Macmillan, 2014), 137–38.
5 For more information about terms and initialisms used by the queer community, consult the Human Rights Campaign's "Glossary of Terms," updated 31 May 2023, https://www.hrc.org/resources/glossary-of-terms.
6 George E. Haggarty, ed., *Gay History and Cultures: An Encyclopaedia* (New York: Routledge, 2012), 553–54.
7 Gary C. Thomas, "Was George Frideric Handel Gay?" in *Queering the Pitch: The New Gay and Lesbian Musicology*, 2nd ed. (New York: Routledge, 2006), 155–204; Ellen T. Harris, *Handel as Orpheus: Voice and Desire in the Chamber Cantatas* (Cambridge, MA: Harvard University Press, 2001), 1–24.
8 Graham Abbott, "The Life and Work of Arcangelo Corelli," Graham's Music, blog, updated 4 August 2021, https://www.grahamsmusic.net/post/the-life-and-work-of-arcangelo-corelli.
9 Marina Kostalevsky, ed., *The Tchaikovsky Papers: Unlocking the Family Archive* (New Haven: Yale University Press, 2018).
10 Paul Kildea, *Benjamin Britten: A Life in the Twentieth Century* (London: Penguin Books, 2013).

11 Howard Pollack, "The Dean of Gay American Composers," *American Music* 18, no. 1 (Spring 2000): 39–49, https://doi.org/10.2307/3052389.
12 Elizabeth B. Crist and Wayne Shirley, eds., *The Selected Correspondence of Aaron Copland* (New Haven: Yale University Press, 2008).
13 Joseph Horowitz, *Classical Music in America: A History of Its Rise and Fall* (New York: W.W. Norton, 2005), 323.
14 Norman Lebrecht, *The Maestro Myth: Great Conductors in Pursuit of Power* (New York: Citadel Press, 2001), 259.
15 Nigel Simeone, ed., *The Leonard Bernstein Letters* (New Haven: Yale University Press, 2013), 294.
16 Donal Henahan, "Leonard Bernstein, 72, Music's Monarch, Dies," *New York Times*, 15 October 1990, https://www.nytimes.com/1990/10/15/obituaries/leonard-bernstein-72-music-s-monarch-dies.html.
17 Eugene Gates, "Damned If You Do and Damned If You Don't: Sexual Aesthetics and the Music of Dame Ethel Smyth," *Kapralova Society Journal* 4, no. 1 (2006): 1–5, https://doi.org/10.2307/3333472.
18 Klaus Müller, "Oral History Interview with Frieda Belinfante," United States Holocaust Memorial Collection, video, recorded 31 May 1994, https://collections.ushmm.org/search/catalog/irn504443.
19 Bateman, "Conductors," 58.
20 Lebrecht, *The Maestro Myth*, 260.
21 Ben Holgate, "Tate à Tate," Review, magazine supplement *The Weekend Australian*, 26–27 September 1998, 17.
22 Geoffrey W. Bateman, "Tilson Thomas, Michael," in *The Queer Encyclopedia of Music, Dance, & Musical Theatre*, 258.
23 "Full Bio," Michael Tilson Thomas, accessed 15 September 2022, https://michaeltilsonthomas.com/about.
24 Terry Gross, "Conductor Marin Alsop Talks about the Joys and Challenges of Leading an Orchestra," Fresh Air, NPR, broadcast 4 April 2022, https://www.npr.org/2022/04/04/1090802924/conductor-marin-alsop-talks-about-the-joys-and-challenges-of-leading-an-orchestra.
25 Politzer, "Black Gay Conductor Heads to Atlanta Symphony."
26 Tom Huizenga and Anastasia Tsioulcas, "James Levine, Former Met Opera Music Director, Is Dead at Age 77," Deceptive Cadence, NPR, broadcast 17 March 2021, https://www.npr.org/sections/deceptivecadence/2021/03/17/834194609/james-levine-former-met-opera-music-director-is-dead-at-age-77.
27 This term, though viewed as outdated by some, refers to the orchestras in New York, Boston, Chicago, Philadelphia, and Cleveland.
28 Zachary Woolfe, "The Met Opera Has a Gay Conductor. Yes, That Matters," *New York Times*, 15 January 2019, https://www.nytimes.com/2019/01/15/arts/music/yannick-nezet-seguin-met-opera-gay.html.

# 20
## VOICES FOR CHANGE
Socially Responsible Programming in Youth Choral Music Education

*Lynsey Callaghan*

For those embarking on a journey of leadership in youth choral music education, two possible paths seem to beckon: one devoted to rigorous skill acquisition and performance, the other to more relaxed group-singing opportunities and social connections. This implies a choice between the music and the people, between musical goals and social aspirations. However, recent social changes demand an alternative approach that combines a people-centred philosophy with intentional music-making. Such an approach recognizes the transformative power of active participation in artistry for children and young people. It calls for a broader definition of excellence in youth choral music education—one that encompasses both artistic and aesthetic experiences that are rooted in, and achieved through, a citizenship-based philosophy that promotes freedom, equality, and dignity for all participants and nurtures the participants' ability to facilitate the same for others. Following an exploration of ideas surrounding the potential for all involved in youth choral music education to practise the values and attitudes underpinning citizenship, this chapter considers ways of rethinking programming within choral contexts. Specifically, it examines the principles and practices that guide the repertoire-selection and decision-making processes, suggesting ways in which they can be harnessed to create a socially responsible and inclusive space that contributes to a more just and inclusive world.

### Engaging the Arts for Citizenship

The potential of the arts to contribute to freedom, equality, and dignity is underscored by the United Nations recognizing cultural and artistic

DOI: 10.4324/9781003299660-25

participation as a fundamental right. Milestones such as the 75th anniversary of the UN's Universal Declaration of Human Rights (UDHR) in 2023 and the 35th anniversary of the UN's Convention on the Rights of the Child (UNCRC) in 2024 give us cause to reflect on the role that the arts and culture could play in moving towards a better world for all. In particular, Article 27 of the UDHR underscores the importance of inclusive participation, affirming that "everyone has the right freely to participate in the cultural life of the community, to enjoy the arts, and to share in scientific advancement and its benefits."[1] Those engaged in youth choral music education are likely familiar with Article 31 of the UNCRC, which recognizes "the right of the child to rest and leisure, to engage in play and recreational activities appropriate to the age of the child and to participate freely in cultural life and the arts."[2] It also declares "the right of the child to participate fully in cultural and artistic life" and encourages "the provision of appropriate and equal opportunities for cultural, artistic, recreational and leisure activity" for young people.[3] This affirms that cultural and artistic participation is an equal and inalienable entitlement of every adult and young person, holding the potential to contribute to the freedom, equality, and dignity of those who participate. Moreover, for some, engaging in cultural and artistic activities fosters the development of values and attitudes associated with artistic citizenship—the notion that artistic practices and arts education promote social competencies related to political, ethical, and moral practices, including the ability to uphold the freedom, equality, and dignity of others.[4] This socially embedded understanding of music highlights the role that the arts and artists play in both responding to and shaping society in a responsible way. Given the myriad significant challenges faced by young people today, such as food and energy insecurity, the climate crisis, global conflict, cost of living, increased risk of pandemics, and socio-political crises, the arts offer a platform for nurturing socially responsible individuals who are capable of enacting change in the world.

To understand how choral music education can facilitate the development of artistic citizenship, it is necessary to delve into the specific competencies that contribute to the cultivation of citizenship, the associated values, and attitudes. Citizenship, itself, is a concept that is subject to contestation, with rights and responsibilities varying subject to time, place, and context.[5] Of particular relevance to artistic citizenship, 'global citizenship' prioritizes an inclusive, non-state-centric approach over the exclusionary legal recognition of nationality. Accordingly, artistic citizenship encompasses a sense of belonging to a common humanity and emphasizes the interconnectedness and interdependency of political, economic, social, and cultural contexts at local, national, and global levels.[6] This positions artistic citizenship as a broad and inclusive concept that transcends national boundaries and resists notions of political exclusion.

Conductors seeking to enact artistic citizenship within choral music education can benefit from consulting recent studies in Global Citizenship Education (GCED), a human-rights-based framework.[7] GCED responds to Goal 4 of the UN's 2030 Sustainable Development Goals (SDGs), which aims to "ensure inclusive and equitable quality education and promote lifelong learning opportunities for all," and specifically to Target 4.7, which calls for the provision of knowledge and skills related to sustainable development, human rights, gender equality, peace promotion, the appreciation of cultural diversity and of culture's contribution to sustainable development, and global citizenship.[8] The concept of GCED aims to be "transformative, building the knowledge, skills, values and attitudes that learners need to be able to contribute to a more inclusive, just and peaceful world."[9] WorldWise Global Schools, funded by Irish Aid in 2013, is one example of a national GCED programme.[10] It defines GCED as teaching and learning through a global justice lens, enabling students to explore and develop the knowledge, skills, attitudes, and values necessary to become global citizens, and empowering them to take actions for a more just and sustainable world. The programme identifies various competencies within GCED, including communication skills, intellectual skills, social skills, and action skills, while emphasizing values and attitudes such as "empathy not sympathy," "solidarity not charity," "respect for self," "respect for others and human rights for all," "social responsibility and belonging," "a commitment to learning," and belief in individual agency for making a difference.[11] Youth choral music education that works towards the cultivation of these skills, values, and attitudes, while also striving for an aesthetic experience, can be understood as a potential site of artistic citizenship.

Citizenship should not be limited to being merely a desired outcome of youth choral music education. Instead, youth choral music education should be a context in which the competencies underpinning citizenship are practised through artistic endeavours. The idea of learning citizenship through participation in social and cultural practices is key to educational researchers Robert Lawy and Gert Biesta's description of citizenship-as-practice, as positioned against citizenship-as-outcome, where students must acquire a set of competencies before participating in society.[12] As a practice, it is crucial to provide young people with opportunities to experiment and develop attitudes, values, and skills that can be applied and adapted to various situations within the choral context. Therefore, youth choral music education should not solely aim to prepare young singers to become citizens, but also offer a space where social responsibility can be nurtured and actioned through music. By wholeheartedly embracing the transformative concept of global citizenship and cultivating its associated competencies within high-quality youth choral music education, every facet of the endeavour—including the recruitment of singers, the development of vocal technique, the mastery of music literacy, and the processes surrounding repertoire choices—is transformed into a platform where artistic citizenship can be practised by everyone involved.

## Programming as/for Change

Choosing repertoire for youth choral music education requires an array of considerations and challenges: young singers need music that has an appropriate range and an ideal *tessitura* for the voices, that displays appropriate musical challenges in relation to the singers' musical development, and that responds to the musical interests of the singers. These are just some of the vocal, pedagogical, and musical criteria that youth choir conductors use to determine the suitability of repertoire for performance. These considerations have serious implications for the singers' continued health and wellbeing, sustained enjoyment, ongoing commitment to the programme, and incremental development of musicianship. However, for youth choral music education to enable both the young people and the facilitators involved to practise and develop the skills, values, and attitudes underpinning artistic citizenship, these aspects become only one part of a multifaceted process of programme planning. The rest of this chapter suggests some of the ways in which programming, both the repertoire itself and the processes surrounding how programmes are designed, can be undertaken as acts of socially responsible artistry.

Through practices such as decentring the choral canon, commissioning and co-creating new music, and engaging with the broader contexts in which the repertoire is created and performed, a diversity of voices can be welcomed into choral programmes. Choosing repertoire that comments on or engages with ideas of empathy, solidarity, respect, responsibility, and belonging, and using the meaning of the texts to engender conversations about the values and attitudes at the heart of global citizenship, enables choral music to be both an entry point into and the language of such conversations. By including young people and cultural experts in decision-making surrounding the repertoire and its performance, the power structure in which decision-making rests solely with the artistic director or conductor is destabilized. This can enable those who have traditionally assumed responsibility for programming to challenge the hegemonic practices that have typically dominated Western youth choral music education. By empowering others to participate in choosing what is performed and how it is performed, choral conductors use their power to develop both their own citizenship and that of others. Collectively, these actions show that rethinking programming in a youth choral music education context can help to develop the values and attitudes that support the cultivation of socially responsible young people, equipped with the language and the tools to effect change. By centring people in all these actions, it is possible to move beyond music-making to true artistry, to the creation of something that is deeply beautiful as both a process and a product.

### Decentring the Repertoire

The historical elevation of Western art music has marginalized other musics and music experiences and processes—and continues to do so in many parts of the world today. Even within Western classical music, certain works and particular composers have been entered into a 'canon,' while others remain peripheral or entirely excluded. This manifests as the repeated programming of certain works and the erasure of many stories and repertoires. Choral literature also has a canon, which favours composers known primarily for their instrumental works.[13] This can clearly be seen in the regular inclusion of Vivaldi, Handel, Bach, Mozart, and Fauré in choral society repertoire. The high 'cultural capital' afforded to these composers means that they appeal to singers, attract audiences, and satisfy long-standing societal expectations. Notwithstanding the high levels of compositional craft and artistic rewards they offer, these are not the only works that display these qualities and, therefore, should not be the only composers given prominence in choral contexts. The act of decentring the choral canon by including non-canonical composers forms part of broader initiatives to expand the status quo.[14] The historical exclusion of women, people of colour, people with disabilities, and other marginalized social and political identities has ensured that the canon of choral music disproportionately represents the music of white, cisgender, mainly deceased males. However, this demographic is not representative of the diversity of composers and creators of choral music, of the people who perform the programmes, or of their audiences. Most significantly, it makes it hard to connect to potential new singers or audience members. But challenging a hegemonic canon often incurs resistance from those who benefit from it.

As youth choral music is less bound by the expectations for choral society programming, it can offer a better arena for expanding the canon. Starting with this age group also supports long-term changes within the choral community as the singers move from youth contexts into adult choral societies, bringing with them the expectation of performing a wider repertoire, and as they become audience members with the power to support concerts that display more diversity in their programming. Therefore, those who choose repertoire for choral music education programmes have an opportunity to exercise their own judgement about what music is right for their own cohorts, while also allowing their programming to reflect how they want to shape the landscape of choral music more broadly. As a first step, conductors can look critically at their own past programmes to understand whose voices are dominating the repertoire and to assess whether these composers are representative of the communities involved in the choir and those who the choir is aspiring to include. Conductors can and should ask questions about the value of the music that they programme and seek to understand whether they have inherited their judgement or have been active participants in evaluating whether the work or piece is suitable for their context.

## Considering the Message

When selecting music for young singers, it is important to recognize that every piece of music, whether it is part of the canon or not, offers an opportunity to develop not only musical skills, but also attitudes and values. The lyrics of songs can serve as a platform for exploring and developing ideas and, therefore, it is imperative that the message of each song aligns with the desired attitudes and values of the choir. When the message aligns with the tenets of global citizenship, the repertoire can engender meaningful conversations in rehearsals, allowing for deeper reflections on the messages embedded in the music. Music can convey complex concepts and emotions while also resonating with the experiences and interests of young people, helping them to develop a wide range of personal emotional expressions. Through these processes, singers can develop a greater understanding of themselves, while also exploring diverse perspectives.

Crucially, it is not only the musical material that demands the attention of those curating programmes for young people. They should also delve into the backgrounds of composers, the communities they represent, and the broader contexts in which the repertoire was created and used. By gaining a thorough understanding of the cultural and historical significance of the potential repertoire, programme selectors can make informed decisions and avoid furthering harmful narratives or reinforcing discriminatory practices. For example, some pieces that still circulate in the repertoire today may have been used historically in ways that caused harm to certain communities by perpetuating discriminatory narratives. By consciously avoiding pieces that lack cultural sensitivity and choosing to include those that celebrate people, it is possible to contribute to a socially responsible agenda and to align with the principles of global citizenship.

## Commissioning and Co-Creating New Music

By intentionally selecting music that challenges young people's preconceptions about composers and their roles, conductors can help to reshape the choral canon. There are many ways to achieve this, including involving young people in the commissioning process and in the creation of new repertoire.

Commissioning a composer to create a new work provides a choir with an opportunity to support and showcase artists who might not have traditionally featured in their programme. This not only expands the diversity of voices within choral music, but also allows choirs to play a part in supporting the creation of new repertoire that aligns with their values and aspirations. By embracing the commissioning process, choirs can instigate change, opening doors for composers who are underrepresented in choral music and amplifying their voices through performance of their music. Securing resources to undertake a commission can be challenging, but there are many funding opportunities that can support choirs in engaging composers.

The co-creation of new repertoire with a composer provides young people with an opportunity to participate in the compositional process. There are many parts of the compositional process that lend themselves well to the participation of young people alongside a composer or songwriter, including the generation of initial ideas and themes, the creation of text, the creation of melodies and harmonic progressions, and the development of paralinguistic features or choreography, to name just a few. Such engagement can give singers a sense of agency and ownership in the creative process. In communicating their ideas, experiences, perspectives, and preferences, and in hearing those around them, singers develop collaborative skills such as communication, listening, negotiation, compromise, and teamwork, while also contributing to the formation of a new piece of music. They develop new artistic skills through their exposure to new artists and they learn how to translate their own thoughts into music.

The successful co-creation of music with young people relies on careful facilitation by the composer. It is essential for participating composers to possess pedagogical skills in addition to artistic capacities. They must know how to scaffold the singers' participation, taking into account their knowledge and skills. Composers must also be mindful of the power dynamics at play, ensuring that they do not undermine the potential for the singers' agency and ownership. Successful co-creation takes time and resources, but the impact of a carefully designed, well-resourced project is significant for all involved. Notably, composers such as Jim Papoulis specialize in co-creating new choral music through collaborative workshops with young people, exemplifying the potential of this approach.[15]

Inviting participating composers into rehearsals, either to meet the singers in advance of writing for them or to co-create with them, can be a transformative experience for young singers, as they speak to composers and gain insights into the creative process. Through these personal interactions, singers can come to realize that they too have the potential to create music and that they can play a part in the world of composition. By interacting with composers from communities that are underrepresented in choral music, young singers begin to recognize that composers can come from diverse backgrounds, challenging historical barriers and exclusionary narratives. This realization can be particularly powerful when young singers also belong to communities that have been traditionally underrepresented in the choral music sphere. Once the belief that they have ability takes root in singers, it becomes vital to provide them with ample opportunities to develop skills and to showcase their music through performances. These practices not only challenge the choral canon by giving young people opportunities to consider what is important, but also cultivate a community of creators and develop audiences for the music of the future.

**Destabilizing the Power**

In youth choral music programmes, artistic directors and conductors are often the ones who are responsible for choosing repertoire. In this paradigm, programming is seen as an expression of the conductor's artistry and expertise. The conductor sits between the repertoire and the singers, with the power to include and exclude certain pieces, works, composers, genres, and styles. This role grants them power over the singers and the audience. There are many methodologies that conductors might enact when creating a programme. Composer David Brunner outlined the dominant programming approaches as: chronological programming; thematic programming, which he described as "music on a certain theme or for a specific occasion, season, or purpose"; and concept programming, which he defined as programming that "assembles and then seeks to unify rather diverse compositions around a general idea or concept."[16] When choosing whether or not to include specific pieces, conductors might look at the qualities of the repertoire in relation to each other. Conductor Hilary Apfelstadt has suggested using criteria such as variety, balance, unity, flow, and music of good quality as a mechanism for deciding on repertoire to be included in a programme.[17] However, as none of these terms are absolute in their meaning, what is included or excluded is highly contingent on the understanding of variety, balance, unity, flow, and quality by the conductor responsible for the decision-making process, as well as the conductor's own positionality, experiences, and expertise.

Rather than attempting to disown their subjectivity, choral conductors and artistic directors can focus on using their positions sensitively and meaningfully to empower others. This is what global development scholar and practitioner Robert Chambers calls the "power to empower": the capacity to redistribute power through the active participation of those affected by the decision-making.[18] In applying Chambers's framework to choral music contexts, a different concept of programming emerges—one where the conductor relinquishes full control of decision-making and acts instead as a facilitator who supports cultural experts and allows young singers to participate in decision-making processes. Such efforts to destabilize persistent power dynamics could impact other areas of young people's lives, and society more broadly.

## Empowering Cultural Experts

In striving to ensure that programmes respond to the array of cultures represented in the choir, conductors can find themselves grappling with repertoires from cultures that are unfamiliar to them, or practices for which they lack training. Western classical music still tends to dominate formal music education and conductor education programmes, leaving many conductors underprepared to utilize pedagogical approaches that are appropriate for the cultural contexts surrounding—and learning styles associated with—diverse repertoires.[19] Encouraging young people to share their own cultures and traditions is one way to move towards more meaningful inclusion of diverse repertoires. Another way is to welcome cultural experts into the rehearsals to curate entire programmes or to engage with specific pieces within a programme. Their understanding of cultural nuances, based on their own lived experiences, is invaluable in a musical context that seeks to develop values such as the appreciation of cultural diversity and empathy. By listening to—and learning from—a cultural expert, a conductor can model the destabilization of traditional power dynamics within the realm of choral music and challenge power dynamics in society more broadly. In a choral context, divesting power to a cultural expert implies the recognition of their expertise, lived experiences, and artistry, and either facilitating a context in which they make decisions or actively involving them in decision-making regarding how a particular piece is taught and performed in an environment of mutual respect. When this happens, singers have an opportunity to experience leaders from different backgrounds; likewise, singers from communities that are underrepresented in choral music can see themselves as potential leaders. In this way, a conductor demonstrates commitment to presenting repertoire and engaging with other cultures in a meaningful and sensitive way that avoids cultural appropriation and promotes cross-cultural understandings.

## Sharing Decision-Making

Participation in decision-making is deeply connected to the rights of the young person as outlined in Article 12 of the UN's Convention on the Rights of the Child, whereby children have a right to have their views given due weight.[20] From a children's rights perspective, young people are viewed as "social actors, as active agents and autonomous, independent human beings in constructing their lives in their own right."[21] In recognition of this, children's rights scholar Laura Lundy created a model of child participation that strives to give the child a meaningful voice in decision-making through the consideration of four interrelated concepts: space, voice, audience, and influence.[22] To incorporate this model into youth choral music education, singers should be provided with a safe and inclusive space to express their views (space). It is imperative that they are given appropriate information and facilitated to articulate their views (voice). Someone should be assigned to the task of listening to and valuing the young people's input (audience), and processes for evaluating and acting on their ideas should be put in place, where appropriate (influence). These processes might be implemented in relation to repertoire selection, concert themes, or other creative projects. Implementing participatory processes, while also recognizing a conductor's artistic vision, might present challenges that will warrant further exploration. Potential tensions and challenges might emerge as conductors incorporate Lundy's model into their artistic practice and attempt to reconcile participatory processes with their own artistic desires. However, for conductors who are serious about developing artistic citizenship in youth choral music education, it is important to configure a purposeful process of youth participation in decision-making relating to programming.

## Conclusion: Rethinking Excellence in Youth Choral Music Education

The exclusionary nature and narrow concepts of excellence found in the conventional paradigms of choral music and choral music education pose a challenge to those involved in youth choral music education today. There is an opportunity to conceive of a new vision for youth choral music education that embraces a multifaceted definition of excellence. Situational excellence allows conductors to respond to their own contexts while rejecting a false dichotomy that forces a separation between skill acquisition and relationship building. Though vocal technique that promotes healthy singing is undoubtedly necessary for lifelong participation in choral music, excellence extends beyond technical capabilities because when basic human rights such as freedom, equality, and dignity are ignored in the name of achieving technical prowess, the potential for true artistry cannot be realized. True artistry is deeply infused with societal concerns because humans and human relationships are central to the art of music, which is a fundamentally social act. By embracing the concept of artistic citizenship, youth choral music education intertwines musical and social aspirations to create a cohesive offering to young people that supports efforts to achieve a better tomorrow. Through profound musical experiences, deep relationships and connections can be built. In turn, through these relationships, true artistry can be enacted. In this way, excellence in youth choral music depends upon its contribution to a more just, inclusive, and beautiful world, created through the voices of young people.

## Notes

1 "Universal Declaration of Human Rights," United Nations, accessed 5 July 2022, https://www.un.org/en/about-us/universal-declaration-of-human-rights.
2 "Convention on the Rights of the Child," United Nations, accessed 5 July 2022, https://www.ohchr.org/en/instruments-mechanisms/instruments/convention-rights-child.
3 "Convention on the Rights of the Child."
4 For a discussion of artistic citizenship, see David Elliott, Marissa Silverman, and Wayne Bowman, eds., *Artistic Citizenship: Artistry, Social Responsibility, and Ethical Praxis* (New York: Cambridge University Press, 2016).
5 For an exploration of the concept of citizenship, see Elizabeth F. Cohen and Cyril Ghosh, *Citizenship* (Cambridge: Polity Press, 2019).
6 UNESCO, *Global Citizenship Education: Preparing Learners for the Challenges of the 21st Century* (Paris: United Nations Educational, Scientific and Cultural Organization, 2014), 14.
7 "What You Need to Know about Global Citizenship Education," UNESCO, accessed 15 October 2023, https://www.unesco.org/en/global-citizenship-peace-education/need-know.
8 "Sustainable Development Goals: Goal 4," UN Department of Economic and Social Affairs, accessed 7 July 2022, https://sdgs.un.org/goals/goal4.
9 UNESCO, *Global Citizenship Education: Topics and Learning Objectives* (Paris: United Nations Educational, Scientific and Cultural Organization, 2015), 15.
10 WorldWise Global Schools, accessed 10 May 2023, https://www.worldwiseschools.ie.
11 "Global Citizenship Education: Skills," WorldWise Global Schools, accessed 10 May 2023, https://www.worldwiseschools.ie/skills; "Global Citizenship Education: Values and Attitudes," WorldWise Global Schools, accessed 10 May 2023, https://www.worldwiseschools.ie/values-and-attitudes.

12 Robert Lawy and Gert Biesta, "Citizenship-as-Practice: The Educational Implications of an Inclusive and Relational Understanding of Citizenship," *British Journal of Educational Studies* 54, no. 1 (2006): 34–50, https://doi.org/10.1111/j.1467-8527.2006.00335.x.
13 Jessica Rickard, "Feeding the Choirs: The Beginner's Recipe Guide to Selecting Repertoire," *The Choral Journal* 56, no. 1 (August 2015): 69–71, https://www.jstor.org/stable/24580585.
14 Susan McClary, *Conventional Wisdom: The Content of Musical Form* (Berkeley: University of California Press, 2000), 30.
15 "Artistic Statement," Jim Papoulis, accessed 11 May 2023, http://www.jimpapoulis.com/index.cfm?view=Artistic%20Statement.
16 David L. Brunner, "Choral Program Design: Structure and Symmetry," *Music Educators Journal* 8, no. 6 (1994): 46–49, https://doi.org/10.2307/3398713. For further perspectives on choral programme design, see also Kari Turunen's chapter in this volume.
17 Hilary Apfelstadt, "First Things First: Selecting Repertoire," *The Choral Journal* 41, no. 7 (2001): 31–35, https://www.jstor.org/stable/23553733.
18 Robert Chambers, "Words, Power and the Personal in Development," in *Language and Development: Africa and Beyond*, ed. Hywel Coleman (Addis Ababa: British Council, 2007), 119–29 (123). Drawing on VeneKlasen and Miller's commonly used framework of "power to," "power over," "power with," and "power within." Chambers adds a fifth type of power: "power to empower."
19 Patricia Shehan Campbell, David E. Meyer, and Edward W. Sarath, "Transforming Music Study from its Foundations: A Manifesto for Progressive Change in the Undergraduate Preparation of Music Majors," in *Redefining Music Studies in an Age of Change: Creativity Diversity, Integration*, ed. Patricia Shehan Campbell, David E. Meyer, and Edward W. Sarath (New York: Routledge, 2016), 45–85.
20 "Convention on the Rights of the Child," Article 12.
21 Didier Reynaert, Maria Bouverne-de-Bie, and Stijn Vandevelde, "A Review of Children's Rights Literature Since the Adoption of the United Nations Convention on the Rights of the Child," *Childhood* 16, no. 4 (2009): 518–34 (521). https://doi.org/10.1177/0907568209344270.
22 Laura Lundy, "'Voice' is Not Enough: Conceptualising Article 12 of the United Nations Convention on the Rights of the Child," *British Educational Research Journal* 33, no. 6 (2007): 927–42.

# INDEX

*2001: A Space Odyssey* (movie) 88

Abbado, Claudio 131, 221, 222
AIDS 247
Alldahl, Per-Gunnar 164
Almila, Atso 11
Alsop, Marin 219, 226n23, 228, 229, 233, 247–48, *see also* Taki Alsop Conducting Fellowship
Alvarado, Arturo 13
Amarillo Symphony 124
American Academy of Arts and Letters 247
American Academy of Arts and Sciences 247
Amsterdam Conservatory *see* Conservatorium van Amsterdam
Arman, Nurhan 124, 126, 127, 130
Armstrong, Mark 57
Army No. 1 Band (Irish Defence Forces) 57
artistic citizenship 253–55, 261, 262
Arts Council of Ireland 142
Association for the Advancement of Creative Musicians 22
Atlanta Symphony Orchestra 98, 226n25, 227n31, 228
atonal music 12, 15, 169–82
attire 73, 222–23, 235
audiation *see* inner hearing

auditions: conservatoire 11–12, 15, 18
aural awareness: in singers 138, 172, 182, 192, 204; in conductors 43, 72–73, 141, 164–65

Bach, C.P.E. 69
Bach, J.S. 50, 68, 70, 256; *Jesu, meine Freude* 155n6; Mass in B minor 47; *St Matthew Passion* 155n6
Bach, Philippe 15
Baltimore Symphony Orchestra 219, 228, 248
Bamberg Symphony 129
Bangor Symphony Orchestra 246
Bard Conservatory 22
Barenboim, Daniel 248
Bartók, Béla 182: Concerto for Orchestra, 15
BBC Philharmonic 227n27
BBC Singers 226n23
BBC Symphony Orchestra 11, 13, 220
Beach, Amy 239n1
Beard, Mary 229–30, 231, 235
Bear Valley Music Festival 248
Beck, Simon 129
Beethoven, Ludwig van 15, 68, 83, 85, 88, 229; *Fidelio* 41; *Leonore Overture No. 3* 41; Symphony No. 5 127; Symphony No. 7 88; Symphony No. 9 102

Belinfante, Frieda 246
Berg, Alban 182
Berlin Philharmonic 31, 221, 244
Berlioz, Hector 89
Berman, John 235
Bern Chamber Orchestra 16
Bernstein, Leonard 4n2, 7, 16, 23n2, 41, 88, 104, 131, 222, 245, 248; *West Side Story* 129–30
Beyer, Bud 141, 142
*Beyond the Grace Note* (documentary film) 228
Bizet, Georges: *Carmen* 39n29, 101
Black Lives Matter 22
Blomstedt, Herbert 104
Boston Symphony Orchestra 244, 247
Boulanger, Lili: *D'un matin de printemps* 89
Boulez, Pierre 247
Bournemouth Symphony Orchestra 220, 226n23, 248
bowings 41, 71, 78
Brabbins, Martyn 19
Brahms, Johannes 68, 83, 86, 88; *Ein deutsches Requiem* 47; Hungarian Dance No. 5 88
Bridge, Frank: *Summer* 89
Britten, Benjamin 244, 246; *Missa Brevis* 175–78
Bruckner, Anton 42
Buffalo Philharmonic Orchestra 247
Bülow, Hans von 30–31, 38n17, 225n3
business: analysis models (SWOT etc) 84–85; strategies 111–17
Bychkov, Semyon 19
Byrd, William 137

Calhoun, Michael D. 247
Canellakis, Karina 226n23
Carnegie Mellon University 234
Chadwick, George 239n1
Chamber Orchestra of Europe 249
Chamorro-Premuzic, Tomas 232, 233, 238
Chan, Elim 223, 226n23
Chang, Tiffany 123, 126
Chicago Symphony Orchestra 227n31, 248
choral blend 136, 158, 204
choral competitions/festivals 47, 57–58, 140

choral/vocal tone 136, 138, 143, 157–58, 160, 163–64
choral warm-up 136–37, 156–68, 192, 194–95
choreography 258
Christina Alexandra, Queen of Sweden 243
City of Birmingham Symphony Orchestra 13, 221, 226n23
City University, London (City, University of London) 7
Cleveland Orchestra 28, 72, 227n31
Clinton, Hillary 235
College of Music Chamber Choir, Dublin 47
Collon, Nicholas 221
commissioning 139–40, 258
conducting gesture 104, 160, 162–63, 192, 202; and gender 236
Conservatorium van Amsterdam 246
contracts 32, 35, 40, 71, 217–218, 225, 226n18, 226n19, 246
Copland, Aaron 88, 244; *Fanfare for the Common Man* 87
Corduroy, Charlotte 19
Corelli, Arcangelo 243
Covid-19 pandemic 13, 22, 87, 96, 100, 141, 209, 210, 219
Culwick Choral Society 46

Dahl, Tone Bianca 143, 158, 166
Dalcroze Method 60n10
Dallas Opera Hart Institute 233
Davis, Sir Andrew 120, 125, 127
Davis, Sir Colin 247
Davydov, Vladimir 243
Debussy, Claude 89, 238: *La Mer* 82–83; *Trois chansons* 46
de la Parra, Alondra 229
Del Mar, Norman 19
Del Tredici, David: *Gay Life* 247
Dervan, Michael 8
DIT Choral Society 46, 58
diversity 22–23, 67, 219–221, 228–29, 238, 250; cultural 260–61; in programming 139, 256–60; *see also* gender
Doherty, Seán: *Snow Dance for the Dead* 51–54
Dohnányi, Christoph von 31, 222
Donizetti, Gaetano: *L'elisir d'amore* 36

Dublin City University (DCU) 3
Dublin Orchestral Players 90n17
Dudamel, Gustavo 131, 221
Dudarova, Veronika 231
Dunboyne Children's Choir 58
Dutoit, Charles 224
Dvořák, Antonín: *Czech Suite* 85; *New World Symphony* 85; Symphony No. 6 105

early music 70, 123, 137, 163, 216, 225
Edlund, Lars 182
Edwards, Anna 228, 232, 236
Edwards, Sian 18–20
Elder, Sir Mark 44n3, 123, 126, 128, 217, 226n15
Elgar, Edward 244; Cello Concerto 90n17; *The Dream of Gerontius* 125
Elizabeth II, Queen of the United Kingdom 244
Emmy Award 245
Erdei, Péter 46
Eriksson, Gunnar 138
European Network of University Orchestras (ENUO) 90n2
European Student Orchestra Festival (ESOF) 90n2

Falletta, JoAnn 121–22, 123, 126, 232, 234
Farberman, Harold 9, 22
Farnham, Alice 3, 19
Farrell, Eibhlís 46
Fauré, Gabriel 89, 256
fees: conductors 218–219; conservatoires 11, 15, 18
Feldenkrais, Moshé 104; Feldenkrais method 104, 142
Fennessy, David 46
film music 83, 88, 89, 101
Finnish Radio Symphony Orchestra 12
fixed-*do* system 49, 173, 183n19, 195
Fontainebleau School of Music 244
French Order of Arts and Letters 247
Fritzsch, Georg 105–06
Furtwängler, Wilhelm 31, 222

Gardner, Edward 18
Gardner, Kay 246
Gateways Music Festival 248
Gatti, Daniele 224

gender 17, 43, 228–39, 242, 243, 246
*Generalmusikdirektor* 31, 33–34, 36, 37, 106
Georgia Arts Council 98
Gergiev, Valery 224–25
German Association of Professional Orchestras 36
German Theatre Yearbook 37
Gershwin, George 130; *Rhapsody in Blue* 86
*Ghostbusters* (movie) 101
Ginsberg, Allen 247
Glassberg, Ben 18, 20
Glazunov, Alexander 89
Global Citizenship Education 254
Graham Cracker, Martha 249
Grainger, Percy 88, 244
Grammy Award 245, 247
*Gramophone* Artist of the Year 247
Græsholm, Niels 202
Gražinytė-Tyla, Mirga 15, 223, 226n23
*The Great Dictator* (movie) 88
Grieg, Edvard: Piano Concerto 85; *Symphonic Dances* 86
Groves, Sir Charles 19
Guido d'Arezzo 61n15
Guildhall School of Music and Drama 19
Gunn, Thom 247

Hagen Philharmonic Orchestra 105–06
Hallé 44n3, 218, 220
Handel, George Frideric 243, 256; *Messiah* 47
Hannigan, Barbara 221, 226n23
HarrisonParrot 14
*Harry Potter* (movie franchise) 101
Hasan, Kerem 15, 16
Haydn, Franz Joseph 124, 247
Helsinki Philharmonic Orchestra 13
Herboly Kocsár, Ildikó 45–46
Herrmann, Bernard: *Psycho Suite* 101
Heyward, Jonathon 18, 20, 221
Hirsh, Jonathan 120–21, 123, 127, 128
Hochschule für Musik Franz Liszt Weimar 20, 39n27, 92, 93–94
Hochschule für Musik Hanns Eisler Berlin 39n27
Hochschule für Musik Karlsruhe 92

Hochschule für Musik und Theater Felix Mendelssohn Bartholdy Leipzig 39n27
Holm, Jesper 201
Holst, Gustav: *The Planets* 101
Homer: *Odyssey* 230
Honeck, Manfred 15
Horstmann, Sabine 137
Hrůša, Jakub 129
Hyflex Curriculum Design (HCD) 210–11

Ilan, Talia 239
Imperial College London 7
improvisation 138–39, 201–208
inclusivity 184, 186, 189–191, 242, 253, 262
inner hearing 47, 50, 56, 59, 104, 123, 167n13, 169
The Intelligent Choir (TIC) 202–08, 211
Internal Revenue Service (IRS) 94
International Conducting Competition, Berlin 28
intervallic hearing 169, 174
intonation/tuning 56, 59, 138, 157–160, 162, 164, 169, 204
Irish National Youth Ballet 87, 91n15
*Irish Times* 8
Ives, Charles: Symphony No. 4 41

Jackson, George 124–25
Janáček, Leoš: Sinfonietta 18
Jansons, Arvīds 13
jazz/pop choir directing 201, 202, 205, 210–11
Jeannin, Sofi 226n23
Joensuu City Orchestra 12
Johansen, Jens 202
Joly, Hubert 115–116
Jurkscheit, Kristin 248

*Kapellmeister* system 2, 27–39, 40, 41; *Chordirektor* 34; First *Kapellmeister* 34, 36; history of 29–31; *Intendant* 36; *Korrepetitor* 35, 39; *Musikvorstände* 37; role of 32–33; Second *Kapellmeister* 28, 34; *Studienleiter* 34; *Vordirigat* 35
Karajan, Herbert von 28, 31, 36, 103, 122, 221, 222, 226n11, 247
Karlsson, Peder 201

Kennedy Center Honors 245, 247
Kidde, W.H. 247
King's Voices 57
Klas, Eri 11
Kleiber, Carlos 36, 222, 247
Klemperer, Otto 31, 40, 43, 222
Koch, Heinrich Christoph: *Musikalisches Lexikon* 29
Kocsár, Miklós 46
Kodály, Zoltán 45, 48–50, 169
Kodály approach 45–51, 55–61
Kodály Institute 3, 45–50, 60
Kodály Ireland 60
Korngold, Erich: Violin Concerto 83
Koussevitzky Prize 247, 248
Kraft, Victor 244
Kuhlemann, Klaus 247

Laetare Vocal Ensemble 157
Lambert, Madeleine 242
Lambert, Michel 242
Lassus, Orlande de 137
Last Night of the Proms 223
*Lavender Jane Loves Women* (album) 246
League of American Orchestras 228
Lebrecht, Norman 215–16, 219, 224, 225
Leeds Conductors Competition 19
lesbian conductors 245–46
Levine, James 131, 224, 247, 249
Lewis, Katherine 87, 91n15
LGBTQ+ 242, 249
Ligeti, György: *Éjszaka* 55; *Clocks and Clouds* 180
Linklater, Kristin 142
Liszt, Franz: *Faust Symphony* 105
Liszt Ferenc Academy of Music 45
Lloyd Webber, Andrew: *Cats* 125; *Jesus Christ Superstar* 125
London Opera Centre 247
London Philharmonic Orchestra 226n23
London Symphony Orchestra 220, 226n23, 247
*Long Haired Hare* (cartoon) 1
Looney Tunes: Bugs Bunny 1, 81, 231
Los Angeles Philharmonic 247
Louis XIV, King of France 242
Lowe, James 16
Low Latency (LoLa) system 209

Lully, Jean-Baptiste 242
Lundy, Laura 261

La Maestra Competition 233
*Maestro* (movie) 4n2
Mahler, Gustav 21, 27, 28, 31, 38n17, 40, 43, 69, 97; Symphony No. 2 41
Mälkki, Susanna 18
Markevitch, Igor 103–06
Markson, Gerhard 46–47
Martín, Jaime 227n27
Martines, Marianna 238
Mathieson, Holly 120, 124, 126, 127
Mattheson, Johann: *Der vollkommene Capellmeister* 27, 29, 37
Mazur, Kurt 131
McFerrin, Bobby 201; circlesongs 202, 205–08
*Mehrspartenhaus* 33
memorization 49, 50, 103, 139–41, 172
Mendelssohn, Felix 27, 30; *Hebrides Overture* 85
Mengelberg, Willem 40
Merkel, Angela 235
metronome marks 68–70
Metters, Colin 18
Minneapolis Symphony Orchestra (Minnesota Orchestra) 244
Mitropoulos, Dimitri 244
Monette, Paul 247
Montealegre, Felicia 245
Monteverdi, Claudio 137; *Beatus vir* 46; *1610 Vespers* 47
Moor, Paul 244
Morgan, Michael 241, 248
Moscow Conservatory 229
movable-*do* system 169–82
Mozart, Wolfgang Amadeus 238, 256: C minor Mass 47; *The Marriage of Figaro* 39n29; Serenade No. 10 18; Symphony No. 40 12
*Mozart in the Jungle* (TV series) 3
Mueller, Christoph-Mathias 15
*Musical America* 247
Musical Chairs 40
musicianship development 48–50, 165, 186–87, 193–96, 202
*Musiktheater* 33
Musin, Ilya 13, 19
Mussorgsky, Modest: *A Night on Bald Mountain* 101

*Nachdirigat* 34
Nachmanovitch, Stephen 142
National Medal of Arts (USA) 247
National Symphony Orchestra (Ireland) 46, 227n27
National Union of Musicians (USA) 98
NBC Symphony Orchestra 23n2, 215
Nevis Ensemble 121
New Dublin Voices 47, 56–58
New England Women's Symphony 246
*New Grove Dictionary of Music* 67
New York Philharmonic 23n2, 244, 245
*New York Times* 245, 249
Nézet-Séguin, Yannick 219, 248–49, 250
Nielsen, Carl: Symphony No. 5 83
Nikisch, Arthur 219
Noone, Eimear 57
Norrington, Sir Roger 13

Oakland East Bay Symphony Orchestra 248
Oakland Youth Orchestra 248
Oliveros, Pauline 145n3
opera houses/companies: Aachen 31, 36; Bad Hall 31; Berlin 31; Cologne 28, 247; Dresden 28, 31, 37, 106; Festival Opera (Walnut Creek) 248; Glyndebourne 20, 128; Hamburg 28, 31, 37; Hannover 31; Kassel 31; Leipzig 28; Ljubljana 31; Meiningen 28, 31; Metropolitan Opera (The Met) 219, 235, 248; Munich 28, 31, 37; Nürnberg 36; Olomouc 31; Riga 28; Rouen 20; Royal Opera House (Covent Garden) 129, 247; Vienna 31; Ulm 31; Würzburg 28: Zurich 30
Oramo, Sakari 11, 13–14
Orange County Philharmonic Orchestra 246
orchestra board 94–98, 224
Orchestra Mozart 224
L'Orchestre Lamoureux 103
Orchestre Philharmonique de Monte Carlo 103
Orff, Carl: *Carmina Burana* 58, 59, 196–99
Oulu Sinfonia 12

Palestrina, Giovanni Pierluigi da 50
Panula, Jorma 11, 13, 14, 16, 21, 238
Papoulis, Jim 258
Pappano, Antonio 131
Parry, Ben 57
Pasquet, Nicolás 13
Paul, Sharon 164
Payare, Rafael 221
Pears, Peter 244
Petrenko, Kirill 31
Petrenko, Vasily 237
Philadelphia Gay Men's Chorus 249
Philadelphia Orchestra 219, 226n25, 227n31, 248, 249
Philharmonia 220
*Philharmonia* (TV series) 3
phrasing 137, 162–63, 199
polyphony 137, 164, 171, 180, 204
Popovich, Gregg 110
Poulenc, Francis: *Un soir de neige* 46; *Gloria* 47
Pouliot, Blake 249
Pritchard, John 247
Prokofiev, Sergei 88, 89; *Autumnal Sketch* 89; Piano Concerto No. 3 244
Puccini, Giacomo: *La Bohème* 39n29
Purcell, Henry 137
*Putty Tat Trouble* (cartoon) 81–82, 90n5

Quality, Resonant, Supported Tone (QRST) 156–57
queer 238, 242
queer conductors 241, 249–50; Baroque 242–43; nineteenth century 243; twentieth century 243–46; twenty-first century 246–49

race 238, 248
RAMA Vocal Center 201, 202, 209
Rastrup Andersen, Svend 202
Rattle, Sir Simon 221, 222
Ravel, Maurice 89; *La Vallée des Cloches* 88; *La Valse* 82–83
The Real Group 201, 202
rehearsal strategies: choral 51–59, 135–45; jazz/pop 202–08, 210–11; orchestral 21–22; university choir 190–99
Reiner, Fritz 28
relative sol-fa *see* sol-fa

Renaissance 137, 14; *see also* early music
repertoire theatre 32
repetiteur 28, 31, 34, 35, 39
Reynish, Timothy 19
Rheinberger, Josef: *Abendlied* 160
Rigtrup, Malene 201
Rodrigo, Joaquín: *Concierto de Aranjuez* 102
Rodgers and Hammerstein: *Carousel* 125
Romantic style: choral 138
Rooke, Chloe 20
Ross, Alvin 244
Rossini, Gioachino: *Il barbiere di Siviglia* 36
Rotterdam Philharmonic Orchestra 249
Rouvali, Santtu-Matias 221
Royal Academic Orchestra, Uppsala 90n2
Royal Academy of Music, London 10, 17–20
Royal Concertgebouw Orchestra 224, 246
Royal Liverpool Philharmonic Orchestra 220
Royal Northern College of Music 8, 19, 20, 25n49
Royal Philharmonic Orchestra 218, 220
Royal Philharmonic Society Women Conductors 3n1
Royal Scottish National Orchestra 218, 220, 226n23
RTÉ National Symphony Orchestra *see* National Symphony Orchestra (Ireland)

Sacramento Philharmonic 248
Saint Petersburg Conservatory 19
Saint-Saëns, Camille: *Organ Symphony* 87
Sallinen, Kristian 14–17
Salonen, Esa-Pekka 11, 13, 24n19
San Francisco Conservatory of Music 248
San Francisco Symphony Orchestra 219, 227n31, 247
São Paulo State Symphony Orchestra 248
Saraste, Jukka-Pekka 11, 13, 14

Sawallisch, Wolfgang 31
*Schauspiel* 33
Schubert, Franz: Symphony No. 5 12
Schumann, Robert: Symphony No. 2 18
Schlaefli, Johannes 13, 15, 21, 25n51; Conducting Academy Johannes Schlaefli 15
Schoenberg, Arnold 79n6, 89, 172, 181, 182; *Friede auf Erden* 150; *Von heute auf morgen* 174–75
Schütz, Heinrich 137; *Selig sind die Toten* 162
*Scott of the Antarctic* (movie) 88
Segerstam, Leif 11
sexual orientation 242–43, 248, 250
Shakespeare, William 68, 89
Sheldrake, Rupert 122, 128, 131
Shostakovich, Dmitri 88; Cello Concerto No. 1 101; Symphony No. 5 68; Symphony No. 10 86
Sibelius, Jean 89; Symphony No. 2 86
Sibelius Academy 10–14, 21
Siemens Hallé International Conductors Competition 44n3
Sinfonia Toronto 124
Sing Ireland 58; International Choral Conducting Summer School 60
Slatkin, Leonard 248
Smith College, Massachusetts 120
Smyth, Ethel 245–46
social media 249
sol-fa 49, 55–56, 61n15, 169, 173–74, 180–82, 195
solfège 45, 49, 56
*The Song of Bernadette* (movie) 88
Sokhiev, Tugan 19
Solti, Sir Georg 222, 247, 248
SonoBus 210
Soundpainting 205
Spohr, Ludwig 29
Spokane Symphony Orchestra 16
Staatskapelle Dresden 224
*Staatstheatern* 33
*Stadttheatern* 33
*stagione* theatre 32
Stalling, Carl 81–82, 90n5
Stasevska, Dalia 223
St Louis Symphony Orchestra 248
Stokowski, Leopold 1, 7, 9, 29, 226n11
Storgårds, John 227n27

Strauss, Johann II: *Blue Danube Waltz* 88
Strauss, Richard 21, 28, 31, 38n17, 41; *Eine Alpensinfonie* 41; *Elektra* 39n29
Stravinsky, Igor 42, 68, 103, 244; *Firebird Suite* 86; *The Rite of Spring* 51, 89; *Symphonies of Wind Instruments* 18; *Symphony in Three Movements* 88
Stutzman, Nathalie 223, 226n25, 228, 229
Swedish Radio Symphony Orchestra 13
Symphony Nova Scotia 121
Szathmáry, Zsigmond: *Fukushima Requiem* 181
Szell, George 28, 72, 131, 222

Taki Alsop Conducting Fellowship 3n1, 233, 248
Tanglewood Music Center 247, 248
*Tár* (movie) 3
Tate, Jeffrey 246
Tchaikovsky, Pyotr Ilyich 83, 89, 124, 243; *Marche Solennelle* 243; *Storm Overture* 86; Symphony No. 1, 'Winter Daydreams' 89; Symphony No. 4 87; Symphony No. 5 85; Symphony No. 6 (*Symphonie Pathétique*) 91n16, 243
Temirkanov, Yuri 19, 238
Thielemann, Christian 29, 36
Thompson, Walter 205
Ticciati, Robin 221, 222
Tilson Thomas, Michael 219, 247, 250
Tippett, Michael: Symphony No. 4 101
Tony Award 245
Toscanini, Arturo 7, 23n2, 215, 217, 222
Touché (vocal ensemble) 201
Tourville, Pierre 249
Trevor, Kirk 16
Trinity College Dublin 45
Tučapský, Antonín 46
TU Dublin Conservatoire 46

UCD Symphony Orchestra 80–81, 90n2, 91n16, 91n17, 91n18
UN Convention on the Rights of the Child 253, 261
unison singing 59, 180

United States Holocaust Memorial Museum 246
University College Dublin (UCD) 3, 80–81, 90n2, 92
University of California, Los Angeles (UCLA) 246
University of Dublin Choral Society 46
University of Galway (NUIG) 7
University of Heidelberg: Collegium Musicum 92
University of Music and Performing Arts Munich 106
University of Music and Performing Arts, Vienna 19, 20
University of Oregon Chamber Choir 164
UN Sustainable Development Goals 254
UN Universal Declaration of Human Rights, 253

Vaughan Williams, Ralph: *Fantasia on Christmas Carols* 46; *Sea Symphony* 47; *Sinfonia Antarctica* 88
Venzago, Mario 16
Verdi, Giuseppe: *Aida* 23n2; *Messa da Requiem* 27, 47
Victoria, Tomás Luis de 137
Vienna Radio Symphony Orchestra 248
Vivaldi, Antonio 89, 256; *Gloria* 46
Vocal Line (choir) 202
Vocal Painting (VOPA) 204–08
vocal technique 135–36, 156–59, 190, 192, 202, 205
vowel unity 158, 192

Wagner, Richard 27, 28, 30–31; *Die Meistersinger von Nürnberg* 30; *On Conducting* 30; *Tristan und Isolde* 30
Walter, Bruno 23n2, 28, 31, 40, 41
Walton, William 244
Weber, Carl Maria von 38n22
Webern, Anton 182
Weingartner, Felix 38n17, 217
Weinstein, Harvey 223
Werfel, Frank 88
*Wiederaufnahme* 38n22
Wigglesworth, Mark 3, 9, 18, 21, 119, 217
Williams, John 88
Wilson, Scott 120, 121, 123–24, 126, 127
women's suffrage 245

Yeats, W.B. 82
Young, Simone 219

Zimmer, Hans 88
Zorn, John: *Aporias: Requia for Piano and Orchestra* 178–79
Zürcher Hochschule der Künste 10, 14–17, 21

Printed in the United States
by Baker & Taylor Publisher Services